The Brazilian Monarchy and the South American Republics
1822–1831

The Brazilian Monarchy
and the South American Republics
1822–1831
Diplomacy and State Building

Ron Seckinger

Louisiana State University Press

Baton Rouge and London

The author gratefully acknowledges permission to reprint the following: parts of
Chapters 4 and 5 and of the Epilogue, which were published in "South American
Power Politics During the 1820s," *Hispanic American Historical Review*, Vol. LVI,
No. 2, copyright © 1976, Duke University Press (Durham, NC), 241–67; and
portions of Chapter 3, which were published in "The Chiquitos Affair: An Aborted
Crisis in Brazilian-Bolivian Relations," *Luso-Brazilian Review*, Vol. XI, No. 1
(© 1974 by the Board of Regents of the University of Wisconsin System), 19–40.

Library of Congress Cataloging in Publication Data

Seckinger, Ron.
The Brazilian monarchy and the South American
republics, 1822–1831.

Bibliography: p.
Includes index.
1. Brazil—Foreign relations—1822–1889. 2. Brazil—
Foreign relations—South America. 3. South America—
Foreign relations—Brazil. I. Title.
F2536.S42   1984   327.8108   83-25588
ISBN 0-8071-1156-2

To My Parents

Contents

Illustrations

Preface and Acknowledgments

This book examines the relations among the South American states during the early years of their existence. The historical moment was an important one. Due to the nature of the colonial regimes and the destructiveness of the wars of independence, the new nations of South America found themselves at a marked disadvantage in the international economy, which was dominated by the industrializing countries—especially Great Britain—of the North Atlantic basin. Moreover, the creole elites that came to power faced the task of building new states—that is, defining and defending claims to the national territory; achieving some degree of consensus with regard to political behavior; and organizing an administrative system, including a monopoly over the means of physical coercion. The problems of state building and of finding a place in the international economy necessarily influenced each nation's conduct of diplomacy.

Brazil serves as the focal point of this study for several reasons. As the largest and most populous country of South America, bordering on all of the other states save Chile (and later Ecuador), Brazil naturally provoked concern among its neighbors. As a monarchy headed by a European-born emperor, Brazil was ideologically isolated in a continent of republics. As the heir of Portuguese culture and language, Brazil faced a broad arc of Spanish-speaking peoples, generally hostile due to the traditional rivalry between the two Iberian crowns in South America. Moreover, Brazil was one of the participants in the most serious international crisis of the period, the long-standing competition with Argentina for possession of the left bank of the Plata estuary.

This study approaches South American international relations by focusing on the organization of the Brazilian government and its diplomatic activities from independence to the abdication of Emperor Pedro I in 1831. As will become obvious, the foreign policies of all the new states were closely intertwined, so that in the event of a dispute between Gran Colombia and Peru, for example, both parties took Brazil into account in their diplomatic maneuvering.

The nature of the Brazilian regime and the international environment were major determinants of the success or failure of Dom Pedro's policy initiatives. The survival of the Portuguese patrimonial state in Brazil gave the emperor a readymade administrative structure staffed by experienced bureaucrats—a clear advantage over the emerging Spanish American nations. His autocratic style, however, sparked domestic opposition that tended to undercut his conduct of foreign affairs. The suspicions of the Spanish Americans and the policies of the Great Powers also limited Brazil's ability to achieve its goals in South America.

Dom Pedro and the Brazilians believed the empire would be preeminent in the continent. They projected a "national image" that assumed Brazil's superiority by virtue of its monarchical institutions and greater territory, population, and natural resources. Some Spanish-American leaders, emphasizing the republican and supposedly democratic nature of their regimes, argued that ideological considerations should be paramount in international relations. Other figures, notably Simón Bolívar, promoted the idea of international cooperation and the peaceful resolution of conflicts by means of the Congress of Panama, but Brazil and most other countries rejected this vision. Underlying both approaches—and surviving their decline at the end of the 1820s—was the principle of national self-interest, by which each country pursued its own narrow goals.

Territorial and commercial issues were other concerns of those who directed foreign policy. The question of boundaries—particularly when involving immediate economic or strategic benefits—was one of the thorniest issues confronted by the new nations of South America. The crucial border conflicts involving Brazil were the Banda Oriental and Chiquitos disputes. Commerce tended to assume critical importance only when it concerned South America's major trading partners in Europe and North America; within the continent, commercial questions were of tangential interest unless linked to territorial and strategic issues.

By their writings and actions, South American leaders revealed their familiarity with prevailing European concepts of competition for relative advantage and of equilibrium-maintenance. Brazil figured prominently in such competition—sometimes as an active participant and sometimes as a potential enemy or ally of neighboring states embroiled in disputes of their own—and in concern over the international equilibrium. Although the new nations of South America constantly competed for relative advantage, they lacked the developed state system that made a balance-of-power or equilibrium model feasible.

By 1830 the South American countries had abandoned grand international designs and cut back their diplomatic contacts because of intractable domestic problems—especially the precarious nature of state organization. Nonetheless, the main characteristics of South American diplomacy were established during the 1820s.

A few technical notes are in order. The topical organization has necessitated some repetition. Whenever possible, I have cited original documents; when the original was unavailable, I have tried to cite the most accessible published copy, and in the absence of the latter I have cited a manuscript copy. Names have been rendered according to the nationality of the individual or the location of the place—for example, Antonio and Río de la Plata in Spanish versus Antônio and Rio de Janeiro in Portuguese. Modern Portuguese orthography has been employed in the text, but the original spelling of authors' names and the titles of publications has been preserved in the notes and bibliography.

Research for this study was sponsored by the American Philosophical Society, the Senior Fulbright-Hays Program, and the University of North Carolina Research Council. Some material on the annexation of Chiquitos and its repercussions was collected during the course of an earlier project funded by the Foreign Area Fellowship Program. Additional research was completed during the two years I was visiting professor of Brazilian history in the Curso de Pós-graduação em História at the Universidade Federal Fluminense in Niterói, Brazil.

Numerous persons have assisted in one way or another. Neill Macaulay, David Bushnell, and Eul-soo Pang offered encouragement and valuable counsel during the entire course of the project. Herbert S. Klein raised a number of provocative issues in conversations and subsequently gave advice on the structure of the book. José Honório Rodrigues, John J. Johnson, and Frank McCann read the manuscript and offered numerous suggestions. Cêurio de Oliveira prepared the maps, and W. James Shaw, the sole figure. Others who helped along the way include Charles W. Bergquist, Lolita Gutiérrez Brockington, Roberto Etchepareborda, Stanley E. Hilton, John W. Kitchens, William L. Lofstrom, F. W. O. Morton, Philip T. Parkerson, and John Hoyt Williams.

Thanks are due also to the custodians of the public archives of South America. I would like to single out a few whose kindness was particularly gratifying: Marta Maria Gonçalves, head of the Arquivo Histórico do Itamarati, whose enlightened stewardship has greatly benefitted Brazilian and foreign researchers alike; Raul Lima and José Gabriel da Costa Pinto, director and vice-director of the Arquivo Nacional in Rio de Janeiro; Gunnar Mendoza, director of the Archivo Nacional in Sucre; and Juan Siles Guevara, chief of the Archivo del Ministerio de Relaciones Exteriores y Culto in La Paz.

Aidyl de Carvalho Preis, coordinator of the Curso de Pósgraduação em História at the Universidade Federal Fluminense, made sure that I had time for research and writing. In addition, several friends and colleagues facilitated my visits to South America: Hebe Clementi and the late Julio César González in Buenos Aires; Alberto Crespo Rodas in La Paz; Ariosto Fernández in Montevideo; and Félix Denegri Luna in Lima.

Georgette Magassy Dorn and Everette Larson, of the Hispanic Division of the Library of Congress, and Dolores Moyano Martin, editor of the *Handbook of Latin American Studies*, also provided valuable assistance. Catherine F. Barton and Mark LaFlaur of Louisiana State University Press made innumerable suggestions for improvement and prepared the manuscript for publication.

Abbreviations Used in Footnotes

AAC	*Annaes do Parlamento Brazileiro: Assembléa Constituinte, 1823*
ACD	*Annaes do Parlamento Brazileiro: Câmara dos Srs. Deputados*
ADI	*Arquivo Diplomático da Independência*
Alvear Ms	Colección Carlos de Alvear
Ar-AGMREC	Archivo General del Ministerio de Relaciones Exteriores y Culto (Buenos Aires)
Ar-AGN	Archivo General de la Nación (Buenos Aires)
ASS	Archivio del Segretario di Stato
Avellán Ms	Colección T. Avellán Moncayo
Bo-AMREC	Archivo del Ministerio de Relaciones Exteriores y Culto (La Paz)
Bo-AN	Archivo Nacional (Sucre)
Bo-BN	Biblioteca Nacional (Sucre)
Bo-UMSA	Universidad Mayor de San Andrés (La Paz)
Br-AHI	Arquivo Histórico do Itamarati, Ministério das Relações Exteriores (Rio de Janeiro)
Br-AHMI	Arquivo Histórico do Museu Imperial (Petrópolis)
Br-AIHGB	Arquivo do Instituto Histórico e Geográfico Brasileiro (Rio de Janeiro)
Br-AN	Arquivo Nacional (Rio de Janeiro)
Br-BN	Biblioteca Nacional (Rio de Janeiro)
Carranza Ms	Archivo de Ángel Justiniano Carranza
Ch-AMRE	Archivo del Ministerio de Relaciones Exteriores (Santiago)
Ch-AN	Archivo Nacional (Santiago)
Co-ADC	Archivo Diplomático y Consular, Ministerio de Relaciones Exteriores (Bogotá)
Co-AHN	Archivo Histórico Nacional (Bogotá)

Abbreviations Used in Footnotes

FAA	Fondo ex Archivo Administrativo
Farini Ms	Colección Dr. Juan A. Farini
FMAHN	Fondo ex Museo y Archivo Histórico Nacional
FO	Foreign Office
García Ms	Colección Jacinto S. García
GB-PRO	Public Record Office (London)
Guido Ms	Archivo del Gral. Tomás Guido
H/AA	Historia/Archivo Anexo
HAHR	*Hispanic American Historical Review*
Herrera Ms	Archivo de Nicolás Herrera
MG/LR	Miscelánea General/La República
MI	Ministerio del Interior
MinNE	Ministério dos Negócios Estrangeiros
MinRE	Ministerio de Relaciones Exteriores
MNE	Brazilian Minister of Foreign Affairs (Ministro dos Negócios Estrangeiros)
MRE	Minister of Foreign Relations (Ministro de Relaciones Exteriores)
Pa-AN	Archivo Nacional (Asunción)
Pe-AMRE	Archivo del Ministerio de Relaciones Exteriores (Lima)
Po-ANTT	Arquivo Nacional da Torre do Tombo (Lisbon)
Ponte Ribeiro Ms	Arquivo Particular de Duarte da Ponte Ribeiro
RIHGB	*Revista do Instituto Histórico e Geográfico Brasileiro*
Rio-Branco Ms	Coleção Rio-Branco
Rück Ms	Colección Ernesto O. Rück
SGM	Secretaría de Guerra y Marina
SH	Sección "Historia"
SM	Seção de Manuscritos
Sp-AGI	Archivo General de Indias (Sevilla)
Sp-AHN	Archivo Histórico Nacional (Madrid)
SPE	Seção do Poder Executivo
Ur-AGN	Archivo General de la Nación (Montevideo)
Va-ASV	Archivio Segreto Vaticano (Vatican City)

The Brazilian Monarchy and the South American Republics
1822–1831

One · Brazil and the International Environment

ON DECEMBER 1, 1822, Pedro de Alcântara Francisco Antônio João Carlos Xavier de Paula Miguel Rafael Joaquim José Gonzaga Pascoal Cipriano Serafim de Bragança e Bourbon was invested as Constitutional Emperor and Perpetual Defender of Brazil. As heir to the Portuguese throne, Dom Pedro took easily to crown and scepter, and most of his subjects welcomed his creation of an independent Brazilian empire. Moreover, continuity in the transition from colony to nationhood facilitated the organization of the state apparatus.

Still, in his pursuit of foreign-policy objectives—such as diplomatic recognition, financial credits, possession of the Cisplatine (present-day Uruguay), supremacy in the Plata region, and protection of the Bragança dynasty's interests in Portugal—Pedro quickly discovered that royal credentials, an imperious manner, and experienced bureaucrats were not enough. In Brazil, he faced the spirited resistance of a liberal faction in the Chamber of Deputies. Abroad, he encountered the suspicions and conflicting goals of the South American republics as well as the determination of the Great Powers of Europe and North America to have their say in Latin American affairs. Pedro, like the leaders of other emerging states, found that challenging the rule of the parent country created as many problems as it resolved.

INDEPENDENCE

The new states of Latin America emerged from the complicated process of decolonization that took place in the American possessions of the Iberian crowns during the late eighteenth and early nineteenth centuries. From the beginning of colonization, the *raison d'être* of the American colonies had been to serve the interests of Spain and Portugal by purchasing goods exclusively from the parent countries and by supplying them with certain primary products—mainly minerals from Spanish America and agricultural commodities from Brazil. In return, the colonies received the putative benefits of metropolitan administration and military protection.[1]

This "colonial pact" began to give way during the eighteenth century under the strains created by changing economic and political conditions in Europe. While England rose to prominence and ultimately bested France in the competition for colonies and trade, the decline of Spain and Portugal continued. British traders aggressively penetrated the colonial markets of the Iberian nations. In the case of Spanish America, this penetration occurred in the face of resistance by the Spanish crown or, after 1713, by means of the *asiento* conceded in the Treaty of Utrecht, which gave the British a legal beachhead in the American trade. In the case of Brazil, the British gained access through a series of treaties with the Portuguese crown, beginning in 1642 and culminating in the Methuen Treaty of 1703. Ships bearing English wares easily marketed their goods in Spanish-American ports through the connivance of corrupt officials and in Brazilian ports by transshipment via Lisbon. Brazilians and Spanish Americans alike welcomed British products, which were cheaper and often of better quality than those supplied by the parent countries.

In the mid-eighteenth century, the Marquês de Pombal in Portugal and the Bourbon dynasty in Spain attempted to reestablish control over the empires through more-liberal trade policies, stimulation of colonial production, and administrative reorganization. Although these reforms yielded spectacular results in the short run, they proved inadequate to arrest the decline of the Iberian countries. What is more, they affected colonial groups and regions unequally, thereby increasing the stresses on the "colonial

1. This section generally follows Tulio Haperín-Donghi, *Historia contemporánea de América Latina* (Madrid, 1969); and Stanley J. and Barbara H. Stein, *The Colonial Heritage of Latin America: Essays on Economic Dependence in Perspective* (New York, 1970).

pact." The entanglement of Spain and Portugal in the wars of the French Revolution and the Napoleonic era completed their ruin and gave disaffected colonials the opportunity to throw off metropolitan domination.[2]

The Spanish-American revolutionaries believed that freer trade and Anglo-French political institutions would usher in a new age of prosperity and freedom. The Brazilian elite was less utopian in its outlook but still expected a bright future. In both Spanish America and Brazil, the new rulers were soon to discover that independence marked merely the first uncertain step toward the construction of a new order.

One of the many problems confronted by the new regimes in the 1820s was the old one of the economic relationship between Latin America and the North Atlantic world. The international division of labor was defined by, and awarded most benefits to, the industrializing nations. With their economies oriented toward the export of primary products, and with many regions suffering the effects of fifteen years of devastating warfare, the new states had little possibility of achieving a balanced development. Independence left unchanged the major characteristics of the Latin American economies: latifundia, monoculture, the export of primary products in exchange for manufactured goods, and periodic victimization by fluctuating prices of those primary products on the world market.

Great Britain, as the world's first industrial nation and mightiest maritime power, benefited enormously from the emancipation of Latin America. During the first years of independence, British traders flooded the Latin American market with manufactured goods of all kinds. Soon, however, the limitations of the market became obvious; with their enormous inequalities of income distribution, Latin American societies were less able to absorb foreign manufactures than first believed. Moreover, practically every government contracted, and then defaulted on, public loans raised in the London capital market during the early 1820s, thereby scaring off British investors for nearly three decades. Fol-

2. John Lynch, *The Spanish-American Revolutions, 1808–1826* (New York, 1973), 1–36. On the eighteenth-century reforms, see Kenneth Maxwell, *Conflicts and Conspiracies: Brazil and Portugal, 1750–1808* (Cambridge, England, 1973); and J. H. Parry, *The Spanish Seaborne Empire* (New York, 1967), 281–326.

3

lowing the initial euphoria, economic relations between the new states and Great Britain stabilized at a lower level of expectations on both sides. British traders continued to market their goods, albeit in reduced quantities, but Great Britain accepted Latin American imports selectively in order to protect production in its own colonial possessions.

The nature of the international economy hindered the organization of the new states. *State building* is used to convey the process by which the people of a defined territory organize themselves politically through the creation and legitimation of a single, coherent politico-administrative system.[3] The new nations of South America tried to accomplish this process, which had taken place over a period of centuries in Europe, within the space of a few years. They drew on their own limited political experience as well as many of the ideas of the eighteenth-century Enlightenment.

The transition from patrimonial to modern bureaucratic organization had proceeded further in the Spanish colonial dominions than in the Portuguese. Within a short time after the conquest of America, the kings of Castile managed to replace the rough-and-tumble conquerors with salaried officials trained in civil or canon law and paid from the royal share of mining revenues. The Spanish crown relied on an elaborate system of checks and balances to guarantee control over its bureaucratic servants. Through such devices as overlapping jurisdictions, periodic visitations by royal investigators, and judicial review of performance in office, the crown contrived to maintain its position as hub of the patrimonial state.[4]

The long wars for independence in Spanish America swept away much of the colonial administrative apparatus and deprived the old institutional order of its power and prestige. Rather than merely replace the Spaniards as rulers, the urban creole elite had to create a new structure, elaborate a new ideology embodying the

---

3. On state building in nineteenth-century Brazil, see Eul-soo Pang and Ron L. Seckinger, "The Mandarins of Imperial Brazil," *Comparative Studies in Society and History*, XIV (1972), 215–44; Fernando Uricoechea, *The Patrimonial Foundations of the Brazilian Bureaucratic State* (Berkeley, 1980); and José Murilo de Carvalho, *A construção da ordem: A elite política imperial* (Rio de Janeiro, 1980).

4. John L. Phelan, "Authority and Flexibility in the Spanish Imperial Bureaucracy," *Administrative Science Quarterly*, V (1960), 47–65.

principles of representative government and presidential succession, and establish the legitimacy of the new order. The political history of Spanish America during the nineteenth century bears witness to the complexity and inherent difficulty of these tasks. Even the most basic issue of all—the choice between monarchical or republican government—was not easily resolved, as shown (among other examples) by the attempted monarchist coup in Bolivia in 1829 and the founding of Maximilian's empire under the auspices of Mexican conservatives in the 1860s.[5]

Moreover, the urban creoles did not assume the mantle without challenge. Although the creoles had chafed under the restrictions of the Spanish colonial system and at the preference shown to peninsulars, they did not envisage an open society in which their social inferiors might compete for the perquisites of power and status. The duration and ferocity of the wars, however, opened the way for individuals from the colonial *castas*—that is, persons of mixed racial ancestry who previously had suffered legal discrimination—to rise to power through military prowess and to maintain themselves there with the army's backing. The Spanish-American nations thus found themselves saddled with voracious military establishments that consumed the lion's share of national revenues and lent themselves to adventurers bent on personal gain. This militarization of society, combined with the dispersion of political power throughout each country, encouraged chronic instability that only Chile and Paraguay managed to suppress by the mid-nineteenth century.[6]

The peculiar course of Brazilian independence partially mitigated the problems of organizing the state. In contrast to the Spanish colonies, the Portuguese empire had few salaried officials, due to the long delay (until the last years of the seventeenth century) in the discovery of precious metals in Brazil. The bureaucracy consisted of a handful of politico-military officials in key cities and a corps of trained magistrates who circulated throughout the empire via a series of appointments. These magistrates

5. See two seminal essays by Richard M. Morse, "Toward a Theory of Spanish American Government," *Journal of the History of Ideas*, XV (1954), 71–93, and "The Heritage of Latin America," in Louis Hartz, *The Founding of New Societies* (New York, 1964), 123–77.

6. See Tulio Halperín-Donghi, *The Aftermath of Revolution in Latin America*, trans. Josephine de Bunsen (New York, 1973).

The Brazilian Monarchy and the South American Republics

theoretically protected the crown's interests against encroachment by local elites, but in reality they often were co-opted by, or absorbed into, the local power structures. Other administrative functions were handled by the recipients of land benefices. Away from the coastal cities, landowners enjoyed more autonomy than their counterparts in Spanish America. In general, the Portuguese colonial administration was more loosely organized and less penetrating than the Spanish.[7]

As a consequence of the flight of the Portuguese court to Rio de Janeiro in 1808 to escape Napoleon's armies, the complete royal administrative structure was reestablished in Brazil. The royal family was accompanied by a retinue of 10,000 to 15,000 nobles, bureaucrats, and other hangers-on. The court's first preoccupation, to use Raymundo Faoro's apt image, lay "in situating the unemployed refugees in the political and administrative world, placing in each mouth a teat connected to the Treasury."[8]

To provide a livelihood for these parasites as well as a growing number of Brazilians hungry for sinecures, Prince Regent João, who would take the throne as João VI in 1816, greatly expanded the size of the bureaucracy in the capital and the captaincies over the next dozen years. He also opened Brazilian ports to friendly (mainly British) shipping, removed various restrictions on manufacturing and agriculture, improved fiscal administration, fostered a scientific and cultural spirit hitherto unknown in the Portuguese colony, and raised Brazil to the status of a kingdom in 1815. His reforms were piecemeal and incomplete, however, and tended to undermine the colonial regime without providing an alternative satisfactory to Brazil or to Lisbon.[9]

In 1820 a liberal revolution broke out in Portugal. Summoned home by the victorious rebels, João departed Rio in April, 1821,

7. Uricoechea, *Patrimonial Foundations*, 8–34. See also Fernando Uricoechea, "Formação e expansão do estado burocrático na Colômbia e no Brasil," *Estudos CEBRAP*, No. 21 (1977), 82–85. On the magistrates, see Stuart B. Schwartz, *Sovereignty and Society in Colonial Brazil: The High Court of Bahia and Its Judges, 1609–1751* (Berkeley, Calif., 1973), especially 171–90.
8. Raymundo Faoro, *Os donos do poder: Formação do patronato político brasileiro* (3rd ed. rev.; 2 vols.; Porto Alegre, 1976), I, 250.
9. Alan K. Manchester, "The Growth of Bureaucracy in Brazil, 1808–1821," *Journal of Latin American Studies*, IV (1972), 77–83; Emília Viotti da Costa, "The

6

leaving his elder son, Pedro, as prince regent. As the Côrtes—the ancient representative body of Portugal, now convened by the liberals—attempted to restore the commercial and political subordination of Brazil, the elite of south central Brazil turned to the idea of independence. Profoundly conservative in social matters, influential Brazilians would tolerate neither the abolition of slavery, on which most production rested, nor significant social change. The presence of the twenty-three-year-old prince regent in Rio de Janeiro offered the elite an opportunity to achieve independence under monarchical institutions and without mobilizing the unpredictable masses.

Dom Pedro accepted the role pressed on him, and during 1822 he increasingly asserted the autonomy of Brazil. In July a Spanish agent in Rio observed, "if there is still some kind of union [between Brazil and Portugal,] it is purely pretense of empty words and entirely contradictory concepts." Dom Pedro proclaimed Brazilian independence in a "manifesto to friendly nations" on August 6, but his more dramatic gesture at Ipiranga on September 7 represented the final break. Proclaimed constitutional emperor on October 12, he formally took the throne on December 1.[10]

The armed struggle with Portugal was relatively minor in comparison with the Spanish-American effort, and through British mediation Dom Pedro obtained Lisbon's recognition of his regime in November, 1825. Since Brazilian independence was realized under the leadership of the prince regent and with a mini-

---

Political Emancipation of Brazil," in A. J. R. Russell-Wood (ed.), *From Colony to Nation: Essays on the Independence of Brazil* (Baltimore, 1975), 51–58. The classic and still valuable study of this period is [Manoel de] Oliveira Lima, *Dom João VI no Brasil, 1808–1821* (3 vols.; Rio de Janeiro, 1945).

10. Antonio Luís Pereyra to Francisco Martínez de la Rosa, July 29, 1822, in Sp-AHN, Estado, legajo 5850. The preceding discussion of Brazilian independence is based on the following works: Octávio Tarquínio de Sousa, *José Bonifácio* (Rio de Janeiro, 1957), 149–234, Vol. I of *História dos fundadores do império do Brasil*; Sousa, *A vida de D. Pedro I* (3rd ed. rev.; 3 vols.; Rio de Janeiro, 1957), I, 136–400, II, 401–493, Vols. II–IV of *História dos fundadores do império do Brasil*; José Honório Rodrigues, *Independência: Revolução e contra-revolução* (Rio de Janeiro, 1975–76), I, 69–272; Tobias Monteiro, *História do império: A elaboração da independência* (Rio de Janeiro, 1927), 242–554; Costa, "Political Emancipation," 63–84; and Carlos Guilherme Mota [ed.], *1822: Dimensões* (São Paulo, 1972).

mum of violence and popular mobilization, the bureaucracy survived virtually intact in configuration and personnel.

THE BRAZILIAN STATE

The Portuguese patrimonial state lived on in independent Brazil. Like his father, Pedro assigned bureaucratic posts as benefices, used the Bank of Brazil as an adjunct of the imperial treasury, and generally ruled as though the political administration were his personal property.[11] The change from absolute to constitutional monarchy had no immediate effect on governance. Indeed, the very history of that change illustrates the underlying continuity. Pedro called for the election of a Constituent Assembly to draft a constitution for the empire; but in November, 1823, incensed by the assembly's baiting of the Portuguese who had remained in Brazil, the emperor dissolved the body, thereby touching off a short-lived republican rebellion in the northeastern provinces. He named ten of his closest advisors to a Council of State, which drafted a constitution to his liking, and he then conferred the charter on his subjects.

The Constitution of 1824 left no doubt concerning the locus of power within the Brazilian state. The government was divided into executive, legislative, and judicial branches, following the prevailing Western political theory, but had a "fourth branch" of sorts. "The moderating power," declared the charter, "is the key of the entire political organization, and is delegated exclusively to the Emperor, as supreme chief of the nation and its first representative, so that he may unceasingly keep watch over the preservation of the independence, equilibrium and harmony of the other political powers [*i.e.*, branches]." The "moderating power" gave the emperor certain prerogatives beyond those he held as head of the executive branch. Among other things, he could dissolve the Chamber of Deputies and call for new elections. In contrast to the British parliamentary system, the chiefs of imperial ministries were accountable to the emperor rather than to the lower house of the legislature.[12]

11. Uricoechea, *Patrimonial Foundations*, 39.
12. Articles 98–101. Floriano de Aguiar Dias (ed.), *Constituições do Brasil* ([Rio de Janeiro], 1975), I, 145–46.

Other powers accrued to Dom Pedro as chief executive, including the direction of foreign relations. The constitution authorized the emperor to name diplomatic and commercial agents, conduct negotiations with other nations, arrange treaties, declare war, and make peace.[13] The legislature was to be advised of treaties, declarations of war, and peace initiatives; otherwise, the legislators had few constitutional prerogatives in the area of foreign affairs. Control over appropriations gave the general assembly a means of influencing the conduct of diplomacy, but the only international act requiring legislative approval was the hypothetical case of a peacetime treaty involving the cession of Brazilian territory.[14]

By temperament as well as law, Dom Pedro dominated the government. The emperor, only twenty-four years old when he took the throne, was a brave, dashing womanizer with supreme self-confidence and a mercurial temper. His own experience in statecraft was limited, for Dom João had excluded him from government deliberations before naming him regent of Brazil. Unlike his timid and indecisive father, Pedro always tried to control events and expand his authority; his attempt to treat the quasi-elective office of senator as a prebend is a prime example of this tendency. He objected to any public demands and chose abdication in 1831 rather than bow to popular pressure to replace his cabinet, declaring: "I will do everything *for* the people, but nothing *by* the people."[15]

Pedro's attitude toward his counselors was equally cavalier. The Council of State—composed of ten lifetime members plus the imperial ministers—advised the emperor on major issues and was the most important body involved in decision-making.[16] The of-

13. Article 102, paragraphs 6–9. *Ibid.*, 146–47.
14. Article 15, and article 102, paragraph 8. *Ibid.*, 93–94, 147. For a discussion of the legal structure of the empire, see João Camillo de Oliveira Torres, *A democracia coroada: Teoria política do império do Brasil* (Rio de Janeiro, 1957).
15. John Armitage, *The History of Brazil from the Period of the Arrival of the Braganza Family in 1808, to the Abdication of Don Pedro the First in 1831* (2 vols., London, 1836), II, 129. On Pedro's personality, see *ibid.*, 104–105, 135–41; Sousa, *A vida de D. Pedro I*, I, 74–88, 136–43; and Rodrigues, *Independência*, IV, 6–13. On Pedro's abuse of Senate appointments, see Afonso de Escragnolle Taunay, *O senado do império* (São Paulo, [1942]), 25–27; and Armitage, *The History of Brazil*, I, 236–37.
16. Analyzing the process of decision making in Brazil during the First Empire is difficult. The internal documentation of the foreign ministry is very poor for this

ficials chosen by Dom Pedro might have contributed effectively to the formulation of domestic and foreign policies, for they had a relatively high degree of administrative experience. The Portuguese crown had never systematically excluded Brazilians from administrative careers.[17] Moreover, no wholesale exodus of Portuguese occurred immediately after independence, and the emperor could call on Portuguese as well as Brazilians who had served in the colonial administration.

The presence of experienced personnel in Brazil provided a sharp contrast with the situation in Spanish America. The Spanish crown had deliberately excluded creoles from higher administrative positions during the last third of the eighteenth century.[18] Peninsular-born Spaniards dominated the colonial bureaucracy when the independence movements began about 1810, and relatively few trained administrators remained after the fighting ceased. The British minister to Bogotá reported in 1826: "It is also said, that not a person is to be found in Peru capable of taking charge of the Department of Foreign Affairs, and indeed that every department is badly administered." He went on to make a general observation about the absence of experienced personnel:

> It will not however appear so strange, that there should in the new States be some difficulty in getting persons qualified to fill these situations properly, when it be considered that under the Spanish regime almost every Government Situation was filled by European Spaniards, and thus the Natives of the Country have now in many instances found themselves called upon to undertake the duties of offices, in the discharge of which they had not the least experience, and to which the bent of their Studies had never been directed. From this difficulty, Colombia it-

period and contains no memoranda discussing options or presenting the opinions of government officials. The records of the Council of State for the years 1824–27 are missing, and those for the period 1828–34 are limited to summaries (*atas*) rather than the lengthy files available for the years after 1841. In the absence of such records, a brief and impressionistic sketch of the different elements involved in formulating foreign policy must suffice. See José Honório Rodrigues' introduction to Brazil, Senado Federal, *Atas do Conselho de Estado* (Brasília, 1973), I, xv–lxiv.

17. Schwartz, *Sovereignty and Society*, 71, 284–86, 296–97, 352–56.
18. Lynch, *The Spanish-American Revolutions*, 1–36.

self, is not exempt, although I beleive [*sic*] in a less degree than the other States.[19]

The disparity in administrative experience may be seen in a comparison of the individuals who directed the foreign ministries of Brazil and Colombia. Of the ten persons who headed the Brazilian ministry of foreign affairs under Pedro I, nine had occupied administrative posts in Portugal and Brazil before 1821. In contrast, not one of the first ten foreign ministers of Colombia (1821–1831) had held an important Crown-appointed position. Domingo Caicedo, who served as secretary of the Spanish Cortes following the forced abdication of Ferdinand VII in 1808, was the only one of the Colombian ministers who could claim any government experience under Spanish rule.[20]

The Brazilian advantage did not guarantee a rational and efficient administration. For one thing, the selection of officials hinged on personal considerations rather than merit. Like his father, Dom Pedro provided for his dependents by giving them government jobs. With the exception of José Bonifácio de Andrada e Silva, who served as minister of the empire and foreign affairs from January, 1822, until November, 1823, none of the emperor's chief advisors distinguished himself by an independent mind or a willingness to disagree with Dom Pedro. One observer, the British merchant John Armitage, commented that, following the dissolution of the Constituent Assembly, "men of integrity were as much as possible excluded from [the emperor's] presence; and the plain and simple language of truth and soberness, was superceded by the vilest adulation."[21]

All of the persons named to the Council of State in 1823 were

19. Joseph Campbell to George Canning (Separate), July 19, 1826, in GB-PRO, FO 18/27, fls. 202–203. For similar comments by United States agents, see William Tudor to Henry Clay (Confidential), May 17 and August 24, 1826, in William R. Manning (ed.), *Diplomatic Correspondence of the United States Concerning the Independence of the Latin-American Nations* (New York, 1925), III, 1796–97, 1807–1808; and Heman Allen to Clay, August 26, 1826, in Manning (ed.), *Diplomatic Correspondence*, II, 1114.

20. A. Tavares de Lyra, "Os ministros de estado da independência á república," *RIHGB*, CXCIII (1946), 13, 33, 42, 49, 53, 62, 66, 68, 76, 86; [José Smith de Vasconcellos and Rodolpho Smith de Vasconcellos], *Archivo nobiliarchico brasileiro* (Lausanne, 1918), 26, 90, 334; Colombia, MinRE, *Historia de la Cancillería de San Carlos*, Vol. I: *Pórtico* (Bogotá, 1942), 111–38.

21. Armitage, *The History of Brazil*, I, 200.

sycophants. Clemente Ferreira França, whom Armitage characterized as "about the most obsequious, abject, and time-serving of the entire council," defended himself against criticism without denying his subservience: "My colleagues (observed he) have not hesitated to tax me with servility, but the charge is utterly unfounded. I am not one whit more servile than they are, but the fact is, I am less hypocritical."[22] Pedro relied particularly on Portuguese courtiers, who often were directly dependent on state employment and less likely to articulate the interests of Brazilian groups; the predominance of less able Portuguese in the highest positions of government was one of the most serious Brazilian grievances and contributed to the erosion of Pedro's popularity.

For another thing, the emperor had little patience with advice contrary to his own thoughts. Sir Charles Stuart, the British minister who negotiated the 1825 treaty between Brazil and Portugal, described Dom Pedro's interaction with his counselors:

> As no one, among His own people dares to contradict Him, the imprudent measures adopted by the Government are the result of the fits of Passion, to which he gives way. . . .
>
> Aware, that His Ministers, either from incapacity, or from the Selfish feeling, which has guided their whole Conduct, take no real interest in the Welfare of the Country, He frequently says, that their Sentiments are of no value with Him, except in as far as they may support His own views, in cases, which affect public opinion, and this feeling is strongly illustrated by His remark, that, notwithstanding the bad Education which he has received, he considers Himself the member of the Cabinet, who is the most equal to the task imposed upon Him.

Stuart further remarked that Pedro was surrounded by "numerous Flatterers" and that "the defects of His Character" compelled "his Council, his family, and all around him to submit blindly to his will."[23]

The Senate, filled by and large with the emperor's aged loyal-

22. *Ibid.*, 359–61.
23. Sir Charles Stuart to Canning (Private, No. 9), September 5, 1825, in GB-PRO, FO 13/20, fls. 58–62. For similar comments, see Condy Raguet to Clay, June 1, 1825, in Manning (ed.), *Diplomatic Correspondence*, II, 820.

ists, was as docile as the Council of State and the cabinet. The Chamber of Deputies, on the other hand, refused to follow the emperor's lead and increasingly attacked his policies, including his conduct of foreign affairs.

By the time the General Assembly convened for the first time in May, 1826, Dom Pedro and his coterie had governed without legislative consultation for two and a half years. During that time, the imperial government had dispatched diplomatic and consular agents to a dozen countries, completed treaties with Portugal and France, and opened negotiations with Great Britain. A group of liberal deputies led by Bernardo Pereira de Vasconcelos sought to assert the authority of the legislature and to check the deficit spending by the government. They found the foreign ministry a convenient target.

In response to repeated demands for information concerning his department, the minister of foreign affairs, the Visconde de Inhambupe, sent an officious letter to the Chamber of Deputies in June, 1826. While denying that imperial ministers were under any constitutional obligation to render accounts to the legislature, he volunteered a brief report on Brazilian relations with other nations. He mentioned that diplomatic agents had been named to the major European courts and asserted the emperor's right to conduct foreign affairs on his own: "His Imperial Majesty will continue to organize the diplomatic corps in such a manner that, without burdening the public treasury with excessive expense, he will not fail to have representatives and political agents in the principal courts and states, in order to preserve with due force, as circumstances permit, those relations of friendship and harmony from which the prosperity of this empire results, just as is done today by other nations."[24]

The deputies were offended by Inhambupe's grudging cooperation, superficial accounting, and affirmation of the emperor's prerogatives. The committee on finance and diplomacy criticized the minister's report and recommended that the Chamber demand copies of the treaties with Portugal and France, reasons for the impasse in the negotiations with Great Britain, and an explanation of the continued naming of diplomatic agents before the passage of a law setting the number of posts and their salaries.

24. *ACD*, 1826, II, 206–207.

13

After a discussion in which several deputies voiced their disapproval of the government's attitude and procedure, the Chamber adopted a resolution incorporating these points.[25] Thus commenced the Chamber's hostility toward the ministry of foreign affairs. Specific issues—the government's involvement in the affairs of Portugal, its conduct of the war against the United Provinces, and the slave-trade treaty with Great Britain, for example—often provoked criticism. But many deputies condemned the foreign service on general grounds, challenging the size and expense of the diplomatic corps whenever the budget was considered. The main charges may be summarized as follows: (1) Given its financial circumstances, Brazil could not afford to maintain a large diplomatic corps. (2) Foreign-service personnel were chosen according to personal considerations rather than merit and were demonstrably incompetent. (3) The government's conduct of foreign affairs without the consent of the General Assembly was unconstitutional. (4) The government should have emphasized relations with other American states rather than with Europe. The foreign ministry had its defenders in the Chamber, but they tended to be on the defensive.[26]

The deputies' disgust with the foreign service ran deep. Bernardo Pereira de Vasconcelos, always the most vociferous critic of Pedro I's regime, asserted in 1827: "I say, and I say again, that our diplomatic corps is the worst possible (*applause*). . . . We have seen loans badly contracted and commissions evilly obtained. (*General applause.*) Treaties badly conducted. (*General applause.*) Negotiations very badly handled (*applause*), and with such fruits can it be said that our diplomatic agents are good? No, Mr. president, they are bad, or, better said, they are awful." Another deputy stated that he had observed Brazilian representatives in action in Europe over several years, leading him to the conclusion "that Brazilian diplomacy was absolutely futile."[27]

25. *Ibid.*, III, 239–42. The minister of foreign affairs furnished the requested information in a more conciliatory tone. Visconde de Inhambupe to José Ricardo da Costa e Aguiar (Copy), July 31, 1826, in Br-AHI, Vol. 291/3/12, fls. 4–5.

26. For the key debates on the foreign ministry, see the following: *ACD*, 1827, IV, 164–75, 200–210; 1828, IV, 91–103; 1829, II, 36–39, V, 25; 1830, I, 88–89, II, 107–112, 335–40, 650–705; 1831, II, 142–56. As already mentioned, the legislature actually had few constitutional prerogatives in the area of foreign relations.

27. *Ibid.*, 1827, IV, 203; 1830, II, 673.

Each year, the liberals attempted to slash appropriations for the foreign service. In a joint session of the Senate and the Chamber of Deputies, Senator Nicolau Pereira de Campos Vergueiro picked up the refrain, asserting that "our diplomacy, instead of bringing us utility, has caused us great harm with the treaties and conventions that it has made to our loss; therefore we should spend the least possible on it, and perhaps we will thereby do ourselves the least possible evil." Two deputies even suggested dispensing with the diplomatic corps entirely, and another proposed a five-year moratorium on international relations to provide relief "from that vulture that gnaws our innards."[28]

As mentioned above, one of the deputies' criticisms of the foreign service had to do with its size. During the years of the First Empire, Brazil dispatched diplomatic agents to twenty-four foreign capitals—more than twice the number sent by Colombia and Peru, and more than three times as many as sent by Argentina, as shown in the accompanying table. The advantage was due partly to greater European willingness to accept Brazil, thanks to its monarchical government and the early recognition of its independence by Portugal. The higher number also reflected Dom Pedro's efforts to preserve the familiar monarchical style in all aspects of his regime. The emperor emulated the European courts and pro-

NUMBER OF CAPITALS TO WHICH FOUR SOUTH AMERICAN
COUNTRIES ACCREDITED DIPLOMATS, 1822–1831

Country	Number of Capitals
Brazil	24
Colombia	10
Peru	10
Argentina	7

SOURCE: Raul Adalberto de Campos (comp.), *Relações diplomáticas do Brasil* . . . (Rio de Janeiro, 1913), 3–128; Antonio José Uribe (ed.), *Anales diplomáticos y consulares de Colombia* (Bogotá, 1900–59), III, 6–62; Arturo García Salazar and Jorge Linch, *Guía práctica para los diplomáticos y cónsules peruanos* (Lima, 1918), I, 89–133; Argentine Republic, Ministerio de Relaciones Exteriores y Culto, *Catálogo de la biblioteca, mapoteca y archivo* (Buenos Aires, 1910), 879–83.

28. *Ibid.*, 1830, II, 691; 1829, V, 25; 1831, II, 150; 1830, II, 338.

claimed Brazil's importance by maintaining a large diplomatic corps. Moreover, the survival of the Portuguese patrimonial state allowed him to organize the foreign service more rapidly than the republican governments of South America.[29] The diplomatic agents of all of the new states were largely on their own, because communications were so slow. A Brazilian diplomat in, say, Paris who requested instructions on a given matter would have to wait months for a reply from Rio, by which time changing circumstances might have rendered the instructions useless. Within South America the situation was even more difficult, since trade and communication between South American countries were limited. The Brazilian government could obtain information quickly only from Montevideo and Buenos Aires; elsewhere, the mails followed the routes of commercial shipping or the British packet boats. In 1830 communication between Rio and Bogotá went via New York and took four or five months, and as late as 1844 the Brazilian minister in Bogotá sent his dispatches by way of London. Loss or misdirection of correspondence sometimes compounded the normal delays. To cite one example, the Colombian government recalled its minister to Rio in December, 1826, but the message did not arrive until February, 1828—about fourteen months later.[30]

THE GREAT POWERS AND LATIN AMERICA

Another of the deputies' criticisms was the Europe-oriented nature of Brazilian diplomacy. As liberals, Dom Pedro's opponents understandably felt an affinity with the Spanish-American revolutionaries, who were seeking to create new societies free of Old World corruption. But even the Spanish Americans, despite their anti-European rhetoric and efforts to form American alliances, could not ignore the reality of Europe's political and economic preeminence. Like the Brazilian emperor, they placed great im-

29. For a more detailed discussion, see Ron Seckinger, "O estado brasileiro e a política externa no século XIX," *Dados*, No. 19 (1978), 111–33.

30. [Monsignor Pietro Ostini] to Cardinal Albani (No. 66), July 3, 1830, in Va-ASV, ASS, rubrica 251, busto 448, fasciolo 3; Ernesto Ferreira França to Manuel Cerqueira Lima, November 22, 1844, in Br-AHI, Arquivo II, tomo 403/2/1; José Manuel Restrepo to Leandro Palacios (Copy), December 7, 1826, in Co-ADC, tomo 50, fl. 32; Palacios to José Rafael Revenga (No. 27), February 28, 1828, in Co-ADC, tomo 158, fls. 46–47.

portance on developing diplomatic and commercial relations with the European courts as well as the rising power in North America. Initially, the Europeans were suspicious of, and in some cases hostile toward, the new states of Latin America. The political climate in Europe was extremely conservative in the years following the defeat of Napoleon. A series of conferences at Chaumont, Vienna, and Paris in 1814 and 1815 had formalized the anti-Napoleonic coalition of Great Britain, Austria, Prussia, and Russia. The resulting Quadruple Alliance, which became the Quintuple Alliance when Bourbon France was admitted in 1818, aimed at maintaining a balanced state system on the war-weary continent. In practice, a preoccupation with "legitimacy"—that is, the legitimacy of monarchical rule in the face of liberal, revolutionary threats—suggested that the Continental Powers pursued reaction above all else. Austria sent troops to stifle a liberal revolution in Naples in 1821, and France did the same in Spain two years later. Interventions also were proposed for Portugal, Greece, and Spanish America.

This antiliberal, anticonstitutionalist policy led many to confuse the Continental Alliance—that is, the Quintuple Alliance minus Great Britain—with the "Holy Alliance." The latter was the creation of the Russian tsar, Alexander I. In 1815 Alexander drafted a treaty by which the signatories agreed to conduct their affairs in accordance with Christian precepts, and most of the European states eventually signed the document. The treaty was not antirepublican per se; the Swiss government ratified it, and the United States declined an invitation to do without showing any horror at the union. In reality, the "Holy Alliance" was no more than a pious declaration of principles, and Russia, like the other monarchies, followed a realistic foreign policy based on self-interest. But the reactionary and interventionist policy of Austria, Russia, and France persuaded liberals in Europe and the Americas that the European monarchs were pursuing some sinister design masked by Alexander's innocuous words.[31] Even though

31. C. W. Crawley, "International Relations, 1815–1830," in *The New Cambridge Modern History* (12 vols.; Cambridge, England, 1964–68), IX, 668–75. For European attitudes toward Latin America, see the following: Manfred Kossok, *Historia de la Santa Alianza y la emancipación de América Latina* (Buenos Aires, 1968); William Spence Robertson, *France and Latin American Independence* (Baltimore, 1939); Russell H. Bartley, *Imperial Russia and the Struggle for*

Brazil retained a monarchical form of government, Pedro's insistence on independence from Portugal and his acceptance of the idea of a constitution discouraged the European powers from recognizing his regime. Fortunately for Brazil and Spanish America, Great Britain operated independently of its allies. Unable to persuade Ferdinand VII to consider any concessions to his subjects in the New World, Prime Minister and Foreign Secretary Lord Castlereagh warned the other European powers in 1817 that Great Britain would not tolerate the use of force against the Spanish-American rebels by any nation other than Spain. British maritime strength thus shielded the insurgents from intervention while they fought against Spanish forces in America. George Canning, who succeeded Castlereagh as foreign secretary in September, 1822, continued his predecessor's policies with regard to Spanish America. At the end of 1824, Great Britain unilaterally recognized the governments of Buenos Aires, Colombia, and Mexico, thereby becoming the first European country to establish diplomatic relations with the Spanish-American republics.[32]

Brazil presented special problems for British policy. On the one hand, Canning did not wish to antagonize Portugal, Britain's client state and oldest ally, by recognizing Dom Pedro's secessionist regime. On the other hand, Canning had good reasons for wanting to preserve and strengthen relations with Rio de Janeiro. First, Brazil was the most important market for British manufactured products in all of Latin America. Trade between the two countries had expanded enormously following the commercial treaty of 1810, which had augmented the British advantage in industrial production and carrying capacity. Unless diplomatic relations were established with the independent government in Rio, Great Britain stood to lose the Brazilian market. Second, Canning hoped that monarchy would be preserved in Brazil, which offered a last opportunity to avoid a polarization between a republican New World and the monarchical Old. And third, Canning believed that he

Latin American Independence, 1808–1828 (Austin, 1978); Ezekiel Stanley Ramírez, *As relações entre a Áustria e o Brasil, 1815–1889*, trans. Américo Jacobina Lacombe (São Paulo, 1968), 28–41.

32. C. K. Webster, "Introduction," in C. K. Webster (ed.), *Britain and the Independence of Latin America, 1812–1830: Select Documents from the Foreign Office Archives* (London, 1938), I, 12–23; William W. Kaufmann, *British Policy and the Independence of Latin America, 1804–1828* (New Haven, Conn., 1951).

could demand an end to the Brazilian slave trade in exchange for recognition of independence.

Canning's solution called for British mediation between Dom Pedro and his father, securing Portuguese recognition of Brazil and protecting Great Britain's interests in both countries. At length, thanks largely to the work of the British negotiator, Sir Charles Stuart, the Portuguese crown officially acknowledged the independence of its former American colony in November, 1825. This opened the way for recognition by Great Britain and the other European monarchies. As compensation for services rendered, Canning demanded and obtained new treaties that ratified Britain's commercial privileges in Brazil and abolished the slave trade.[33]

United States policy toward Latin America was hamstrung neither by antirepublican sentiment nor by obligations to the Spanish crown, and Washington's official neutrality generally favored the insurgents. President James Monroe extended formal recognition to Gran Colombia and Mexico in 1822 and to the other new states over the next few years.[34]

Brazil, as usual, presented a unique problem. Relations between Washington and the Portuguese court in Rio de Janeiro had been troubled for years, and the retention of monarchical institutions by Brazil was viewed with some distaste by the Monroe administration. But the United States had already recognized the Mexican regime of Agustín I, and this precedent, coupled with a quickening commercial interest in Brazil, overcame the lingering antimonarchical sentiment in Washington. In May, 1824, Monroe received the Brazilian representative, signifying formal acceptance of Dom Pedro's government.[35] The promulgation of the

33. On British policy toward Brazil, see Webster, "Introduction," in Webster (ed.), *Britain and the Independence of Latin America*, I, 53–66; Kaufmann, *British Policy*, 182–200; Alan K. Manchester, *British Preëminence in Brazil: Its Rise and Decline. A Study in European Expansion.* (Chapel Hill, 1933), 136–58; and Leslie Bethell, *The Abolition of the Brazilian Slave Trade: Britain, Brazil and the Slave Trade Question, 1807–1869* (Cambridge, England, 1970), 27–61. On British mediation of the treaty between Brazil and Portugal, see Caio de Freitas, *George Canning e o Brasil: Influência da diplomacia inglêsa na formação brasileira* (São Paulo, 1958), II, 169–337. The Brazilian government did not enforce the ban on the slave traffic until after 1850.

34. Arthur Preston Whitaker, *The United States and the Independence of Latin America, 1800–1830* (Baltimore, 1941), 100–392.

35. Stanley E. Hilton, "The United States and Brazilian Independence," in Russell-Wood (ed.), *From Colony to Nation*, 109–129; João Pandiá Calógeras, *A política exterior do império* (Rio de Janeiro, 1927–28), II, 3–396.

Monroe Doctrine in 1823, warning the European powers against attempts to acquire territory in the Western Hemisphere, had no serious impact at this time.[36]

By 1825, then, the United States and Great Britain had taken the lead in recognizing the new states. As mentioned earlier, Dom Pedro wasted no time in sending diplomatic representatives to Washington and the capitals of Europe. Brazil's relations with the other nations of South America developed more slowly. The emperor had little interest in the rest of the continent, with the exception of the Plata region.

THE NEW STATES OF SPANISH SOUTH AMERICA

At the time of Brazilian independence, relatively stable regimes were emerging in several neighboring countries. Although this stability proved ephemeral, the revolutionary elites seemed to be justified, during the early 1820s, in believing that prosperity and orderly self-government were at hand. All of the new regimes had, to a greater or lesser extent, an authoritarian cast.

Argentina was to be Dom Pedro's nemesis. The creole elite of Buenos Aires, which headed the independence movement, tried to maintain control over the entire territory of the viceroyalty of the Río de la Plata, but Upper Peru (Bolivia), Paraguay, and the Banda Oriental (Uruguay) went their separate ways. The dispersion of power in the ill-named United Provinces of the Río de la Plata was such that, by 1820, no national administration could be said to exist. During that year, the government in Buenos Aires changed hands on the average of twice a month, and ever afterwards "1820" would symbolize the nadir of national fortunes. Soon, however, the province of Buenos Aires entered a period of peace and prosperity under Martín Rodríguez and Bernardino Rivadavia. The administration inaugurated an ambitious program of economic development, relying on British capital, free trade, and the export of hides, tallow, and jerked beef. The *caudillos* (political bosses) of the interior, however, resented the preeminence of the *Porteños*—as the inhabitants of Buenos Aires were known—and resisted many of the capital's economic and liberal reform policies. An unsuccessful attempt to secure the reincorporation of

36. Dexter Perkins, *A History of the Monroe Doctrine* (Boston, 1955), 27–64.

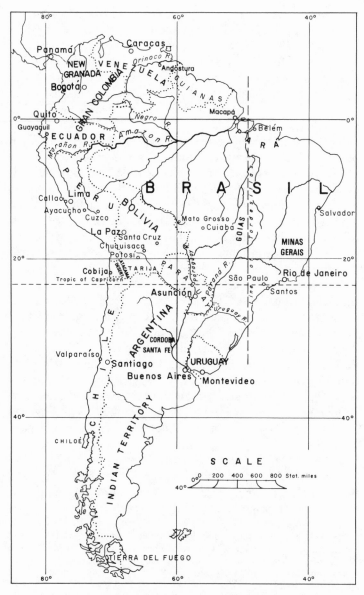

South America in 1830
(All borders approximate and in dispute)

the Banda Oriental into the United Provinces contributed to the government's financial dilemma and to the erosion of its popularity. After 1827 federalism triumphed in Argentina and became the banner of Juan Manuel de Rosas, who dominated the political scene from 1829 until 1851. Argentina was the only country in which "public opinion" may be said to have carried much weight, and even there it was limited to the city of Buenos Aires and to the pre-Rosas period.[37]

The Paraguayan elite early established its independence from Buenos Aires, declaring Paraguay an autonomous republic in 1811. A few years later, Dr. José Gaspar de Francia emerged as the dominant figure and ruled with brutal efficiency until his death in 1840. His dictatorial regime gave Paraguay stability without any pretense of representative government. He responded to hostility from his neighbors by maintaining his fiefdom in diplomatic isolation and by permitting only a controlled trade with Brazil and the littoral provinces of Argentina.[38]

Revolution in the Banda Oriental took on an aspect of agrarian radicalism under José Gervasio Artigas. To eliminate his threat to southern Brazil, Portuguese troops occupied the region in 1811–1812 and again in 1816—the latter time with the acquiescence of the Buenos Aires government. After chasing Artigas into exile, the Portuguese crown incorporated the Banda Oriental into the Kingdom of Brazil in 1821, and, after declaring Brazilian independence, Pedro I determined to maintain possession of the territory. Following an inconclusive war, Brazil and the United Provinces agreed to the creation of the independent state of Uruguay in 1828.[39]

In Chile, liberated by the Argentine General José de San Martín's army of Argentines and Chilean exiles in 1818–1819, Bernardo O'Higgins took the title of supreme director and undertook a reform program similar to those of the other republics.

37. Tulio Halperín-Donghi, *Politics, Economics and Society in Argentina in the Revolutionary Period*, trans. Richard Southern (Cambridge, England, 1975); Miron Burgin, *The Economic Aspects of Argentine Federalism, 1820–1852* (Cambridge, Mass., 1946), 3–159; Ricardo Piccirilli, *Rivadavia y su tiempo* (2nd ed.; Buenos Aires, [1960]).

38. John Hoyt Williams, *The Rise and Fall of the Paraguayan Republic, 1800–1870* (Austin, 1979), 24–99.

39. John Street, *Artigas and the Emancipation of Uruguay* (Cambridge, England, 1959).

O'Higgins' inability to consolidate his authority resulted in his overthrow in 1823, which was followed by a series of regional uprisings and abortive constitutions. In 1829–1830 a conservative coalition succeeded in taking power.[40] In the north, the Republic of Gran Colombia was the creation of Simón Bolívar, greatest of the revolutionary leaders. Based on the territorial boundaries of the viceroyalty of New Granada, it included New Granada proper (present-day Colombia plus Panama), the captaincy general of Venezuela, and the presidency of Quito (present-day Ecuador). Consolidation of the state was difficult because of a virulent regionalism, the divergent economic interests of different groups, financial problems common to all of the new regimes, and the division of the elite's allegiance between Bolívar and his vice-president, Francisco de Paula Santander. While the Liberator—as Bolívar was known in northern South America—led the campaign against the Spanish in Peru from late 1821 until 1825 and headed the independent Peruvian government until mid-1826, Santander attempted to carry out basic liberal reforms against insuperable odds. When Bolívar returned to assume the administration, he found Gran Colombia disintegrating under the stress of sectional interests. His personal prestige, more conservative policies, and concessions to regionalism held off the centrifugal forces for a few more years, but, in 1829 and 1830, Venezuela and Ecuador proclaimed their independence, leaving the truncated state of New Granada in the center.[41]

Peru had vested interests that only reluctantly accepted the idea of independence from Spain. Not until a combined Argentine-Chilean expeditionary force landed on the Peruvian coast did the war turn in favor of the insurgents. Following unfruitful experiments in government by San Martín and subsequently by Peruvian creoles, the area around Lima acclaimed Bolívar dictator. After defeating the last Spanish forces, the Liberator gave Peru an authoritarian constitution he had originally written for Bolivia. He hoped to create a powerful Andean Federation, composed of

---

40. Simon Collier, *Ideas and Politics of Chilean Independence, 1808–1833* (Cambridge, England, 1967).

41. David Bushnell, *El régimen de Santander en la Gran Colombia*, trans. Jorge Orlando Melo (Bogotá, 1966), and "Santanderismo y bolivarismo: Dos matices en pugna," *Desarrollo Económico*, VIII (1968), 243–61; Gerhard Masur, *Simon Bolivar* (Albuquerque, N.M., 1948).

Gran Colombia, Peru, and Bolivia; but, after his departure for Bogotá, a coup in Lima overturned his constitution and removed Peru from his orbit. A series of military strongmen ruled Peru thereafter.[42]

Upper Peru was the last region to be liberated from the Spaniards. In 1825 the creole elite honored Bolívar by offering him the lifetime presidency and bestowing his name on the new republic. The constitution he drafted for Bolivia reflected his growing conservatism; the hallmark of the new state was to be political and social stability, guaranteed by a centralized, authoritarian political system. In January, 1826, the Liberator left Bolivia to tend to his duties in Peru and Gran Colombia, leaving Antonio José de Sucre in his place as president. A reluctant administrator, Sucre nonetheless attempted to carry out his mentor's program, which called for administrative reorganization, fiscal and educational reform, and the destruction of the Church's power. Only the last of these had been accomplished, however, when a Peruvian invasion enjoying the tacit support of the Bolivian elite overthrew Sucre's regime in mid-1828.[43]

These were Dom Pedro's neighbors. Inattentive at first, he eventually came to understand that his destiny was bound up with theirs.

42. Jorge Basadre, *Historia de la república del Perú, 1822–1933* (6th ed. rev.; Lima [1968]), I–III.

43. William Lee Lofstrom, *The Promise and Problem of Reform: Attempted Social and Economic Change in the First Years of Bolivian Independence* (Ithaca, N.Y., 1972).

Two • Ideology, Internationalism and Self-Interest

ON DECEMBER 8, 1824, some 6,000 insurgents under the command of General Antonio José de Sucre, Bolívar's youthful lieutenant, faced 9,300 Spanish royalists at Ayacucho, a small plain 10,000 feet high in southern Peru. Sucre's Peruvian troops checked the royalist attack while his Colombians rolled up the enemy's left flank and captured the last Spanish viceroy in America. After fifteen years of struggle, the revolutionaries had made good their bid for independence. Ferdinand VII might wrap himself in pipe dreams of reconquest, but his heirs would have to be content with Cuba and Puerto Rico. The mainland was gone forever.

With Spanish power eliminated, the successor states now could turn their attention to other international projects. They might enlist in Bolívar's effort to create a cooperative organization, or, in pursuing their individual interests, they might fall to fighting among themselves. Another possibility was alignment along ideological lines.

During the first half of the nineteenth century, the overriding ideological issue throughout the Western world was the degree of popular participation in government. Proponents of absolutism, constitutional monarchy, liberalism, and socialism had their own different—and unyielding—perspectives.[1] In South America, the ideological issue stood out most clearly in the wariness between monarchy and republic. Since the outbreak of the independence movement in Spanish America, numerous projects for the estab-

---

1. E. J. Hobsbawm, *The Age of Revolution: Europe, 1789–1848* (London, 1962), 234–52.

lishment of autonomous monarchies—under Bourbon princes, a descendant of the Inca dynasty, or various creole generals—had been aired, and such schemes still had their advocates in the 1820s.

As the United States consul in Buenos Aires wryly observed in 1824, "Monarchy is the *pill* that the political doctors of Europe prescribe to purge these countries of *absurd and dangerous theories*, and although it may upset a few stomachs, the majority is going to swallow it with good appetite."[2]

Without European intervention, however, European preferences counted for little. After Ayacucho, Brazil was the only territory in South America still under monarchical institutions. All the other nations of the Western Hemisphere—save Haiti under Dessalines and Christophe and, for less than a year, Mexico under the reign of Agustín de Iturbide—adopted republican forms. The Brazilian empire stood alone.

THE BRAZILIAN NATIONAL IMAGE

Monarchical institutions figured prominently in the "national image" held by the Brazilian elite.[3] The choice of monarchy was expected to confer both internal and international legitimacy on the independent Brazilian regime. Since 1815 Brazil had enjoyed the status of kingdom, coequal with Portugal and sharing the same monarch. When Dom Pedro severed ties with Lisbon, he intended that Brazil take its place among the European monarchies on a basis of equality.

Luís José de Carvalho e Melo, foreign minister from November, 1823 to October, 1825, asserted Brazilian prerogatives in the extreme. George Canning irritably reminded the Brazilian ministers in London that Brazil was still an upstart in the community of nations. He objected to Carvalho e Melo's hubris as well as to certain "arbitrary acts, which seem to imply an opinion, on the part of the Brazilian Gov[ernmen]t, not only that Brazil is on a footing with all other Gov[ernmen]ts in the World, but that it is somewhat superior to them." Although Great Britain had "been

2. John Murray Forbes to John Quincy Adams (Personal), June 3, 1824, in John Murray Forbes, *Once años en Buenos Aires, 1820–1831: Las crónicas diplomáticas*, comp., trans., and ed. Felipe A. Espil (Buenos Aires, 1956), 301.

3. On this concept, see K. E. Boulding, "National Images and International Systems," *Journal of Conflict Resolution*, III (1959), 120–131.

content to overlook Such instances of assumed Superiority," Canning served notice that, once Brazil had been recognized as an independent state, "We shall look for the same observance of the usual rights of Courtesies of Nations, from Brazil as from any of the ancient Nations of the World."[4]

With regard to the other South American countries, the Brazilian national image contained two components. The first was a belief in Brazilian superiority, based on its monarchical form of government and concomitant stability, as well as its greater territory, population, and natural resources. One writer contrasted Brazilian unity with Spanish America's political fragmentation: "Do we not already see one State in Chile, another in Cuzco, another in Paraguay, and in Buenos Aires another that by all appearances will be the cradle of a thousand others more or less as mighty as Lucca, Florence, Mantua, [and] Ragusa?" The official newspaper of Dom Pedro's regime, the *Diário do Govêrno* (later retitled the *Diário Fluminense*), boasted in early 1823 that the empire was "[more] powerful, respected, and already at its birth [more] solidly based, as it is, than any other [Latin American] state."[5]

This presumption of superiority emanated partly from confidence in Brazil's monarchical institutions. Liberal thought had contributed to the coming of Brazilian independence, but the liberalism that eventually triumphed in Brazil was monarchist and antidemocratic in nature. Thus, Brazilian leaders tended to look on the political life of the republics as near anarchy and to draw odious contrasts between the Spanish-American countries and their own. José Bonifácio painted such a contrast in the Constituent Assembly when arguing that the constitution should guard against the perils of democracy: "What a picture unhappy [Spanish] America shows us! For fourteen years its peoples have torn themselves to pieces, because, after having known a monarchical government, they aspire to establish a licentious liberty. And, after

---

4. Canning to Felisberto Caldeira Brant Pontes and Manuel Rodrigues Gameiro Pessoa (Confidential, Draft), May 5, 1825, in GB-PRO, FO 13/15, fls. 197–99.

5. "Consideraciones politico-mercantiles sobre la incorporacion de Montevideo, Por I.S.V. Natural de Minas Gerais," 1822 (MS in Br-BN, SM, 1–31, 22, 17); *Diário do Govêrno* (Rio de Janeiro), March 29, 1823, pp. 307–308.

having swum in blood, they are no more than victims of disorder, poverty, and misery."[6]

The official newspaper also asserted the preferability of monarchy. In early 1823 the *Diário do Govêrno* suggested that Spanish America summon a prince from one of the ruling houses of Europe and submit to his rule, since republican government did not suit "the physical and moral qualities of the inhabitants and the country." Otherwise, Spanish America "will continue to be the victim of unbridled ambition, and, torn by different factions, its days will be numbered by its misfortunes."[7]

The second component of the Brazilian national image derived directly from the first. By virtue of its vast territory and the presumed superiority of its resources, population, and political institutions, Brazil was destined to be the dominant power in South America. Brazilians frequently employed the image of a giant to convey the size and strength of their country in comparison to the republics. The Brazilian ministers in London, anticipating a war with the United Provinces, confidently predicted: "Brazil is the giant that will triumph, even if our Pigmy neighbors are aided and favored [by Europe]." In response to an Argentine's assertion that Buenos Aires should tolerate neither the monarchical government nor the territorial unity of Brazil, the *Diário Fluminense* replied scornfully: "This will make every Brazilian split his sides with laughter, seeing the vain posture of the *dwarf at the foot of the giant!*"[8]

To the Brazilian elite, the empire was a great power and respectable monarchy in an "Anthill of Republican Governments," to use the expression of one of Dom Pedro's diplomatic agents.[9] This open contempt for the republics, coupled with ideological differences, held the danger of uniting the Spanish Americans against Brazil. Many of the Spanish-American leaders were as suspicious of monarchies as Pedro and his advisors were of republics.

6. Vicente Barreto, *A ideologia liberal no processo da independência do Brasil, 1789–1824* (Brasília, 1973), 109–149; AAC, I, 53.

7. *Diário do Govêrno*, February 5, 1823, pp. 113–14. The article was continued in the issue of March 20, 1823, pp. 270–72.

8. Brant and Gameiro to José Bonifácio de Andrada e Silva (No. 1, Secret), July 14, 1824, in Br-AHI, tomo 217/3/1; *Diário Fluminense*, January 5, 1826, p. 15.

9. Antônio Manuel Corréia da Câmara to MNE, July 28, 1823, in Br-AHI, tomo 205/2/14.

Ideology, Internationalism, and Self-Interest

MONARCHY VERSUS REPUBLIC

The Brazilian government attempted to use the ideological issue to its advantage in both America and Europe. In the Western Hemisphere, Dom Pedro and his ministers emphasized the American character of the regime and pledged solidarity with the other nations that had broken free of European domination. Until Portugal accepted Brazilian independence, the court in Rio de Janeiro explored the possibility of a formal alliance—most energetically with the United States but also, for a while, with Buenos Aires.[10] Brazilian officials and newspapers frequently used such phrases as "American system" to indicate that Brazil adhered to certain principles that irrevocably separated the New World from the Old.[11] Spanish America figured prominently in the ministerial newspaper, which carried articles on the war against Spain and on conditions in the various republics, and which reprinted treaties, official documents, and articles from other newspapers. Despite the prevailing sense of superiority and the frequently supercilious treatment of the republics, the Brazilian press generally sympathized with the Spanish Americans in their efforts to win independence.[12]

Simultaneously, the imperial government stressed its monarchical nature while seeking the recognition of the European states. A few months after Dom Pedro had declared independence, José Bonifácio suggested to Baron von Mareschal, the Austrian representative in Rio, that prompt recognition would guarantee the permanence of monarchy in Brazil and touch off a chain reaction in the South American republics. The Brazilian foreign minister asserted that "Bolívar was ready to declare himself Emperor and to introduce the monarchical system, that Chile had the same tendency, and that Buenos Aires—squeezed between that state, which it fears, and Brazil—probably will see itself obliged to bind

10. José Bonifácio to Bernardino Rivadavia, June 10, 1822, in *ADI*, V, 239–40; Carvalho e Melo to José Silvestre Rebelo, January 31 and September 15, 1824, January 28, 1825, *ibid.*, 10–12, 24, 30.

11. *Diário do Govêrno*, March 20, 1823, p. 270, and April 4, 1823, pp. 329–330; *O Tamoio* (Rio de Janeiro), September 23, 1823, p. 56. See also Francisco de Assis Barbosa, "José Bonifácio e a política internacional," *RIHGB*, CCLX (1964), 260–62.

12. For example, *Diário do Govêrno*, February 3, 1823, pp. 105–106; and *Diário Fluminense*, September 10, 1824, p. 304.

itself, more or less, to the latter."[13] Although the imperial government never again construed the issue in such outrageously optimistic terms, it continued to argue that recognition would protect the interests of the European monarchies. By sustaining Dom Pedro's regime, Brazilian officials claimed, Europe would preserve the monarchical principle in the Americas and avoid the separation of the Old World and the New on the basis of ideology.[14]

Many Brazilians perceived the difficulty of maintaining an American monarchy, although Antônio Manuel Corréia da Câmara clearly exaggerated the numbers and strength of the empire's enemies. A paranoid reactionary, Corréia da Câmara undertook diplomatic missions in the Plata region, pursued (he said) by spies, assassins, Masons, and Carbonari. So unrelenting was his hatred and fear of the republics that, in August, 1825, almost ten months after the Battle of Ayacucho, he insisted that Bolívar's victory was "fictitious." The Marquês de Barbacena was less prone to fantasy but nonetheless worried about Brazil's ideological isolation. "Ah, Sir," he wrote Dom Pedro, "the Imperial Throne is surrounded by Republics, and as long as It does not have England's guarantee . . . Your Imperial Majesty's faithful Servants will rightly fear the traumas of Democracy."[15]

Dom Pedro himself did not feel comfortable among his republican neighbors. He probably gave them little thought until Ayacucho, but the elimination of the Spanish and the sudden emergence of Bolívar and his army as the most powerful military force on the continent quickly captured the emperor's attention. Condy Raguet, the United States consul in Rio, reported that news of

---

13. Baron von Mareschal to [Count Metternich] (No. 42), December 21, 1822, in Jeronymo de A. Figueira de Mello, "A correspondencia do Barão Wenzel de Marschall (Agente diplomatico da Austria no Brasil, de 1821 a 1831)," *RIHGB*, LXXX (1916), 145–47.

14. Gameiro to José Bonifácio (No. 3), November 19, 1822, in Br-AHI, tomo 224/4/13; Raguet to Adams, January 20, 1824, in Manning (ed.), *Diplomatic Correspondence*, II, 775; Domingos Borges de Barros to Carvalho e Melo (No. 2, Secret), June 10, 1824, in Br-AHI, tomo 225/4/7; Carvalho e Melo to Antônio Teles da Silva, June 15, 1824, in Br-AHI, Arquivo II, tomo 427/1/1. Both Canning and the Austrian foreign minister, Count Metternich, wanted the Brazilian monarchy to endure for this very reason.

15. [Corréia da Câmara to MNE?], August 29, 1825, in Br-BN, SM, Rio-Branco Ms, I–29, 26, 10, doc. 29; Marquês de Barbacena to Pedro I, April 4, 1827, in Br-AHMI, II-POB 16.1.827 Hor.c 1–9. See also Viconde da Pedra Branca to Marquês de Aracati (No. 53, Secret), February 3, 1828, in Br-AHI, tomo 225/4/7.

Ayacucho "produced an astonishing excitement" in the Brazilian capital, where "many people for the first time began to reflect upon the possibility of maintaining a monarchy in the midst of Republicks [*sic*]. The Government, or at least some of its members, were known to be well wishers of the success of the [Spanish] Royal cause, and it is even said that Don [*sic*] Pedro expressed himself in exultation when he heard a former report of the defeat of Bolívar." According to Raguet, the new geopolitical realities prompted the Council of State to mend fences. On the day after the Council discussed the insurgent victory, the government newspaper hailed Ayacucho as the triumph of "the cause of justice and reason" and Bolívar as "that immortal Champion of the independence of Spanish America."[16]

In private conversations with Baron von Mareschal, Dom Pedro deplored Bolívar's victory. The emperor predicted that Ayacucho would encourage insurrection in the Cisplatine and give heart to Brazilian republicans. Mareschal informed Count Metternich, the Austrian foreign minister: "His Royal Highness is far from unaware of the real danger with which he is menaced by the republican form of the rest of the Governments of South America. Well to the contrary, Bolívar's latest victories have inspired in him a veritable terror."[17] If his neighbors were to combine against him, Dom Pedro would be hard pressed to sustain his throne.

The initial reaction of the republics to the creation of an independent Brazilian monarchy generally had been friendly. During 1822 newspapers in Bogotá and Buenos Aires favorably anticipated the separation of Brazil, under Dom Pedro's leadership, from Portugal. The government of Buenos Aires received an agent from Rio, and that of Chile indicated its willingness to accept a Brazilian consul.[18] Following the establishment of the empire, the Peruvian and Colombian ministers in London urged their govern-

---

16. Raguet to Clay, March 11, 1825, in Manning (ed.), *Diplomatic Correspondence*, II, 811–12; *Diário Fluminense*, March 4, 1825, p. 201.
17. Mareschal to Metternich (No. 16, Copy), May 21, 1825, in Br-AIHGB, lata 349, doc. 8. See also Mareschal to Metternich (No. 9-A, Copy), March 17, 1825, *ibid.*; and José Delavat y Rincón to Francisco Zea Bermúdez (No. 71), April 6, 1825, in Sp-AHN, Estado, legajo 5851.
18. *Gaceta de Colombia* (Bogotá), August 25, 1822; *El Argos de Buenos Aires*, February 16, 1822, p. 3, March 9, 1822, p. 1, August 31, 1822, p. 2, and September 7, 1822, p. 3; Joaquín de Echaverría to Barão da Laguna, September 30, 1822, accompanying Laguna to José Bonifácio, November 22, 1822, Br-AHI, tomo 309/4/10.

ments to open relations with the new regime in Rio de Janeiro.[19] Events soon eroded this sense of solidarity with Brazil. Dom Pedro's conflict with the Constituent Assembly made him an absolutist in the eyes of the Spanish Americans. José Rafael Revenga, the Colombian representative in London, was disquieted by the emperor's apparent desire to exercise "an absolute veto even over the fundamental laws. This pretension places him in agreement with the Monarchical principle that is flaunted now on the [European] Continent. It places him in opposition to the will of the people to whom he owes his elevated rank . . . and shows that we are not as far as it might seem from those who assert, as political dogma, that all conduct has to be dictated by the Prince."[20] In mid-1824 Daniel Florence O'Leary, Bolívar's Irish-born aide-de-camp, raised the possibility that Bolívar might intervene to overthrow the emperor: "Pedro's name is detested in the capital itself. At times I ask myself, will the Amazon be the route that restores the Liberator to Colombia?"[21] This issue soon faded away, however. In July, 1824, the official newspaper *Gaceta de Colombia* reported that "the emperor has given the nation a rather liberal constitution. The Brazilian people have received it with joy and have approved it without opposition."[22]

Far more serious was a territorial dispute that one party sought to cast in ideological terms. The Buenos Aires government intended to regain possession of the Banda Oriental, which had been occupied by Portuguese troops since 1816 and formally incorporated into the kingdom of Brazil in 1821. By determining to retain the Cisplatine province, as the territory was called in Brazil, Dom Pedro placed his government on a collision course with that of Buenos Aires. As the emperor's intention became clear, the Argentine press began to attack him and his subjects in scathing terms.

19. J. García del Río and Diego [i.e., James] Paroissien to Peruvian MRE (no. 73), Janaury 4, 1823, in Pe-AMRE, 1823, carpeta 5–17, no. 4; Revenga to Colombian MRE (No. 46), May 27, 1823, in Co-ADC, tomo 475, fl. 56.

20. Revenga to Colombian MRE (No. 71), October 4, 1823, in Co-ADC, tomo 475, fl. 179.

21. Daniel Florence O'Leary to Simón Bolívar, June 29, 1824, in Vicente Lecuna (ed.), *Relaciones diplomáticas de Bolívar con Chile y Buenos Aires* (Caracas, 1954), I, 245.

22. *Gaceta de Colombia*, July 4, 1824. Apparently the editors had not yet heard of the rebellion in the northeastern provinces of Brazil, provoked by the emperor's actions.

By January, 1824, another change could be detected in the attitude of *El Argos de Buenos Aires*, the leading Argentine newspaper, toward Brazil. *El Argos* ceased treating the Brazilians themselves with contempt and instead struck out at the monarchical form of government and the emperor's personal and ideological bonds to the "Holy Alliance." "His Majesty the emperor," read one article, "does not want to lend his royal attention to the humble republicans who, throughout the American continent, shout at him to leave, to leave a hemisphere predestined to be (among other things) the tomb of tyrants." The editors of *El Argos* cheered the republican rebels of the northeastern provinces and repeatedly expressed hope that the monarchy would fall. In October, 1825, on the eve of war between the United Provinces and the empire, the Argentine newspaper portrayed the rift in these terms: "Brazil constituted as a Republic, governed by American principles, and without private adherence to Europe—Brazil under this happy aspect is the complement of the American system. Otherwise, it is an enemy we must fight, an enterprise that one day will be appreciated by true Brazilians."[23]

Thus, the territorial dispute had come to represent a transcendental, ideological conflict: America versus Europe, republic versus monarchy, and (implicitly) good versus evil. Whereas *El Argos* had first welcomed the movement for Brazilian independence as completing the separation of the New World from the Old, it now viewed the empire as an atavistic political system that imperiled republicanism in the Americas. With this viewpoint, Buenos Aires sought to isolate Brazil and win the support of the Spanish-American republics on ideological grounds.[24]

By the beginning of 1825 Bolívar also had begun to dwell on the danger posed by an American monarchy. Dom Pedro was the only surviving monarch in the Western Hemisphere, and Bolívar wished him ill: "Iturbide's death is the third volume of the history of American princes. Dessalines, Christophe, and he have all ended the same. The emperor of Brazil may follow them, and the devotees [of monarchy] should take heed." Since the Battle of Ayacucho, the Liberator had come to fear that the Brazilian em-

23. *El Argos de Buenos Aires*, February 7, 1824, p. 4, and October 29, 1825, p. 3.

24. See, for example, Carlos de Alvear to José María Salazar, December 3, 1824, in Co-AHN, MG/LR, tomo 24, fl. 236.

pire was a stalking horse for the Continental Alliance. The victory over Spain had not eliminated the danger of intervention by the monarchies, and Dom Pedro might assist his European kinsmen. Bolívar wrote Santander: "This emperor of Brazil and the Holy Alliance are one. And if we, the free people, do not form another [union], we are lost."[25]

Soon afterwards, another border conflict, this time on the frontier with Bolivia, fanned suspicions of Brazil. A short-lived attempt by the Mato Grosso government to annex the Upper Peruvian province of Chiquitos, undertaken without the emperor's knowledge, persuaded many Spanish Americans that their worst fears were all too true. After war broke out between Brazil and the United Provinces at the close of 1825, some continued to express concern that Dom Pedro would carry out the sinister designs of the Continental Alliance.[26]

In addition to Brazil's overt actions in the Banda Oriental and Chiquitos, rumors of Brazilian complicity in reactionary plots contributed to the republicans' disquiet. The Colombian foreign minister understood that Dom Pedro had proposed to the defeated Viceroy José de la Serna, when the latter arrived in Rio in March, 1825, en route to Europe, that La Serna return to fight again in Peru with Brazilian arms and troops.[27] Although this story was surely false, the Brazilian government did maintain contact with representatives of Ferdinand VII—contact that could only raise suspicions in Spanish America. Since the beginning of the independence movement, Brazil had served as a principal way station for royalist officers moving between Europe and Spanish America. Numerous royalists had traveled overland from Rio de Janeiro to reach the viceroyalty of Peru. Moreover, the Spanish

25. Bolívar to Francisco de Paula Santander, January 6, 1825, in [Simón Bolívar], *Cartas del Libertador* (2nd ed.; Caracas, 1964–70), IV, 238; Bolívar to Santander, February 9, 1825, *ibid.*, 251–52. See also Nestor dos Santos Lima, *La imagen del Brasil en las cartas de Bolívar* [Caracas, 1978].

26. [Mariano Egaña to Chilean MRE] (No. 104, Copy), January 14, 1826, in Ch-AN, MinRE, vol. 13; Ventura Blanco Encalada to Egaña (No. 232, Copy), January 31, 1826, in Ch-AMRE, Argentina, vol. 10, fl. 1; doc. accompanying José María de Pando to Hipólito Unánue and José de Larrea y Loredo, June 29, 1826, in Simón B. O'Leary (ed.), *Memorias del general O'Leary* (Caracas, 1879–88), XXIV, 8.

27. Revenga to José Manuel Hurtado (No. 87), February 19, 1826, in Co-ADC, tomo 488, fl. 18. See also Gregorio Funes to Bolívar, August 26, 1825, in O'Leary (ed.), *Memorias del general O'Leary*, XI, 140.

legation in the Brazilian capital provided a steady stream of information about events in the rebellious colonies.

For their part, Spanish officials tried to involve Brazil in their plans of reconquest. After Ayacucho, Ferdinand's representative in Rio sought to persuade the Brazilian foreign minister to sell arms via Mato Grosso to the tiny band of royalists waging a last-ditch resistance in Upper Peru. The foreign minister promised to present the suggestion to Dom Pedro, although it is unlikely that either of them could have seriously considered such collaboration. At any rate, the prompt liquidation of the royalists removed the issue from discussion.[28]

Quixotic schemes, however, were not wanting in Madrid. In August, 1825, the Council of Ministers commissioned Mariano de la Torre y Vera, bishop-elect of Charcas (Upper Peru), to promote an insurrection there on behalf of the Spanish king. Although the Brazilian foreign minister promised his representative in London that the imperial government would not get involved, Torre y Vera was permitted to take up residence in Rio de Janeiro when he arrived from Spain. With a foolish optimism all too characteristic of Ferdinand's loyalists, Torre y Vera wrote the Spanish government that Dom Pedro "would happily enter into treaties with Our Sovereign to operate in unison against the Enemies of every crowned head."[29]

In 1826 the Spanish government shifted its attention to the Plata region. Two additional agents were sent to help the bishop-elect obtain Brazilian assistance in restoring Spanish dominion over Buenos Aires and the other Platine provinces. From Rio de Janeiro, Torre y Vera wrote Madrid that 7,000 or 8,000 men would be sufficient to conquer Buenos Aires, Córdoba, and Santa Fe, as well as open the road to Peru, and that both Brazil and Paraguay might aid in the campaign.[30] In the meantime, the former gover-

28. José Delavat y Rincón to Francisco Zea Bermúdez (Nos. 71 and 78), April 6 and May 7, 1825, in Sp-AHN, Estado, legajo 5851.

29. [Marqués de] Zambrano to Mariano de la Torre y Vera (Copy), August 9, 1825, in Sp-AGI, Estado, legajo 76, doc. 76; Carvalho e Melo to Gameiro (No. 79, Copy), September 23, 1825, in Br-AHI, tomo 268/1/14, fls. 139–40; Torre y Vera to Spanish secretary of state (Secret), December 16, 1825, in Sp-AGI, Estado, legajo 76, doc. 76. The Spanish representative in Rio also suggested that Brazil would collaborate with Spain. Delavat y Rincón to Zea (No. 117, Secret), December 8, 1825, in Sp-AHN, Estado, legajo 5838.

30. Francisco Viola to [Ferdinand VII], June 22, 1826, in Sp-AGI, Estado, le-

nor of Chiquitos awaited Ferdinand's orders in Mato Grosso, ready to lead a royalist resurgence in Bolivia.[31]

Although the Spanish Americans were aware of Torre y Vera's mission, his overtures to Dom Pedro caused no undue alarm in the republics. What did disturb republican leaders was the prospect of Brazilian involvement with two men operating in Europe; one was a shadowy figure who claimed to represent Dr. Francia, and the other was a former president of the Peruvian republic.

The self-styled representative of Paraguay was a Spanish-born cavalry captain named José Agustín Fort y Yegros, who called himself the Marqués de Guaraní. This adventurer arrived in Lisbon in mid-1823, armed with a document—probably forged—by which Dr. Francia pronounced him "fully authorized for all affairs of this Province of Paraguay in Europe." Ostensibly, Fort's mission was to follow up an opening by Portugal's liberal regime, which in 1821 had pronounced itself ready to recognize the independent states of Spanish America.[32]

The Paraguayan agent was unable to make any headway with the Portuguese government because he could present no credentials. At the request of the Spanish court, the Portuguese police prepared to expel Fort from the country, but he managed to win the protection of Queen Carlota Joaquina by giving her the sum of 30,000 *pesos duros* and by telling her that Paraguay was ready to resubmit to the authority of her brother, Ferdinand. Through the queen's intercession, Fort provoked the interest of the Spanish court and obtained permission to go to Madrid. The agent procrastinated with claims of ill health, however, till in April, 1824, he was implicated in the *Vilafrancada*, an unsuccessful revolt headed by Prince Miguel and Carlota Joaquina—with the backing of France and Austria—and directed against Dom João's pro-British government. After holding Fort in prison for almost a year, the Portuguese yielded to constant pressure from Madrid and turned him over to Spanish authorities at the frontier in April,

gajo 104, doc. 84; Council of the Indies to [Ferdinand VII], September 6, 1826, and Torre y Vera to [Ferdinand VII] (Copy), September [10], 1826, both *ibid.*, legajo 76, doc. 76.

31. Delavat y Rincón to Duque del Infantado (No. 173), August 4, 1826, in Sp-AHN, Estado, legajo 5852.

32. [José Gaspar de] Francia to Silvestre Pinheiro Ferreira (Copy), February 18, 1822, in Br-AHI, Ponte Ribeiro Ms, lata 286, maço 6, pasta 15. The original has not been located.

1825. In Spain the self-styled Marqués de Guaraní immediately got into trouble again, conspiring with Portuguese refugees linked to Dom Miguel's party and contributing funds to the abortive uprising of General Bessieres. Arrested in August, 1825, Fort still languished in prison in mid-1828.[33] Apparently he never presented Francia's purported wishes for reconciliation with Ferdinand, and these were most likely fabricated anyway.

Fort's appearance in Spain caused consternation in the other South American republics. Throughout 1826 the Colombian minister in London received frequent reports from a secret agent in Madrid, many of them focusing on Fort's mission and speculating on Dom Pedro's involvement with Francia and Ferdinand in a reactionary plot.[34] Suspicions of Brazilian complicity presumably arose because of a Brazilian overture to Paraguay in 1825, when Corréia da Câmara succeeded in penetrating Dr. Francia's realm and became the first diplomatic agent to reach Asunción in twelve years. The missions of Fort and Corréia da Câmara intersected in the imaginations of the Spanish-American leaders to form a frightening but ephemeral conspiracy. Warnings of the imminent forging of an Asunción-Rio-Madrid axis radiated from Bogotá to the other republican capitals.[35]

The second agent allegedly conspiring against the republics was José de Riva Agüero, who had served briefly as president of Peru in 1823. Afterwards he had fought against Bolívar more fiercely than against the Spanish royalists until sent into exile by his own troops. The Peruvian aristocrat was said to be the ringleader of a reactionary club headquartered in Brussels. During 1826 and 1827 the representatives of several Spanish-American republics re-

33. This summary is based on documents in Po-ANTT, MinNE, maço 139 and caixas "Legação de Portugal em Hespanha," 1824 and 1825; *ibid.*, Ministério do Reino, Intendência Geral da Polícia, livros 21, 22, and 223, and maços 47, 49, 50, and 226; Sp-AHN, Estado, legajos 219, 4525, 4528, 4529, 4828, 4829, and 5388; and [? to ?] (Copy), Madrid, July 20, 1828, and accompanying doc., in Br-AHMI, I-POB 20.7.828 Par.do.

34. Many of Manuel José Hurtado's dispatches from London to the Colombian MRE, found in Co-ADC, tomo 481, contain excerpts from the reports.

35. Revenga to Peruvian MRE (Copy), September 21, 1826, *ibid.*, tomo 259, fl. 69 bis; Restrepo to Argentine MRE, December 22, 1826, in Ar-AGN, Sala X, legajo 1-9-11. Other reports told of two Paraguayan agents in France involved in the alleged plot of Riva Agüero. [? to Manuel de Sarratea, 1826], and Sarratea to Argentine MRE (No. 32, Secret), August 19, 1826, in Ar-AGN, Sala X, legajo 1-1-8.

ported from London that Riva Agüero and his associates, who supposedly enjoyed the support of the Brazilian emperor, planned to travel to Peru and organize a monarchist insurrection. Although one Brazilian in Brussels suggested that Riva Agüero might be of help to the empire in the war with the United Provinces, the Peruvian's putative connection with Dom Pedro was as specious as Fort's.[36]

The ideological cleavage between Brazil and the republics fostered such suspicions, which were further compounded by historical experience. Centuries of Spanish and Portuguese rivalry in Europe and the New World had added a psychological dimension to the cultural differences between the two peoples, and the emerging nations inherited this tradition of mutual distrust. When fearful of or angry at the Brazilians, Spanish Americans called them "Portuguese," a label that carried a great deal of contempt in the former colonies of Spain. Sucre, irate over the incursion into Chiquitos in 1825, referred to them as "those Portuguese, infinitely more barbarous and degraded than the Spaniards." If Sucre went to extremes in comparing the Brazilians unfavorably to the hated Spanish overlords, he nonetheless gave voice to a sentiment widely held in the republics.[37]

Spanish-American suspicions of Brazil raised the possibility of a clear division between monarchy and republics in South American relations. This possibility seemed especially strong in 1825 when concern over Brazilian actions in the Banda Oriental and Chiquitos reached its peak, accompanied by renewed fears of Eu-

36. Hurtado to Colombian MRE (No. 6, Secret), March 7, 1826, in Co-ADC, tomo 481, fls. 99–100; untitled doc. [June 1826], in Pe-AMRE, 1826, carpeta 5-17, no. 1; circular no. 22 from Pando to Peruvian prefects, September 11, 1826, in Antonio Gutiérrez de La Fuente, *Manifiesto que di en Trujillo en 1824* . . . (Lima, 1829), xxv–xxvi; José Fernando Madrid to Colombian MRE (No. 161), August 17, 1827, in Co-ADC, tomo 488, fl. 326; José Anselme Corréia to [Visconde da Pedra Branca] (Copy), Brussels, May 14, 1826, accompanying Pedra Branca to Inhambupe (No. 37, Secret), May 19, 1826, in Br-AHI, tomo 225/4/7.

37. [Sucre] to Agustín de Otondo (Draft), May 14, 1825, in Bo-AN, MI, tomo 8, no. 63. See also the following: Funes to Pedro Gual, March 16, 1825, in Co-AHN, MG/LR, tomo 152, fls. 454–57; Bolívar to Santander, May 30, 1825, in [Bolívar], *Cartas del Libertador,* IV, 340; Unánue to Bolívar, July 10, 1825, in O'Leary (ed.), *Memorias del general O'Leary,* X, 320–21. On the historical development of separate Brazilian and Spanish-American nationalisms, see M[anuel José do] Bomfim, *O Brasil na América: Caracterização da formação brasileira* (Rio de Janeiro, 1929), 392–442.

ropean intervention. The Argentine government, in searching for allies in the coming war with Brazil, proposed a grand coalition of the republics to guarantee Spanish-American territorial claims and to destroy the monarchy. But, in spite of their apprehensions, the other republics left Buenos Aires to fight alone. The fears engendered by ideological differences were not strong enough to serve as a basis of alignment.

INTERNATIONALISM

Although the republics disdained the formation of an antimonarchical bloc, multinational collaboration remained a potential keystone for diplomacy in postwar South America. The struggle against Spain had been an international enterprise. Argentine troops had contributed to the liberation of Chile and Peru, and Venezuelans had fought from their homeland to Upper Peru. Fledgling national governments had financed the extension of the campaign to other regions. Nationality was no litmus test for office-holding in the new states; Britons and Spaniards as well as other Spanish Americans held important civil or military posts in many countries. Bolívar and Sucre, to cite two of the most conspicuous examples, were natives of Venezuela but occupied the presidencies of Peru and Bolivia. There existed a sense of Spanish-American citizenship that to some extent transcended national boundaries and loyalties.

In 1815, at the nadir of the independence movement, Bolívar had articulated a vision of permanent cooperation among the nations that were to emerge from Spain's American dominions. United in a loose federation, he suggested, the new states should send representatives to a congress that would provide for a common defense and foreign policy, resolve disputes among member nations, and handle other matters of mutual interest. The federation was to be an American answer to the Concert of Europe; if one alliance system could uphold the legitimacy of monarchies in the Old World, then another could safeguard republics in the New. After the establishment of Gran Colombia in 1819, the Liberator set out to implement his dream. In 1821 he dispatched agents to Mexico, Peru, Chile, and Buenos Aires to negotiate bilateral treaties of alliance and obtain commitments to support the forthcoming American Congress. The missions were ostensibly successful, but cooperation proved elusive.[38]

Bolívar originally conceived of the federation as a league of Spanish-American nations. His formal invitation to the American Congress, issued as dictator of Peru in December, 1824, went only to Gran Colombia and Mexico. After the Liberator left Lima, the Peruvian government invited Chile, Buenos Aires, and Central America. Santander and Pedro Gual, the Colombian vice-president and foreign minister, also invited Great Britain, the United States, and the Netherlands, all of which agreed to send observers, and France, which rejected the overture out of hand.[39]

In addition, the Colombian government decided to include Brazil in the American league. In February, 1825, Gual instructed the Colombian minister in London, Manuel José Hurtado, to approach his Brazilian counterpart to this end.[40] Hurtado conveyed the invitation to Manuel Rodrigues Gameiro Pessoa in June. If Dom Pedro were willing to send representatives to the assembly in Panama, Hurtado informed the Brazilian agent, the Colombian government would take "the liveliest satisfaction and would employ all its influence with its allies so that the Representatives of His Imperial Majesty would be received with the proper honor and distinction." Gameiro replied in equally cordial terms and promised to give a definitive answer as soon as the emperor responded.[41]

Some Brazilians favored participation as a means of gaining influence in South America. The publicist Hipólito da Costa had so counseled the imperial government in 1823 after discussing the

38. Víctor Andrés Belaúnde, *Bolívar and the Political Thought of the Spanish American Revolution* (1938; rpr. New York, 1967), 259–67; Masur, *Simon Bolívar*, 410–414; Harold A. Bierck, Jr., *Vida pública de don Pedro Gual*, trans. Leopoldo Landaeta (Caracas, 1947), 323–32.

39. Bierck, *Vida pública*, 445–513, *passim*.

40. Gual to Hurtado (No. 45), February 28, 1825, in Co-ADC, tomo 476, fl. 106. The Santander regime later cited the inclusion of Brazil as proof that the American alliance would not be antimonarchical. J. Campbell to Canning (No. 15), August 19, 1825, in GB-PRO, FO 18/14, fls. 152–53; Gual to Hurtado (No. 70), September 9, 1825, in Co-ADC, tomo 476, fls. 191–94; Revenga to Gual and Pedro Briceño Méndez, January 9, 1826, in Co-ADC, tomo 606, fl. 94.

41. Hurtado to [Gameiro], June 7, 1825, in Br-AHI, Arquivo II, tomo 413/1/387; Gameiro to Hurtado (Copy), June 18, 1825, accompanying Gameiro to Carvalho e Melo (No. 64), June 24, 1825, in Br-AHI, tomo 271/4/1. See also Pedro A. Zubieta, *Apuntaciones sobre las primeras misiones diplomáticas de Colombia: Primero y segundo períodos—1809–1819–1830* (Bogotá, 1924), 457–63.

projected American league with the Colombian minister in London: "[I]f the gathering of the Envoys of all those Powers is held in Rio de Janeiro, that will no doubt be the beginning of the supremacy that the Empire of Brazil in the future will exercise in all South America, without those States' perceiving the consequences, just as the United States will do in North America. That Congress in Rio de Janeiro will have in America the same preponderance that the Congress of Vienna has in Europe."[42]

Domingos Borges de Barros, the Brazilian representative in Paris, took a similar view two years later. He argued that, by participating in the Panama Congress, Brazil could check the excesses of the republicans. "I can see the Empire taking part in the American cause," he wrote, "overturning frightful revolutionary plans, cutting off their authors from the means of deceit, and at the same time, shielded by the greatness of the [European] Thrones, gaining preeminence in the Congress."[43]

From London, Gameiro also advocated participation in and domination of the assembly:

> The Dignity of Brazil demands that the Emperor's Plenipotentiary to the Panama Congress serve as President, following the example of what is done in the German Diet by the Plenipotentiary of His Majesty the Emperor of Austria. Since it is perhaps intended to deny him this primacy, however, he must fight for the observance of the practice adopted at the Congress of Vienna, which is that the Plenipotentiaries sign all acts in alphabetical order of the names of their respective countries. In this way the Emperor's Plentipotentiary will always sign first, because by its initial letters Brazil precedes all the other States assembled in the Congress. In a conversation with the Colombian Minister, I put forth the proposition that, the City of [Belém do] Pará being the most central point of America and the closest to Europe, it was there that future American Congresses should be installed. It seems to me that this idea should be repeated at the Congress of Panama,

42. Hipólito José da Costa Pereira Furtado de Mendonça to José Bonifácio (No. 18), July 8, 1823, in Br-AHI, tomo 216/1/1.

43. Borges de Barros to Carvalho e Melo (No. 29, Secret), November 8, 1825, *ibid.*, tomo 225/4/7.

and that at least the principle of alternating the site of subsequent assemblies should be accepted.[44]

In mid-1826 Gameiro, now graced with the title of Barão de Itabaiana, reported that diplomats from several countries had suggested Brazil send delegates to the American assembly and work for a joint mediation with the United States to arrange a settlement between Spain and her former colonies. Itabaiana endorsed this proposal which, he said, would place Brazil in a position superior to that of the republics.[45] In all of these cases, Brazilian participation in the Panama Congress was seen as a means of securing a strategic advantage in South America.

Dom Pedro had more immediate reasons for responding favorably to the Colombian overture. The invitation to send a representative to Panama arrived in Rio in early August, 1825, almost simultaneously with news of the misadventure in Chiquitos. Realizing that Gran Colombia and Peru would blame him for the incident, the emperor could hardly pass up the opportunity to demonstrate his goodwill. He thus notified the Colombian government, again through the ministers in London, of his intention to name a representative to the American Congress as soon as Brazilian independence had been recognized by the European powers. True to his word, Dom Pedro appointed Teodoro José Biancardi plenipotentiary to the Panama assembly in January, 1826.[46] At this time, Brazil was at war with the United Provinces, and the imperial government knew of an Argentine mission that was seeking Bolívar's military support.

Biancardi's appointment seems to have been no more than a gesture calculated to placate Bolívar and reassure the republics. The British consul general in Rio commented: "It is not intended that he should set off immediately. In fact, from what the Minister [of foreign affairs] has told me, confidentially, the nomina-

44. Gameiro to Carvalho e Melo (No. 6, Secret), November 30, 1825, in Br-AHI, tomo 217/3/1. Gameiro probably had not yet learned of the creation of Bolivia, or he may have counted on its following Brazil in alphabetical order by its name at that time, República Bolívar.

45. Barão de Itabaiana to Inhambupe (Nos. 13 and 14, Secret), May 10 and June 13, 1826, *ibid.*

46. Carvalho e Melo to Gameiro (No. 58), August 18, 1825, in *ADI*, I, 118–19; Gameiro to Hurtado (Copy), October 30, 1825, in GB-PRO, FO 13/14, fls. 56–57; decree of January 25, 1826, in *Diário Fluminense*, February 6, 1826.

tion may be considered as having been announced to the Publick [*sic*] more for the sake of saving appearances than for any other practical effect." Moreover, the consul general understood that Biancardi had declined the post. In June the imperial government announced that Biancardi would not proceed on his mission due to ill health and that a substitute would soon be named.[47]

When the first Colombian minister to Rio arrived in early 1827, one of his tasks was to see this promise fulfilled. The Peruvian representative in the Brazilian capital gave him little chance of success: "Perhaps he will not achieve it for a long time, because to tell the truth this Government still lacks a perfect idea of the object for which that Congress has been formed. It is no exaggeration to say that there reigns here an ignorance of what is happening in the other States of America as great as [the ignorance] of their geographical situation." In January, 1829, Dom Pedro finally made good on his pledge by appointing a minister to Bogotá and instructing him to represent Brazil at Tacubaya, Mexico, to which city the American Congress had removed in 1827.[48] But compliance came too late, for the assembly had already terminated its deliberations in October, 1828, in an atmosphere of disillusionment and failure.

Both the Spanish minister in Rio and the Chilean minister in London had interpreted Dom Pedro's acceptance of the Colombian invitation as a ploy to avoid antagonizing the republics.[49] In retrospect, this judgment seems warranted. The emperor and his advisors apparently never took seriously the possibility that Brazil might manage to dominate the assembly. On the contrary, the Spanish-American nations were likely to unite on the Banda Oriental question and demand that Brazilian troops evacuate that

47. Henry Chamberlain to Canning (No. 20), February 9, 1826, in GB-PRO, FO 13/22, fl. 139; Chamberlain to Canning (No. 56), June 19, 1826, *ibid.*, FO 13/23, fl. 260. In *Diccionario bio-bibliographico brasileiro de diplomacia, politica externa e direito internacional* (Rio de Janeiro, 1938), 70–71, Argeu Guimarães writes that Biancardi traveled as far as Bahia before being recalled by the imperial government, but no documentary evidence has been found to support this assertion.

48. José Domingo Cáceres to Pando, February 20, 1827, in Pe-AMRE, 1827, carpeta 5-2; Marquês de Aracati to Luís de Sousa Dias (No. 2, Copy), January 24, 1829, in Br-AHI, Arquivo II, tomo 403/2/1.

49. Delavat y Rincón to Infantado (Nos. 145 and 185), March 9 and November 20, 1826, in Sp-AHN, Estado, legajo 5852; [Egaña to Chilean MRE] (No. 126, Copy), May 17, 1826, in Ch-AN, MinRE, vol. 13.

territory. As the largest country in South America, Brazil had an advantage in pursuing a divide-and-rule strategy.[50] An institutionalized system of international relations could have facilitated the coalescense of its weaker neighbors on specific issues, such as common boundaries with the empire. Therefore, the imperial government shrewdly disarmed the republics by pretending to participate but did nothing to make the Panama Congress a success.

Immediate strategic advantage also governed the response of the United Provinces to the American assembly. The Buenos Aires government had refused to pledge its attendance in the 1823 treaty with Gran Colombia. At that time the United States' agent in the Argentine capital predicted that Buenos Aires would never join the other republics in such an enterprise.[51] During 1825, however, the Argentine leaders seemed willing to reconsider, despite their fears that Bolívar would use the Panama Congress to establish Colombian hegemony (or his personal dominance) over the entire continent.

The possibility of Argentine participation materialized only because of the Banda Oriental dispute and was linked to the prospect of Colombian aid against Brazil. In instructions to General Carlos de Alvear, named minister to Gran Colombia in January, 1825, the Buenos Aires government underlined the urgency of securing an agreement for the mutual guarantee of the borders of the new states at the time of emancipation. If pressed on Argentine attendance at the Congress, Alvear was to dissemble, avoiding a commitment but leaving the door open while pursuing an accord on the territorial question. The general declined to accept this mission, but in May he agreed to go to Upper Peru with José Miguel Díaz Vélez as emissary to Bolívar. Again, Buenos Aires' support for the Panama Congress was to be dangled as bait while Alvear endeavored to obtain the Liberator's participation in a Brazilian campaign.[52] Before the emissaries arrived, the Argentine

50. John H. Hann, "Burr's Model Applied: The Balance of Power in the Río de la Plata, Brazil's Role," *Proceedings of the Pacific Coast Council on Latin American Studies*, III (1974), 31–44.

51. Forbes to Adams (Nos. 42 and 43), January 23 (January 27 postscript) and February 22, 1823, in Forbes, *Once años*, 217, 221.

52. [Manuel José García?] to Alvear (Draft), January 15, 1825, in Ar-AGN, Sala X, legajo 1-5-2; M. J. García to Alvear and José Miguel Díaz Vélez, June 16, 1825, in Ernesto Restelli (comp.), *La gestión diplomática del general de Alvear en el Alto Perú (Misión Alvear-Díaz Vélez, 1825–1827): Documentos del Archivo del Ministerio de Relaciones Exteriores y Culto.* (Buenos Aires, 1927), 17–18.

president formally notified the Peruvian government in September that the United Provinces would send delegates to Panama. The Argentine foreign minister then informed Alvear and Díaz Vélez of the decision, commenting that it should facilitate their negotiations with the Liberator.[53]

This conciliatory attitude was clearly calculated to gain the Liberator's goodwill. Woodbine Parish, the British minister in the Argentine capital, asserted that the opposition of the Buenos Aires government to the American Congress "is perhaps rather strengthened than diminished" since 1823, and he explained the volte-face in the following terms:

> The Policy of Columbia [*sic*], to which may now be added the strength of Peru, appears to these People to be tending very much to an overbearing military System; as such, this Government has no inclination to commit itself to any connexion with them which might hereafter perhaps warrant an interference in their particular Affairs.
>
> But, on the other hand, the question of the Banda Oriental is one in which they are most anxious to induce Columbia especially, if not the rest of the new States, to become a party, and, they are unwilling at this moment, when that question is pending, to appear to separate themselves from all their Allies upon any consideration of their general Interests.[54]

Manuel Moreno, at one time approached privately to represent the United Provinces at Panama, concluded that "it may be inferred that there is no intention of participating in that Congress, nor was there ever." Rather, Buenos Aires wished "to create a momentary illusion about this important matter, to evade the weight of opinion of the sovereign States of our Continent with an apparent deference, and to continue under a system of aloofness." In early 1826 the Colombian delegates to the assembly at Panama offered an identical interpretation of Buenos Aires' new attitude. "This sudden change in the policy of that Government," they wrote, "which has so much thwarted the goals of the Colom-

53. Gregorio de Las Heras to Peruvian supreme council, September 9, 1825, in Restelli (comp.), *La gestión diplomática,* 68–69; M. J. García to [Alvear and Díaz Vélez], September 10, 1825, *ibid.,* 67–68.
54. Woodbine Parish to Canning (No. 59), September 10, 1825, in GB-PRO, FO 6/9, fls. 178–80.

bian [government] concerning the federation of American States, induces us to believe that its object is to engage us in the war that, so it is said, it plans to declare on the Emperor of Brazil." In fact, Buenos Aires temporized through 1825 and 1826 with one delay after another, and no Argentine representative attended the congress.[55]

The Chilean government repeatedly expressed its interest in participating in the assembly but said that the national legislature must authorize the naming of a delegate.[56] Like their counterparts in Buenos Aires, the members of the Chilean regime suspected that Bolívar harbored Napoleonic ambitions. This was among the reasons cited by the Chilean minister to Washington in explaining Chile's absence from the assembly to Secretary of State Henry Clay: "[T]he fears that were conceived in our countries that this Congress convoked at Panama might be a Machine that General Bolívar would make use of for his personal designs, the difficulty of its resolutions' having any effect given the disorganization in which all the new Republics find themselves, and finally the enfeebling and neglect of this assembly after its removal to Mexico had been the motive for which the dispatch of the Minister of Chile had not been carried out."[57]

By February, 1826, Bolívar already had despaired of seeing either Chile or the United Provinces take part in the deliberations at Panama, and even Bolivia—a nation bearing his name, governed under his constitution, and presided over by his protégé, Sucre—was unrepresented. The Bolivian legislature elected a delegate to the Panama Congress in the last quarter of 1825, but the first two candidates declined and the third never took his seat. The

55. Manuel Moreno to Bolívar, December 9, 1825, in Lecuna (ed.), *Relaciones diplomáticas*, II, 227; [Gual and Briceño Méndez to Revenga] (No. 6, Copy), February 20, 1826, in Co-ADC, tomo 608. Julio César González treats the stalling tactics of the Buenos Aires government in detail but stops short of calling them a deliberate policy. See his lengthy article, "Las Provincias Unidas del Río de la Plata y el Congreso de Panamá," *Trabajos y Comunicaciones*, XII [1964], 29–91.

56. Juan de Dios Vidal [del Río] to Peruvian MRE, July 4, 1825, in Lecuna (ed.), *Relaciones diplomáticas*, II, 74–75; Blanco to Peruvian MRE (Copy), February 27, 1826, in Ch-AMRE, Perú, vol. 12, fl. 1; Blanco to [Gual and Briceño], April 8, 1826, in Co-ADC, tomo 607, fl. 404.

57. Joaquín Campino to Chilean MRE (No. 3), April 21, 1828, in Ch-AMRE, Perú, vol. 9. See also Allen to Clay, March 20 and August 26, 1826, and March 12, 1827, in Manning (ed.), *Diplomatic Correspondence*, II, 1111, 1114, 1116; and Tudor to Clay (Confidential), June 15, 1827, in Manning (ed.), *Diplomatic Correspondence*, III, 1834.

government made yet another appointment in mid-1826, again without success.[58]

Whether Bolívar also invited Paraguay to send a delegate to Panama is unclear. Two letters attributed to the Liberator suggest that he did. One, undated but supposedly written from Cuzco, asked Dr. Francia to end his neutrality and join the other republics in seeking European recognition together; this was published in *El Comercio de los Dos Mundos* of Cádiz, Spain, in January, 1826. The second, dated at La Plata (Chuquisaca, or present-day Sucre) on July 15, 1825, implored that the Paraguayan dictator take part in the "very necessary union" of Spanish-American states but did not mention the Panama Congress.[59] In reply, Francia allegedly vowed that Paraguay would remain isolated "until there is restored to the New World the tranquility that it enjoyed before revolutionary apostles appeared in it, covering the perfidious dagger with an olive branch in order to irrigate with blood the liberty that the ambitious proclaim."[60] Since neither of the letters attributed to Bolívar appear in his published correspondence, and since they were supposedly written at a time when Bolívar was contemplating an invasion of Paraguay, they are most likely apocryphal. But, like the rumors of Brazilian complicity in reactionary plots against the republics, the tale of Bolívar's overture to Dr. Francia found currency among some contemporaries.[61]

Ultimately, only Gran Colombia, Peru, Mexico, and Central America sent ministers to Panama; a British agent attended in the capacity of observer, and a United States delegate arrived in time

58. Bolívar to Santander, February 17, 1826, in Co-ADC, tomo 606, fl. 92; José Ignacio de San Ginés to [Felipe Santiago Estenós], November 23, 1825, in Lecuna (ed.), *Relaciones diplomáticas*, II, 219–220; José Mariano Serrano to Facundo Infante (No. 42), August 18, 1826, in Bo-AN, MinRE, Bolivia-Argentina, tomo 1, no. 4.

59. A Portuguese translation of the first letter appeared in *Diário Fluminense*, May 18, 1826, p. 440. The second is quoted in Francisco Wisner [de Morgenstern], *El dictador del Paraguay, José Gaspar de Francia* (2nd ed.; Buenos Aires, 1957), 128–29. The editor of these memoirs, Julio César Chaves, dismisses the letter as a fraud.

60. Francia to Bolívar (Copy), August 23, 1825, in Ar-AGN, Sala VII, Guido Ms, legajo 16-1-8. This letter was published in *El Comercio de los Dos Mundos* and reprinted in *Diário Fluminense*, May 18, 1826, p. 440, and in Wisner, *El dictador del Paraguay*, 129–130.

61. Hurtado to Colombian MRE (No. 63), March 1, 1826, in Co-ADC, tomo 481, fl. 140; Torre y Vera to [Ferdinand VII] (Copy), September [10], 1826, in Sp-AGI, Estado, legajo 76, doc. 76.

for the sessions at Tacubaya. The Peruvian representatives clashed with the Colombians and did not proceed to Mexico once the first round of meetings ended. Only the government of Gran Colombia ratified the treaties and conventions drafted by the assembly. Other than giving expression to an enduring sentiment for inter-American cooperation, the Panama Congress achieved nothing. An Argentine likened the assembly to "Plato's Dreams" and made a penetrating observation even before the first deliberations at Panama: "The idea of the American federation approaches the sublime in thought, but is next to impossible in practice."[62]

NATIONAL SELF-INTEREST

Neither ideology nor internationalism provided the basis for intra-South American relations in the first years after independence. Buenos Aires could not organize an anti-Brazilian coalition founded on republican solidarity, and Bolívar could not organize an American system founded on the notion of mutual benefit. Instead, it soon became apparent that the principle of national self-interest was the dominant principle of foreign policy.

This was so even during the wars for independence, when, despite their common hatred of Spain, both the Colombian and Buenos Aires governments negotiated separate armistices with Madrid, regardless of the consequences for their fellow insurgents in other regions. Once the rebels had defeated Spain and the threat of European intervention faded, the main stimulus for collaboration among the new states faded, too. At the very time an ecstatic population celebrated Ayacucho in the streets of Buenos Aires, Argentine leaders uneasily considered the implications for their own power. The contemplation of Bolívar, perched with his victorious army in the highlands of Upper Peru and surveying the southern half of the continent, could only discomfit those who ruled in the United Provinces and Chile.

Independence won, each state looked after its own interests. Protonationalism made such a course of action easier, and diverging foreign policies reinforced the sense of separateness. The

62. [Tomás Guido?] to Juan Manuel de Luca (Draft), November 13, 1825, in Ar-AGN, Sala VII, Guido Ms, legajo 16-1-8.

origins of the Latin American nationalities lay in the past but were strengthened by more recent experiences. Regional differentiation began during the colonial period. Geographical barriers such as towering mountain ranges, tropical jungles, and vast deserts separated widely divergent ecological zones, each with its own economy and mode of social relations. Moreover, the peoples of different areas varied according to the nature of the aboriginal inhabitants, the flow of voluntary and forced immigration from Europe and Africa, and the pattern of racial intermingling. The efforts of the Spanish crown to inhibit trade among the colonies contributed to this process of differentiation. The ethnic composition and social structures of the new states were dissimilar, in spite of their common Iberian heritage.[63]

Travel and communication within South America had never been greater than during the wars for independence, but increased contact tended to confirm rather than dissolve long-standing prejudices. Bolívar, for example, denigrated the residents of Quito and Peru compared to those of Venezuela and Guayaquil: "The Venezuelans are saints in comparison with those malicious [*Quiteños*]. The *Quiteños* and the Peruvians are identical: vicious to the point of infamy and base in the extreme. The whites have the character of Indians, and the Indians are all cheats, all thieves, all liars, all deceitful, with no moral principle to guide them. The *Guayaquileños* are a thousand times better." He also had little faith in the inhabitants of Buenos Aires and his native Caracas: "The *Porteños* and the *Caraqueños*, who are found in the extremes of South America, are unfortunately the most turbulent and seditious of all the men in the whole of America."[64]

Colombians had no monopoly on drawing national distinctions based on race. After invading Bolivia in 1828 to overthrow Sucre's regime, the Peruvian general Agustín Gamarra commented: "Without Peru, Bolivia would still be respecting and even adoring the Negroes of Colombia, who brought their African huts

63. See Gonzalo Vial Correa, "La formación de las nacionalidades hispano-americanas como causa de la independencia," *Boletín de la Academia Chilena de Historia*, No. 75 (1966), 110–31; Halperín-Donghi, *Historia contemporánea*, 11–73; and Nicolás Sánchez-Albornoz, *The Population of Latin America: A History*, trans. W. A. R. Richardson (Berkeley, 1974), 129–45.

64. Bolívar to Santander, January 7, 1824, and May 8, 1825, in [Bolívar], *Cartas del Libertador*, IV, 13, 316.

from the Orinoco to rule over [the Bolivians] as they would over some degraded Sharecroppers."⁶⁵ The first Brazilian diplomat in Peru described the inhabitants of that country as "the most stupid of America, but also the most docile and least bloodthirsty."⁶⁶ Such stereotypes show that the citizens of each country thought of themselves as separate and distinct from their neighbors despite a shared cultural heritage and commitment to "the cause of America." The sense of a common American citizenship yielded quickly to protonationalism.

Moreover, the wars for independence generated tensions as well as stimulated collaboration among the regions of Spanish America. The occupation of one region by troops from another invariably led to friction. The Argentines, for example, mounted three expeditions to Upper Peru between 1810 and 1815. Each time they secured the area from Spanish control, they alienated the local population by exacting levies to support the army and enacting mining and Indian policies that threatened the interests of the elite. The Upper Peruvians came to look on the Argentines not as liberators but as oppressors and drove them out each time. These experiences left a lingering prejudice against the Argentines that Sucre encountered in 1825: "Last night, a young lady told me, speaking of those gentlemen, that during their campaigns in Upper Peru they had shown how to converse and dress very well; but that in combat they received the first volley from the enemy and by the second they had already fled to their homes."⁶⁷ Similarly, the Peruvians took offense at the supercilious conduct of the Colombian officers and troops in their country.⁶⁸

The wars for independence heightened strains between the new

---

65. Agustín Gamarra to [?] Macedo (Copy), August 27, 1829, in Bo-AN, Rück Ms, no. 447. Gamarra referred to the Colombian troops—mostly Venezuelan *pardos* (mulattoes)—who had remained in Bolivia to support Sucre's government.

66. Duarte da Ponte Ribeiro to [Francisco Gomes da Silva?], October 24, 1829, in Br-AHMI, I-POB 24.10.829 Rib.c. See also Vial Correa, "La formación de las nacionalidades hispanoamericanas," 131–42.

67. Sucre to Bolívar, August 3, 1825, in O'Leary (ed.), *Memorias del general O'Leary*, I, 289. See Halperín-Donghi, *Politics, Economics and Society in Argentina*, 241–45; and Charles Arnade, *The Emergence of the Republic of Bolivia* (Gainesville, Fla., 1957), *passim*.

68. Thomas S. Willimot to Joseph Planta, Jr., May 21, 1825, in GB-PRO, FO 61/6, fl. 57; Delavat y Rincón to Zea (No. 91), September 6, 1825, in Sp-AHN, Estado, legajo 5851.

states in another way. Governments that financed the liberation of neighboring regions tried to recover the costs of the campaigns from the beneficiaries, who accepted these debts in the euphoria of organizing their independent governments. Bolivia, for example, owed Peru 725,000 *pesos*, while Peru was indebted to Gran Colombia in the amount of 6,000,000 *pesos* and to Chile in the amount of 3,000,000 *pesos*, in addition to internal debts. Just as the Spanish loyalists in the viceroyalty of Peru had been squeezed in a pincers movement from north and south, so the successor states of Peru and Bolivia found themselves caught in a similar pincers formed by promissory notes.[69]

The indebtedness of the new states to Great Britain further complicated the discharging of obligations to each other. Between 1822 and 1825 all of the South American governments—except in Paraguay and Bolivia—contracted huge loans on the London capital market. These credits were obtained on the faulty assumption of rapid economic recovery and political consolidation; the chances of an orderly amortization were always tenuous, and they evaporated completely in the European economic crisis of 1825. As each regime struggled with its fiscal problems, demands for repayment flowed along the entire chain and further strained relations among the new states.[70]

The participation of foreigners in administration was another source of tension. William Miller, the English general who fought with Bolívar's army, had a premonition of future troubles the night after he helped rout the Spaniards at Ayacucho. Writing letters in a little hut near the battleground while heavy rains fell outside, Miller suddenly exclaimed to his companion, the Irish-born officer Francis Burdett O'Connor: "The last cannon shot fired today on this field should serve warning to all foreigners to leave this country, because there will be nothing for us here."[71]

Within a few years the Englishman's prophecy became reality in much of South America. Foreigners found themselves vulner-

69. Basadre, *Historia de la república del Perú*, I, 135–36, 220–222; Lofstrom, *The Promise and Problem of Reform*, 459–460.

70. Jaime E. Rodríguez O., *The Emergence of Spanish America: Vicente Rocafuerte and Spanish Americanism, 1808–1832* (Berkeley, Calif., 1975), 120–128. For a list of the British loans, see *ibid.*, 113.

71. F[rancis] Burdett O'Connor, *Independencia americana* (Madrid, n.d.), 150–51.

able in the competition for public office, which represented a scarce resource contested by different factions of the national elite, and often were ousted from positions of responsibility. In Brazil, for example, the nativist attack on Portuguese influence in the imperial government led in 1828 to a request by the Chamber of Deputies that each minister ascertain the number of foreigners—legally, all persons who were neither native Brazilians, nor naturalized citizens, nor Portuguese who had sworn allegiance to the 1824 constitution—in his department. A few months after the abdication of Pedro I, the Regency ordered that all foreigners holding civil posts in the provinces be dismissed.[72]

Bolivia, which had the highest degree of participation by foreigners in the government, also had the most far-reaching purge. The Treaty of Piquiza, imposed on Bolivia by the Peruvian army in July, 1828, required the withdrawal of Sucre and all foreign-born soldiers save those married to Bolivian women and holding a rank no higher than captain.[73] Subsequently, the Bolivian elite eliminated foreigners from civil posts as well. The Argentine-born ecclesiastic Gregorio Funes, for example, had represented Bolivia (as well as Gran Colombia) in Buenos Aires for some time. Soon after the change of regimes in Chuquisaca, the new foreign minister relieved Funes of his diplomatic commission, stating his certainty that the Argentine would understand "how humiliating it is for Bolivians that a foreigner, no matter how illustrious . . . be their Chargé d'Affaires in a Country to which he belongs by blood and opinion." The Bolivian government also canceled Funes's ecclesiastical appointment as dean of the cathedral chapter of La Paz.[74]

72. The foreign minister reported in 1828 that three foreigners served in his department, all as consular officials. Aracati to José Carlos Pereira de Almeida Torres (Copy), August 11, 1828, in Br-AHI, tomo 291/3/12, fls. 22–23. For the dismissal order, see decision no. 252, August 18, 1831, Collecção das Decisões do Governo do Imperio do Brasil, 1831, pp. 190–91.

73. "Tratado preliminar de paz y desocupación militar," July 6, 1828, in Peru, MinRE, *Colección de los tratados, convenciones, capitulaciones, armisticios y otros actos diplomáticos y políticos celebrados desde la independencia hasta el día* (Lima, 1890–1919), II, 171–76. Concerning Sucre's reliance on foreigners to staff his bureaucracy, see William L. Lofstrom, "From Colony to Republic: A Case Study in Bureaucratic Change," *Journal of Latin American Studies*, V (1973), 177–97, and *The Promise and Problem of Reform*, 89–96.

74. Casimiro Olañeta to Funes (No. 14, Copy), August 30, 1828, accompanying Funes to Guido, October 18, 1828, in Ar-AGN, Sala X, legajo 1-9-5. See also Vial Correa, "La formación de las nacionalidades hispanoamericanas," 142–44.

Such purges were never total; the Bolivian Andrés Santa Cruz served as president not only of Bolivia but also of Peru from 1836 to 1839, and the Venezuelan Juan José Flores was in and out of the presidency of Ecuador from 1830 till 1845. But, generally speaking, foreign birth was a liability in the political life of the new states after the early years.

Similarly, some countries attempted to limit the role of foreign merchants in their commerce. Peru provides the most conspicuous example, perhaps owing to the monopolistic tradition established during the colonial period, which had particularly benefited the merchants of Lima. The Peruvian government placed various restraints on the commercial activities of foreigners, much to the annoyance of those traders and their own governments.[75] In Chile, the restrictions were not as onerous, but by the early 1830s, foreign merchants could deal only through Chilean agents.[76]

Such actions both reflected and fostered protonationalism. Quite apart from emotional reactions toward foreigners and other countries, however, elites attempted to formulate policy on the basis of rational evaluations of national interests. The calculated manner in which the Brazilian and Argentine governments responded to the Panama Congress reveals the primacy of this principle, and dozens of other examples could also be offered.

Mariano Egaña, the Chilean minister in London during the mid-1820s, articulated the axiom of self-interest more clearly than any of his contemporaries. In objecting that the sale of naval vessels to Buenos Aires might involve Chile in the war with Brazil, Egaña observed:

A nation never sacrifices itself romantically for another, nor imperils its tranquility and happiness save for its own, direct benefit. Neither are they sacrificed to sustain grand principles in the abstract if its forces are too weak to lay down the law to the human race, or to an entire continent, or to a powerful State. Those who have followed the pol-

75. See, for example, Charles Milner Ricketts to Canning (No. 25), December 20, 1826, in GB-PRO, FO 61/8, fl. 240; José de Riglos to Argentine MRE, February 20, 1830, in Ar-AGN, Sala X, legajo 1-9-3; Tomás Manuel de Anchorena to Riglos (Copy), August 31, 1830, in Ar-AGN, Sala X, tomo 1-10-13, fls. 73–74.

76. Duarte da Ponte Ribeiro, "Memoria sobre as Republicas do Pacifico," April 7, 1832 (MS in Br-AHI, Ponte Ribeiro Ms, lata 269, maço 3, pasta 1).

icy of the Buenos Aires Cabinet during these last years will have observed that its Government took this maxim far beyond the rational, disdaining to take part in the war against the Spaniards and almost affecting neutrality, despite the fact that in America one could not lend oneself to a more worthy, more urgent, and more essentially necessary principle than that of shaking off the Spanish yoke. A smile cannot but appear on the lips of the politician who observes that the people that today calls for a crusade to sustain the principle of respecting the ancient borders of the United Provinces is the same people that did not lend itself to sustain that of expelling the ancient masters of those borders.[77]

By 1830 the international order in South America had taken shape. The republics had accepted coexistence with the Brazilian monarchy. The possibility of a permanent system of cooperation had been dampened by the failure of the Panama Congress, although it would emerge again in time of crisis. International disputes might find expression in ideological terms, but ideology had proved itself weak in comparison with national self-interest as a basis of foreign policy. More concrete issues, such as territory or strategic concerns, prevailed over abstractions in decision-making.

77. [Egaña to Chilean MRE] (No. 137, Copy), September 18, 1826, in Ch-AN, MinRE, vol. 13.

Three • Territory and Trade

"I AM, then," General Antonio José de Sucre wrote to the commander of a small detachment of Brazilian troops in 1825, "instructing the commandant-general of Santa Cruz that, if you do not withdraw immediately from the province of Chiquitos, he march against you and not content himself with liberating our frontiers but penetrate the territory that has declared itself our enemy, carrying desolation, death, and terror to avenge our country."[1] Sucre's fulminations were prompted by a Brazilian attempt to seize lands in what soon was to become the Republic of Bolivia.

Territorial disputes historically have been the most emotional issues of Latin American politics and the most frequent cause of war. The resolution of conflicting claims has proceeded slowly, and the passions associated with them rarely die. Argentina's disastrous attempt in 1982 to reassert by force its claim to the Malvinas or Falkland Islands—after 149 years under British rule—is merely the most recent example.

Such issues were of particular concern to the new nations of South America, for one of the first and most basic tasks of state building is the definition of the national territory. The idea of state or nation implies a specific territorial expanse—the space within which a people organize themselves politically. Contiguous nations in South America needed to establish mutually recognized frontiers so that each government knew what people owed it allegiance, what resources could be exploited, and what borders had to be policed.

During the colonial period, vast and ill-known regions sepa-

1. Sucre to Manuel José Araújo e Silva (Copy), May 11, 1825, in Vicente Lecuna (ed.), *Documentos referentes a la creación de Bolivia* (Caracas, 1924), I, 209–210.

rated the main areas of settlement; the administrative divisions of the Spanish and Portuguese empires in America had little need for distinct boundaries. The new states thus inherited a situation of potential conflict. During the early years of independence, the question of borders—that is, the possession of valuable lands— overshadowed almost all other issues in South American international relations. Since Brazil shared common borders with all of the other South American states save Chile (and later, Ecuador), many of the disputes of the early years involved the empire.

Trade also occupied the attention of South American statesmen during the period of this study. Since customs duties accounted for the lion's share of government revenues in most countries, every regime had a direct interest in stimulating commerce. Since many countries exported the same products, they competed for the same markets. To a certain extent, however, the South American economies complemented one another, and the trade among them—limited by the Iberian crowns during the colonial era—presumably expanded somewhat following independence. Commercial issues occasionally complicated relations between South American states, but, in general, trade was secondary to territorial and strategic concerns.

DEFINING BOUNDARIES

The division between Portuguese and Spanish America dated from the earliest years of discovery. During the Middle Ages the popes, as the vicars of Christ on earth, had often mediated between Christian princes and coordinated the work of proselytization. When Portuguese explorers began opening up the West African coast in the fifteenth century, the papacy awarded Lisbon a monopoly over Christianization and commerce there. Following these precedents, the monarchs of Spain and Portugal maneuvered in the wake of Columbus' first voyage to obtain control over as much of the new lands as possible.

In 1493 the papacy issued a series of bulls that assigned different zones of commercial and missionary activity to the two Iberian crowns. These bulls were superceded the following year by the Treaty of Tordesillas, the result of direct negotiation between Spain and Portugal. By this agreement, the Iberian monarchs accepted a north-south meridian 370 leagues west of the Cape Verde

Territory and Trade

Islands as the dividing line between their respective spheres. The exact location of the imaginary meridian remained ambiguous, because of the imprecise state of American geography, but it clearly cut off the eastern "hump" of Brazil from the rest of South America. The lands to the east of the meridian pertained to Portugual; those to the west, to Spain. Ratified by a papal bull in 1506, the Tordesillas line constituted a legal boundary between Spanish and Portuguese America.[2]

In practice the Portuguese paid little attention to the treaty. Spanish settlement was limited largely to the Pacific coast and to the Andean highlands, save some nuclei in the Plata basin. The Luso-Brazilians sprawled across the Tordesillas line during the seventeenth and eighteenth centuries, blazing trails through the lands that ostensibly belonged to Spain. Portuguese expansion in South America was at times sponsored by the crown, most notably in the Amazon basin and toward the Plata in the south, but usually it was the work of free lancers in search of precious metals, Indian slaves, or forest products. The discovery of gold and diamonds in Minas Gerais, Goiás, and Mato Grosso between 1695 and 1722 ensured the Portuguese occupation of the heart of the continent. During the eighteenth century the royal government in Lisbon elaborated and implemented a continental strategy for making good its claim to the western lands in the Amazon and Plata basins.[3]

In 1750 Spain recognized Portuguese gains in South America by the Treaty of Madrid. The Iberian monarchs accepted the principle of *uti possidetis de facto* (effective occupation) as the determinant of territorial ownership, except for a few specific adjustments of the frontier. Neither side tried seriously to carry out the agreement, however, and it was abrogated by mutual consent in 1761. The Treaty of San Ildefonso (1777) represented a second attempt to settle territorial claims, but the demarcation of bound-

2. Charles Gibson, *Spain in America* (New York, 1966), 14–18.
3. On territorial expansion, see Basílio de Magalhães, *Expansão geographica do Brasil colonial* (2nd ed. rev.; São Paulo, 1935); and João Capistrano de Abreu, *Caminhos antigos e povoamento do Brasil* (2nd ed.; [Rio de Janeiro], 1960). On the strategy of the Portuguese crown, see David Michael Davidson, "Rivers and Empire: The Madeira Route and the Incorporation of the Brazilian Far West, 1737–1808" (Ph.D. dissertation, Yale University, 1970), 2–107; and João Gualberto de Oliveira, *Gusmão, Bolívar e o princípio do "uti possidetis"* (São Paulo, 1958), 7–36.

57

aries by binational commissions was never completed, largely because of Portuguese foot-dragging. At the time of independence, the Spanish-Portuguese frontier in South America remained nebulous, although the acceptance of the principle of ownership by effective occupation provided a potential basis for the eventual resolution of the problem.[4]

Since Brazil did not fragment into several autonomous states, boundary disputes between internal administrative units (provinces under the empire, states under the republic) could be settled peacefully within the national juridical system. In Spanish America, however, independence represented the assertion of local political control and resulted in the foundation of a number of states, corresponding roughly to the administrative divisions of the colonial era. When Gran Colombia was established in 1819, Bolívar proposed that all of the new nations accept the principle of *uti possidetis juris* of 1810; that is, the administrative boundaries of the Spanish empire at the start of the independence movement should serve to delineate the successor states. In championing this idea, Bolívar sought to prevent territorial disputes and to enhance Gran Colombia by giving it a strong claim to Guayaquil and other lands near the frontier with Peru. Eventually, all of the new countries embraced the principle of *uti possidetis juris* of 1810.[5]

Disagreements were not so easily avoided, however. Boundaries between different regions of the Spanish empire were hazy because of frequent administrative reorganization and because they fell in sparsely populated and often economically unimportant areas. Thus, every one of the new nations became embroiled in border disputes. The annexation of Guayaquil by Gran Colombia disregarded the claims of Peru and Chile, and the rivalry over debatable lands contributed to the outbreak of war between Colombia and Peru in 1828. The Argentines were loath to accept the

4. On the problem of boundaries, see José Carlos de Macedo Soares, *Fronteiras do Brasil no regime colonial* (Rio de Janeiro, 1939); Gordon Ireland, *Boundaries, Possessions and Conflicts in South America* (Cambridge, Mass., 1938), 321–29; and Oliveira, *Gusmão*, 59–99.

5. B[enigno] Checa Drouet, *La doctrina americana del uti possidetis de 1810: Un estudio de derecho internacional público americano* (Lima, 1936), 15–63; John William Kitchens, Jr., "Colombian-Chilean Relations, 1817–1845: A Diplomatic Struggle for Pacific Coast Hegemony" (Ph.D. dissertation, Vanderbilt University, 1969), 169–83.

inclusion of Tarija in Bolivia. Paraguayan claims in the Chaco region conflicted with those of Bolivia and Argentina. The border between Peru and Bolivia long remained a matter of controversy, and Brazilian claims along its extensive frontier were challenged by its neighbors. It was a territorial controversy involving Brazil and the United Provinces of the Río de la Plata that led to the first international war in postindependence South America.

THE BANDA ORIENTAL DISPUTE

The Plata region had been the lodestar of Portuguese ambitions in the New World since the sixteenth century. In the 1620s forays of *bandeirantes*—slave-raiding frontiersmen from São Paulo—began assaulting the missions that Spanish Jesuits had established among the Indians in the Uruguay and Paraná valleys. Within two decades the *bandeirantes* threw back the line of Spanish settlement. In 1680 the Portuguese government founded Colônia do Sacramento on the northern shore of the Plata estuary in an effort to renew a profitable contraband trade between Brazil and the silver mines of Potosí in Upper Peru. During the eighteenth century the crown promoted the colonization of Santa Catarina and Rio Grande do Sul to shorten Colônia's supply lines and ensure that Brazil would extend to the mouth of the Plata. Neither armed conflict nor the treaties of 1750 and 1777 settled the question of possession. The lands on the left bank of the Uruguay River—called the Banda Oriental or the province of Montevideo by the Spaniards, and the Cisplatine by the Portuguese—remained in Spanish hands at the beginning of the nineteenth century but were still coveted by Lisbon.[6]

On arriving in Rio de Janeiro, Dom João endeavored to extend Portuguese influence in the Plata. After the independence movement began in Buenos Aires in May, 1810, the Portuguese court conspired to detach the provinces of Paraguay, Entre Ríos, Corrientes, and Montevideo from the insurgent government. This undertaking, implemented in part by the armed occupation of the Banda Oriental in 1811–1812, aimed at insulating Brazil from the revolutionary fervor of Buenos Aires or at preventing the trans-

6. Calógeras, *A política exterior*, 151–281; Dauril Alden, *Royal Government in Colonial Brazil* (Berkeley, Calif., 1968), 59–275.

formation of the viceroyalty into a single independent state that might threaten Portuguese interests in the Plata.[7]

In 1816 the court again sent troops into the Banda Oriental to stifle Artigas' democratic movement, and this time the Portuguese forces remained. Absorption of the territory offered several advantages: a natural, more easily defended border; suppression of political turmoil that undermined the stability of southern Brazil; access to the Uruguay and Paraná rivers, and the possibility of access to Mato Grosso via the Paraguay River; commercial opportunities, including use of the port of Montevideo; and, by preventing the incorporation of the Banda Oriental into the United Provinces, a check on the power of Buenos Aires. Nonetheless, Dom João maintained a flexible policy and never made a firm commitment to retain the disputed lands. Early in 1821 the new liberal regime in Lisbon undertook to improve relations with the republican governments of South America before the king's return to Europe. The regime intended to recognize the independence of Buenos Aires, Chile, and Colombia, and to grant self-determination to the Orientals. The inhabitants of the Banda Oriental were to choose, via free elections guaranteed by the occupying troops, whether they preferred union with Brazil, complete independence, or union with some other state.

Although Dom João and his advisors fully expected the Orientals to opt for independence, the Portuguese commander in Montevideo—General Carlos Federico Lecor, the Barão da Laguna—manipulated the selection of delegates to ensure that the Cisplatine Congress was dominated by elements that had collaborated with the government of occupation. A small minority of Orientals—wealthy landowners who feared a return to the "anarchy" of Artigas' agrarian radicalism and merchants who benefited from Lecor's commercial policies—wanted to make the association with Brazil permanent. On July 31, 1821, the hand-picked congress dutifully voted in favor of incorporation into the kingdom of Brazil.[8]

Dom Pedro's first reaction was one of disgust at Lecor's ac-

7. John Henry Hann, "Brazil and the Rio de la Plata, 1808–1828" (Ph.D. dissertation, University of Texas, 1967), 98–99, 452–53.

8. Hann, "Brazil and the Río de la Plata," 240–251, 337–47; Street, *Artigas*, 279–335. On the pro-Portuguese element in the Banda Oriental, see Rosa Alonso Eloy *et al.*, *La oligarquía oriental en la Cisplatina* (Montevideo, 1970).

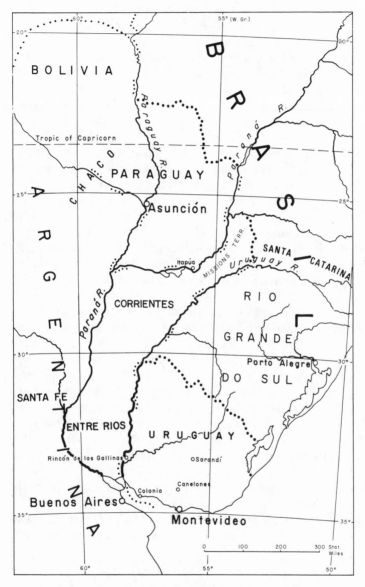

The Plata Region in 1828
(All borders approximate and in dispute)

tions, or so he told the indignant Spanish minister in Rio de Janeiro, and he proposed to let his father handle the affair from Europe. Indeed, the government in Lisbon disavowed Lecor's machinations late in 1821 and continued to do so during the following year.[9] But by that time it had no control over events in South America.

Expansion to the Plata appealed to some Brazilians' sense of grandeur. The *Revêrbero Constitucional Fluminense* hailed the resolution of the Cisplatine Congress with this vision: "We . . . who are Brazilians cannot but feel true jubilation, when, with this acquisition, born of a spontaneous and legal choice, we see our Continent enclosed by its natural limits, by those corpulent Rivers that extend their arms through an immense, fertile, rich territory, the envy of all the world."[10] More important, the idea appealed to the prince regent and future emperor. Unlike his father, Pedro decided that personal and national honor required the retention of the Cisplatine, and his South American policy during the early years of his reign was limited almost entirely to pursuing this end.

The Argentines had had no choice but to acquiesce in the Portuguese occupation of the Banda Oriental in 1816. With its resources committed to the liberation of Chile and Peru, Buenos Aires lacked the ability to quiet the troubled province and do away with Artigas' influence; thus, the *Porteño* leaders were momentarily content to allow the Portuguese to accomplish these goals for them. The political disintegration that culminated in the disastrous events of 1820 precluded any attempt to obtain a withdrawal of the occupying forces. But, as relative peace returned to the Plata and a stable administration was erected in the old viceregal capital, the recovery of the Banda Oriental became the Argentines' principal concern. War against the Portuguese "is the great talisman of popularity in these Provinces," wrote the United States agent in Buenos Aires in early 1821, "and those who manage to be at the head of the government when hostilities com-

9. Conde de Casaflores to Eusebio Bardaji y Azara (Nos. 655 and 660), August 18 and September 4, 1821, in Sp-AHN, Estado, legajo 5849; Pinheiro Ferreira to Laguna, December 22, 1821, in Br-BN, SM, I-31, 22, 17; Pinheiro to governor of Buenos Aires, March 31, 1822, and Pinheiro to M. J. García, August 30, 1822, in Ar-AGN, Sala X, legajo 1-7-11.

10. *Revérbero Constitucional Fluminense* (Rio de Janeiro), February 5, 1822, p. 156.

mence will no doubt acquire a very solid and permanent authority." Lecor's manipulation of the Cisplatine Congress enraged the
Argentines and enhanced the likelihood of conflict. From early
1822 until the outbreak of war in 1825, the provincial governments of Entre Ríos and Santa Fe impatiently pressed for united
action against the Luso-Brazilians in the Banda Oriental, while
Buenos Aires continued to explore all avenues to a peaceful settlement.[11]

During 1822 Dom Pedro obtained the allegiance of many of
the Oriental leaders, as well as that of Lecor, but most of the Portuguese officers remained loyal to the liberal government in Lisbon and ignored the prince regent's orders to sail for Europe. Lecor maintained the Brazilian headquarters in the interior at
Canelones, while the Portuguese forces controlled Montevideo
until November, 1823. Disaffected Orientals, in the meantime,
sought help from Buenos Aires and the other Platine governments.[12]

Dom Pedro hoped that the absorption of the Banda Oriental
would not be contested. In May, 1822, José Bonifácio commissioned Antônio Manuel Corréia da Câmara to represent Brazil in
Buenos Aires, Santa Fe, Entre Ríos, Paraguay, and Chile. Ostensibly, Corréia da Câmara's mission was to replace the recently de-
ceased consul of Portugal and promote Brazilian commercial interests. He also carried secret instructions to acquire partisans in
the Buenos Aires and Paraguayan governments and seek an alliance with the United Provinces against Portugal and Spain. In addition, he was to refute "any erroneous notion" that Brazil would
abandon the Banda Oriental; on the contrary, the prince regent
intended to maintain the disputed territory even if Lisbon ceded
it to Spain or Buenos Aires.[13]

In his delicate mission, Corréia da Câmara found himself out-
matched by the Argentine minister of government and foreign relations, Bernardino Rivadavia—a shrewd, forty-two-year-old

11. Forbes to Adams (No. 8), February 9, 1821, in Forbes, *Once años*, 89–90;
Martha Campos Thévenin de Garabelli, *La revolución oriental de 1822–1823:
Su génesis* (Montevideo, 1972), I, 31–71; Juan Beverina, *La guerra contra el imperio del Brasil: Contribución al estudio de sus antecedentes y de las operaciones
hasta Ituzaingó.* (Buenos Aires, 1927), 65–81; Alonso Eloy et al., *La oligarquía
oriental,* 151–61.

12. Thévenin de Garabelli, *La revolución oriental,* I, 238–81, 370–93.

13. José Bonifácio to Corréia da Câmara, May 30, 1822, in *ADI,* V, 235–38.

merchant turned politician. Rivadavia handled the Brazilian emissary with finesse, stalling for time while carefully avoiding any categorical assertion of Argentine rights to the disputed territory. After almost two months in the Argentine capital, Corréia da Câmara still felt confident that the Buenos Aires administration would not aid the anti-Brazilian faction in Montevideo. By late October, however, the Oriental rebels' public appeals for aid and the positive reaction of the Argentine press made such optimism increasingly difficult to sustain. In November, Rivadavia informed Corréia da Câmara that Buenos Aires, as head of the United Provinces, could no longer hesitate to protest the occupation of the Banda Oriental. The Argentine said he hoped that the issue could be resolved without "bloodshed and war," but he made it clear that Brazil's claim to the territory would not go unchallenged. Having failed to accomplish any of the goals of his mission, the Brazilian agent departed Buenos Aires in January, 1823, and returned to Rio de Janeiro without visiting any of the other capitals to which he was accredited.[14]

According to John Murray Forbes, the United States representative in the Argentine capital, the Buenos Aires administration believed that Dom Pedro would withdraw his troops from the Banda Oriental to prop up his shaky throne, making armed conflict unnecessary. While Uruguayan émigrés conspired with the governments of the littoral provinces and fomented interprovincial war in their attempt to raise an army, Rivadavia tried diplomacy. In May, 1823, he appointed a cleric, Valentín Gómez, to try to persuade the emperor to surrender the province of Montevideo.[15]

Gómez arrived in the Brazilian capital in early August. The moment was inopportune for any sort of negotiation, for the at-

---

14. Corréia da Câmara to José Bonifácio (No. 48, Secret, and No. 61), September 25 and November 13, 1822, in Br-AHI, tomo 205/2/14. The correspondence dealing with the Corréia da Câmara mission is published in Brazil, Ministério das Relações Exteriores, *Annaes do Itamaraty* (Rio de Janeiro, 1936–42), II, and *ADI*, V, 233–98. See also Thévenin de Garabelli, *La revolución oriental*, I, 115–73; R. Antonio Ramos, *La política del Brasil en el Paraguay bajo la dictadura del Dr. Francia* (2nd. ed.; Buenos Aires, 1959), 65–72; and Hann, "Brazil and the Río de la Plata," 351–53.

15. Forbes to Adams (Nos. 41 and 43), January 3 (January 9 postscript) and February 22, 1823, in Forbes, *Once años*, 215, 221–22; Emilio Ravignani, *Historia constitucional de la República Argentina* (Buenos Aires, 1926–27), II, 222–24.

tention of the emperor and his advisors was distracted by their differences with the Constituent Assembly. Moreover, Dom Pedro would brook no discussion of giving up the Cisplatine, and his government used the same dilatory tactics Corréia da Câmara had encountered in Buenos Aires. For weeks at a time, the Brazilian foreign minister ignored Gómez's frequent requests for a conference, claiming that additional information was necessary before profitable conversations could begin.

The Argentine came to hope the Constituent Assembly might resolve the issue. During the last two weeks of September, several deputies expressed opposition to the retention of the Cisplatine province on political or legal and moral grounds. José Antônio da Silva Maia of Minas Gerais, for example, put the issue in these terms:

> It is said that the Río de la Plata can be taken as the dividing line [*i.e.*, the southern boundary of the empire]. But this does not suit me; because, if it is because this is a natural and very visible line, then by the same token we should take the Amazon River as the northern dividing line. Such would be to the great detriment of Brazil, and the nation would remain greatly prejudiced without the possessions beyond the river. But just as we should not lose what certainly belongs to us, neither should we covet what belongs to our neighbors, extending ourselves to the Río de la Plata.[16]

One of the opposition deputies visited Gómez privately and encouraged his hopes for legislative action. This possibility evaporated with the emperor's dissolution of the assembly on November 11, but Gómez predicted that the ensuing political turmoil would oblige Dom Pedro to surrender the Banda Oriental or risk the secession of the northern provinces and perhaps some of the southern ones as well.[17] In late November, however, the Argentine minister was informed privately that Dom Pedro would not give up the disputed territory under any circumstances. The emperor, Gómez reported, "was firm on the idea of conserving that

16. *AAC*, V, 149–150. See also *ibid.*, 119–22, 143–58, 163–80, 267–68.
17. Valentín Gómez to Bernardino Rivadavia, September 21, October 8, and November 18, 1823, in Ar-AGN, Sala X, legajo 1-7-4.

place at all costs, to the extreme of being indifferent to the separation of the Northern Provinces, which he considered inevitable but which he intended to resist only by means of a blockade of the ports, abandoning the provinces to themselves until, devoured by anarchy, they seek reincorporation into the Empire and the protection of His Majesty as the remedy to their problems."[18]

The new Brazilian foreign minister, Luís José de Carvalho e Melo, kept putting off substantive talks on the pretext of inadequate information. Eventually Gómez decided his mission was futile. He obtained Rivadavia's authorization to demand a categorical reply from the Brazilian cabinet, failing which he would break off the negotiations. On February 6, 1824, six months after his arrival in Rio, the Argentine envoy finally pried an answer out of the imperial ministry. Carvalho e Melo informed Gómez that the emperor, after careful consideration, had determined that Buenos Aires' pretensions to the Cisplatine were untenable, since the Orientals had freely chosen union with Brazil in 1821. With this, the Argentine agent requested his passports and departed.[19]

Following the failure of the Gómez mission, Buenos Aires concentrated on obtaining the diplomatic support of Great Britain, the United States, and the other South American republics in the hopes of pressuring Dom Pedro into giving up the Banda Oriental. If the emperor remained intransigent, the Argentine government planned to organize a republican coalition to liberate the Orientals.[20]

The Buenos Aires public, the Oriental émigrés, and the provinces of Santa Fe and Entre Ríos continued to clamor for war, and the administration—now headed by Governor Juan Gregorio de Las Heras and Minister of Government and Foreign Relations Manuel José García—slowly moved in that direction. Woodbine Parish, the British representative in the Argentine capital, reported in mid-1824 that "one of the most difficult tasks of the new administration here has been to restrain that zeal and spirit of the

18. V. Gómez to Rivadavia, November 29, 1823, *ibid.*

19. V. Gómez to Rivadavia, February 9, 1824, and accompanying doc., Carvalho e Melo to V. Gómez (Spanish trans.), February 6, 1824, in Ar-AGN, Sala X, legajo 1-7-4. The correspondence between Gómez and the Brazilian government is published in *ADI*, V, 335–42.

20. Thomas Brabson Davis, *Carlos de Alvear, Man of Revolution: The Diplomatic Career of Argentina's First Minister to the United States* (Durham, N.C., 1955), 18–83.

Buenos Ayreans which would have driven them long ago to an armament and to forcible measures for the expulsion of the Brazilians. It has indeed been hardly possible for the Government to avoid commencing upon hostilities, and they have only been able to pacify public opinion upon the subject by a promise to refer the consideration of the question and the measures to be taken upon it to the General Congress as soon as it is convoked."[21]

In the aftermath of Ayacucho the pressures for war mounted. During the celebration of Bolívar's victory the crowds in Buenos Aires shouted "Death to the Brazilian Emperor, and long live the liberty of the Orientals!" The newly arrived Brazilian consul showed his disapproval of the republican triumph by refusing to illuminate his residence, and then fled the city temporarily when an angry mob smashed his windows.[22] The governments of Entre Ríos and Santa Fe began mobilizing their forces, and the Oriental exiles in Buenos Aires reportedly wrote Bolívar to ask for his help.[23]

The incident that ensured the outbreak of war between Brazil and the United Provinces occurred in mid-April, 1825. The Oriental rancher Juan Antonio Lavalleja led a small band of Orientals, Argentines, and others across the estuary from Buenos Aires and called on the inhabitants of the Cisplatine to rise up against the Brazilians. Woodbine Parish considered it a quixotic, "utterly hopeless" enterprise that would "seriously tend to increase the Public Irritation already existing on both sides upon this question, and make it a more difficult task than ever for this Government to maintain a peaceable Course." Actually, the expedition of the "Thirty-three Orientals" turned out to be both a symbolic

21. "General report on the rise and progress of the present government of Buenos Ayres," accompanying Parish to Canning (No. 31), June 25, 1824, in R. A. Humphreys (ed.), *British Consular Reports on the Trade and Politics of Latin America, 1824–1826* (London, 1940), 19.
22. Sinfônio Maria Pereira Sodré to Laguna (Copy), February 5, 1825, accompanying Laguna to Carvalho e Melo, February 12, 1825, in Br-AHI, tomo 309/4/13; Raguet to Clay, March 11, 1825, in Manning (ed.), *Diplomatic Correspondence*, II, 812.
23. [Juan Francisco] Seguí to Bonifacio Isas Calderón (Copy), February 6, 1825, in Br-AHMI, II-POB 14.1.826 Cam.do 1–8; Guillermo Gil to Diego Espina (Copy), April 2, 1825, accompanying Laguna to Carvalho e Melo, April 10, 1825, in Br-AHI, tomo 309/4/13; Laguna to Carvalho e Melo, April 26, 1825, and accompanying doc., León Solá to Laguna (Copy), April 17, 1825, in Br-AHI, tomo 309/4/13.

event and the beginning of effective military action against the Brazilians. Fructuoso Rivera, a powerful landowner and *caudillo* who had supported the occupying forces for a number of years, went over to the invaders, and his followers provided the nucleus of the insurrectionary army. The guerrilla tactics of Lavalleja and Rivera soon paid off with several minor victories against Lecor's troops. Wealthy citizens in Buenos Aires furnished arms and munitions to the Orientals, and *El Argos* persistently called for intervention.[24]

In June, Parish made a prophetic statement about the manner in which the Orientals could force the hand of the Argentine government. "It is reported," he wrote, "that Lavalleja means to convoke immediately assemblies in the Districts which he has occupied, for the election of Deputies for the General Congress of these Provinces: if this be true, and such Persons arrive here, the Congress will be placed in a most embarrassing Situation; considering that the Banda Oriental was a part of the Old Union, I know not how they can positively refuse to admit them, and if they do admit them, it appears to me that the Nation is at once compromised in defense of their Cause."[25]

Despite the worsening situation in the Plata, the Brazilian cabinet took no decisive measures to prepare for war. The imperial government neither sent substantial reinforcements to Lecor nor tried to conciliate the disaffected Orientals, who had always been treated like a conquered people despite the fact that they had been made Brazilian citizens in 1822. Dom Pedro and his advisors relied on Brazil's superior manpower and resources, and on the unenviable Argentine history of political instability and fractiousness, to overcome any military threat in the Cisplatine. The sense of Brazilian superiority appeared clearly in the correspondence of several diplomats, who smugly predicted that the emperor's forces would make short work of whatever challenge the Argentines might pose.[26]

24. Parish to Canning (No. 31), May 1, 1825, in GB-PRO, FO 6/8, fls. 210–213; Beverina, *La guerra*, 93–130; Street, *Artigas*, 341–44; *El Argos de Buenos Aires*, May 14, 18, and 21, June 4, 8, 11, and 15, 1825, all p. 1.

25. Parish to Canning (No. 38), June 10, 1825, in GB-PRO, FO 6/8, fls. 272–73.

26. Brant Pontes and Gameiro to Carvalho e Melo (No. 1, Secret), July 14, 1824, in Br-AHI, tomo 217/3/1; Rebelo to Carvalho e Melo (No. 19), March 26, 1825, *ibid.*, tomo 233/2/19; Teles da Silva to Pedro I, July 29, 1825, in Br-AHMI,

The emperor's single firm act backfired. Dom Pedro sent Admiral Rodrigo José Ferreira Lobo and a naval squadron to Buenos Aires to protest Lavalleja's expedition as a violation of the ostensible neutrality of the Argentine government. Arriving in early July, Lobo carried out his mission in a haughty manner that, coupled with the ominous presence of the war fleet, was taken as an attempt to intimidate the Las Heras administration. García refused to discuss anything with Lobo, who could present no diplomatic credentials. After a few days, the admiral abandoned the effort, having succeeded only in aggravating anti-Brazilian sentiment and prodding Las Heras into hurried preparations for the defense of the Argentine capital.[27]

While mobilizing its forces and appealing to Bolívar for assistance, the government of the United Provinces continued to explore diplomatic channels in seeking restitution of the Banda Oriental. In September, García named Manuel de Sarratea to replace Rivadavia, who had been serving as minister to the Court of Saint James since the previous year. Sarratea's principal task was to persuade the British cabinet to use its influence on Dom Pedro. Sarratea was ordered to tell Canning that the Argentine government wished to settle the question through negotiation, but under no circumstances would the territory be left in Brazilian possession. García also told the agent to cite the other republics' concern over the emperor's behavior and to emphasize the ease with which Buenos Aires could organize a coalition to recover the province of Montevideo by force.[28]

Simultaneously, García sent Manuel Irigoyen to present a new proposal for negotiations to the emperor. If Dom Pedro were willing to ratify the statements of his father at the time of the Portuguese occupation of the Banda Oriental—that is, if Dom Pedro

I-POB 26.2.825 Men.c 1–6. Raguet thought such confidence ill founded; see his dispatch to Clay, May 12, 1825, in Manning (ed.), *Diplomatic Correspondence*, II, 816.

27. The correspondence between Lobo and M. J. García was published in *Diário Fluminense*, August 10, 1825, pp. 134–36. See also J. R. Posey to [William Miller], July 18, 1825, in Ar-AGN, Sala VII, Carranza Ms, legajo 7-3-10; and Beverina, *La guerra*, 131–38.

28. M. J. García, "Instrucciones que deberá seguir el Sor Encargado de Negocios cerca de S. M. B.–D. Manuel de Sarratea" (Copy), September 7, 1825 (MS in Ar-AGN, Sala X, tomo 1-10-12, fls. 20–21); [M. J. García] to Stuart (Confidential, Copy), September 12, 1825, in GB-PRO, FO 13/18, fls. 44–45.

would agree that the intention of the Portuguese court had been to occupy the region temporarily until order had been restored in the Plata—the government of the United Provinces would commission plenipotentiaries to work out the details for the surrender of the province, presumably on the basis of a pecuniary reimbursement to Brazil.[29] Irigoyen, however, never proceeded farther than Montevideo. For reasons that remain obscure, he tarried there for three weeks, passing up several opportunities to sail for Rio de Janeiro. On learning of the Portuguese recognition of Brazilian independence, he returned to Buenos Aires in October.[30] Las Heras and García briefly considered yet another mission to Rio, but the pressures for war forced them to abandon diplomatic approaches once and for all.[31]

The Brazilian government also brought up the possibility of a negotiated settlement. In mid-August, the Rio chancery abruptly asked the British cabinet to mediate and instructed its representative in Vienna to persuade the Austrian government to support the idea in London.[32] This was almost certainly an artifice. The suggestion occurred soon after news of the annexation of Chiquitos reached the Brazilian capital; it formed part of a public-relations campaign, which included also the acceptance of the Colombian invitation to the Panama Congress, designed to placate the republican regimes and dampen enthusiasm for an anti-Brazilian coalition. In reality, Dom Pedro remained obstinate in his determination to retain possession of the Cisplatine.

The Oriental rebellion soon brought matters to a head. On August 25 the assembly organized by Lavalleja declared the Banda Oriental reincorporated into the United Provinces and named

29. M. J. García to Carvalho e Melo (Copy), September 12, 1825, in GB-PRO, FO 6/9, fls. 288–89; Forbes's notes on conference with M. J. García, September 15, 1825, in Forbes, *Once años*, 380–81.
30. Laguna to Carvalho e Melo, September 28, 1825, in Br-AHI, tomo 309/4/13; Parish to Canning (No. 68), October 10, 1825, in GB-PRO, FO 6/9, fls. 270–73; Thomas Samuel Hood to Planta (No. 28), October 13, 1825, in GB-PRO, FO 51/1, fls. 250–251.
31. Forbes to Clay (No. 25), October 15 (October 20 postscript), 1825, in Forbes, *Once años*, 390; Parish to Stuart (Copy), October 31, 1825, in GB-PRO, FO 13/20, fl. 89.
32. Carvalho e Melo to [Stuart] (Copy), [August 17, 1825], in GB-PRO, FO 13/4, fls. 113–15; Carvalho e Melo to Gameiro (No. 59), August 18, 1825, in *ADI*, I, 119–21; Carvalho e Melo to Teles da Silva (No. 27), August 18, 1825, in Br-AHI, Arquivo II, tomo 427/1/1.

delegates to the national congress, an action calculated to oblige Buenos Aires to join the military effort. The Argentine government at first avoided a public response and side-stepped a direct inquiry from the Brazilian political agent.[33] But victories by the Oriental rebels at Rincón de las Gallinas on September 24 and Sarandí on October 12 galvanized public opinion in Buenos Aires. The Argentine congress had already been debating in secret session whether to seat the Oriental delegates, and the exalted state of public sentiment carried the issue. On the night of October 20 a mob assaulted the residence of the Brazilian agent, who demanded his passports the following day, thereby severing relations between the two countries.[34] At about this time, Rivadavia arrived from London and began to excoriate the government for its procrastination and to demand an immediate declaration of war on Brazil. From the Banda Oriental came Tomás de Iriarte, bearing Lavalleja's plea for more substantial support. Dissatisfied with the response of Las Heras and García, Iriarte approached two influential members of congress and persuaded them to press for a decision to seat the Oriental delegates.[35]

On October 25 the congress officially declared the Banda Oriental reincorporated into the United Provinces and authorized the executive to provide for the defense of that territory. Notifying the imperial government of the congressional act, García tried even at this late date to be as conciliatory as the circumstances permitted. He affirmed that his government would preserve its "spirit of moderation and justice," and that "it will not attack except to defend itself and to obtain the restitution of the points still occupied, reducing its pretensions to conserving the integrity of the territory of the United Provinces and solemnly guaranteeing for the future the inviolability of its borders against force or sedition." Hoping that Dom Pedro might yield in the face of his military reverses in

33. Beverina, *La guerra*, 181–83; Antônio José Falcão da Frota to Carvalho e Melo (Nos. 10 and 11), September 13 and 14, 1825, in Br-AHI, tomo 205/2/15.

34. Falcão da Frota to Carvalho e Melo (No. 15), October 24, 1825, and accompanying docs., in Br-AHI, tomo 205/2/15; Forbes to Clay (No. 26), October 26, 1825, in Forbes, *Once años*, 292. On the two battles, see Beverina, *La guerra*, 159–180.

35. Funes to Bolívar, October 26, 1825, in O'Leary (ed.), *Memorias del general O'Leary*, XI, 150; Forbes to Clay (No. 27), November 16 (November 17 postscript), 1825, in Forbes, *Once años*, 396; Tomás de Iriarte, *Memorias* (Buenos Aires, 1944–69), III, 256–61.

the Cisplatine, the firm attitude of the United Provinces, and the possibility of Bolívar's involvement, García intended to avoid direct conflict while giving the emperor time to reconsider.[36]

As a matter of fact, the victories of the Oriental rebels had given pause to the imperial government. In a belated attempt to redress some of the grievances of the Orientals, Dom Pedro removed Lecor from command, reorganized the administration of the Cisplatine, and ordered that the port of Montevideo be opened in January, 1826. The Brazilian court was also reported to have decided, until dissuaded by military advisors, to propose new negotiations.[37]

Still, the emperor had no intention of giving up the occupied territory, and news of the reincorporation of the Banda Oriental into the United Provinces only stiffened his resolve. Henry Chamberlain, the British consul general in Rio, pictured the Brazilian cabinet as eager for war: "The proceedings of the Government and Congress of the River Plate Republick, have not in reality displeased the Brazilian Government; all of whose Members, as I have fully ascertained in my occasional Conversations with them during the last Month, were entirely disposed towards War, and are thankful to their Opponents for having spared them the odium of being the first to begin Hostilities, and the necessity of justifying them." On December 10 the imperial government formally declared war on the United Provinces and issued a lengthy memorandum explaining its rationale. A Spanish version of the memorandum was published, presumably for dissemination in the Banda Oriental and in the republics.[38]

The often-predicted war had come at last, for neither party would yet consider the expediency of creating an independent state. Although Brazil tried to forge an alliance with Paraguay, and

36. M. J. García to Carvalho e Melo, November 4, 1825, in *El Argos de Buenos Aires*, November 5, 1825, p. 1; Parish to Stuart (Copy), November 18, 1825, in GB-PRO, FO 13/11, fls. 212–13; Forbes to Clay (No. 28), November 29 (December 11 postscript), 1825, in Forbes, *Once años*, 402.

37. Stuart to Canning (No. 91), November 18, 1825, in GB-PRO, FO 13/6, fls. 197–99; "Noticias," November 30, 1825 (MS in Ar-AGN, Sala X, legajo 1-7-11).

38. Chamberlain to Canning (No. 145), December 5, 1825, in GB-PRO, FO 13/11, fl. 172; Brazil, *Manifiesto o exposición fundada, y justificativa del procedimiento de la Corte del Brasil con respecto al gobierno de las Provincias Unidas del Río de la Plata; y de los motivos que le obligan a declarar la guerra al referido gobierno* (Rio de Janeiro, 1825).

Buenos Aires sought the aid of Gran Colombia, Chile, and Bolivia, the conflict remained restricted to the original belligerents.

On paper, the Brazilian forces were far superior to the Argentine. The Brazilian navy managed to maintain an effective blockade of the Plata until a severe setback in February, 1827. On land,
however, Dom Pedro's troops did not gain even a temporary advantage. The army suffered from poor leadership, inadequate
supplies, corruption, disease, low morale, and a high desertion
rate. The Brazilian forces remained inactive for an entire year, al-
lowing the enemy time to prepare for battle. When the Brazilians
finally went into action in December, 1826, they proved no match
for the Argentines and Orientals. Moreover, opposition to the war
mounted in Brazil. Rio Grande do Sul bore the brunt of the war,
while forcible conscription caused hardships in other provinces.
By 1827 the liberals dominated the Chamber of Deputies and
ceaselessly attacked the government's prosecution of the war.[39]

After two years of stalemate in the Banda Oriental, both sides
came to realize the impossibility of settling the dispute by force of
arms, and the long-standing offer of British mediation was accepted. In 1828 the territorial question was resolved by creating
the independent state of Uruguay. The erection of a buffer state
in the Cisplatine extinguished neither the problem of borders nor
the Brazilian-Argentine competition for influence in the Plata. But
it did settle the thorniest issue of the period—possession of the
Banda Oriental—and provided the basis for a new status quo in
southern South America.

THE ANNEXATION OF CHIQUITOS

A second territorial issue involved the province of Chiquitos, a
sparsely populated and economically unimportant region in the
eastern lowlands of Bolivia, bordering on the Brazilian province
of Mato Grosso. On March 13, 1825, the governor of Chiquitos,
Sebastián Ramos, followed the lead of many other Upper Peruvian royalists in the wake of Ayacucho and defected to the insur-

39. Michael Charles McBeth, "The Politicians vs. the Generals: The Decline
of the Brazilian Army During the First Empire, 1822–1831" (Ph.D. dissertation,
University of Washington, 1972), 8–100, 112–32, 156–74; Beverina, *La guerra*,
249–362; Enrique de Gandía, *Los treinta y tres orientales y la independencia del
Uruguay* (Buenos Aires, 1939); Hann, "Brazil and the Río de la Plata," 407–425.

gent cause. A week later, however, he reversed himself on hearing that the republican chief in Santa Cruz had ordered his arrest for having served the royalists.[40] On March 20 Ramos sent his adjutant to negotiate an agreement with the government of Mato Grosso, asking that Brazil extend its protection to Chiquitos until King Ferdinand could reestablish his authority in South America. After some vacillation, the offer was accepted on April 13, and a party of sixty Brazilian soldiers was sent into Chiquitos to assist Ramos in defending the province against Sucre's army.[41]

The provisional government of the Brazilian province was dominated by residents of the city of Mato Grosso (formerly Vila Bela), who, with good reason, feared that their city would lose the status of provincial capital to Cuiabá. The economic decline of the old capital made the retention of its administrative functions essential to its continued survival. The desire to protect the status and economic welfare of their city thus induced the leaders of Mato Grosso to annex Chiquitos at Ramos' request. The city of Mato Grosso would be the geographical center of the enlarged province, and the townspeople would presumably gain the gratitude of the emperor by adding new lands to his domain. On the arrival of other members of the provisional government, however, the decision was reversed on May 13 and the Brazilian troops were recalled. The abrogation of the annexation agreement thus came about because of reconsideration by the Mato Grosso authorities, and not as a direct result of imperial or Spanish-American disapproval.[42]

On learning of Ramos' action, Sucre dispatched 200 men from

40. Sebastián Ramos to Sucre, March 13, 1825, in *El Cóndor de Bolivia* (Chuquisaca), January 19, 1826; [José] Videla to [Sucre], April 25, 1825, in Lecuna (ed.), *Documentos*, I, 188–190; *representación* of Ramos, June 10, 1832, accompanying Diego de la Riva to Bolivian minister of the interior (No. 99), October 25, 1832, in Bo-AN, MI, tomo 41, no. 33.

41. *Ata* of Mato Grosso provisional government, April 13, 1825, in "A anexação da província de Chiquitos," *Revista do Instituto Histórico de Mato Grosso*, IX (1927), 29–31; José Saturnino da Costa Pereira to Carvalho e Melo (No. 2), September 14, 1825, in Br-AHI, tomo 308/2/8. Sucre and other officials in Upper Peru mistakenly put the number of Brazilian soldiers at two hundred.

42. *Atas* of provisional government, May 13 and 21, 1825, in "A annexação da província de Chiquitos," 38–41; Ron L. Seckinger, "The Chiquitos Affair: An Aborted Crisis in Brazilian-Bolivian Relations," *Luso-Brazilian Review*, XI (1974), 22–23. The origins and consequences of the annexation of Chiquitos are treated in detail *ibid.*, 19–40.

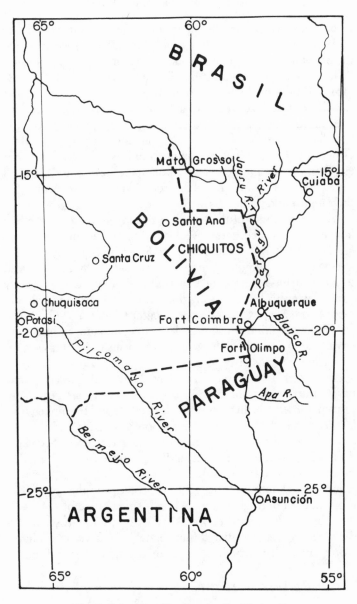

The Bolivian-Brazilian Border Region in 1825
(All borders approximate and in dispute)

Chuquisaca to reinforce the garrison at Santa Cruz, which was under the command of Colonel José Videla. Sucre suspected that the Brazilian invasion might be no more than another rumor; but he instructed Videla that, if Brazil had indeed violated the province of Chiquitos, he should politely ask the enemy commander to withdraw at once, and in case of intransigence should send his entire force against the intruders. The general planned not only "to throw them out of Chiquitos, but also to penetrate Mato Grosso and revolutionize the whole countryside, proclaiming liberty, republican and democratic principles, license itself, and all the elements of confusion and disorder that will make them regret their unjust and perfidious aggression."[43]

The commander of the Brazilian occupying force, which had not yet been recalled, soon revealed that the incursion was indeed real. On April 26 he sent a letter to Sucre, notifying him of the annexation of Chiquitos and the consequent absence of any need to move against the royalists there. In addition, with only sixty comrades at his back, the Brazilian warned Videla that, should forces from Santa Cruz attempt to enter Chiquitos, "I will proceed to destroy all the troops under your command, and also that city of Santa Cruz. I will leave only fragments of what it was, for the memory of posterity."[44]

The Brazilian commander's bravado was misplaced. Sucre, barely thirty years old and already a general for six years, had proven himself a brilliant military leader. He had triumphed over Spanish arms throughout northern South America and was not one to back away from a fight. Angrily, he retorted that Sebastián Ramos had no authority to surrender Chiquitos to Brazil and that the occupation of the province by Brazilian troops was "the most scandalous violation of the rights of peoples and the laws of nations, and an outrage that we will not suffer tranquilly." It was then that he threatened to wreak havoc on Mato Grosso unless the territory were evacuated immediately. To back up his harsh words, Sucre dispatched more troops to Santa Cruz and sent to

43. Sucre to Videla (No. 5, Copy), May 7, 1825, in Lecuna (ed.), *Documentos*, I, 200–201.

44. Araújo e Silva to Videla (Spanish trans., Copy), April 26, 1825, *ibid.*, 193; Araújo e Silva to Sucre (Copy), April 26, 1825, accompanying Sucre to Colombian secretary of war and navy (No. 30), May 24, 1825, in Co-AHN, SGM, tomo 374, fls. 797, 801.

Potosí for guns and munitions. He also ordered Videla to form guerrilla bands in Chiquitos and send agents to foment insurrection in Mato Grosso.[45]

Seasonal rains had inundated the road from Santa Cruz to Chiquitos and forestalled any immediate attempt to recover the occupied province and seek vengeance across the border. Before the road became passable, Videla and Sucre reassessed the Brazilian threat. Videla correctly guessed that the annexation was strictly a local affair, without the sanction of the emperor and even without the participation of Cuiabá. Sucre himself wrote Bolívar that "the Brazilians' little war near Santa Cruz does not amount to anything," but he was ready to retaliate if the Liberator so ordered.[46]

Bolívar reacted with similar reserve. Through his secretary, the Liberator overruled any consideration of an invasion of Brazil; if the conduct of the Spanish Americans were correct, he wrote from southern Peru, the "execration of nations" would fall wholly on the Brazilian commander. Like Videla, Bolívar doubted that the annexation had been undertaken with the emperor's blessing, and he conjectured that the Continental Alliance might take advantage of an invasion of Brazil to accuse the republics of trying to destroy the only monarchy in America. The Liberator authorized the recovery of Chiquitos, but only under the strictest discipline and without the use of guerrilla forces. Not wanting to involve the government of Gran Colombia in a conflict with Brazil, he ordered that only Peruvian troops be used in the operation.[47]

Despite Bolívar's caution, the possibility of a retaliatory invasion apparently was the subject of much discussion among the officers of his staff. One wrote a correspondent in Bogotá: "If present circumstances do not change their aspect, it is not altogether impossible that our next campaign will be against Brazil." The anonymous officer reviewed the events of the Chiquitos affair and concluded, with a confidence betraying his ignorance of Brazilian

45. Sucre to Araújo e Silva (Copy), May 11, 1825, in Lecuna (ed.), *Documentos*, I, 209–10; Sucre to [Videla] (No. 4, Copy), May 11, 1825, *ibid.*, 210–212; [Sucre] to prefect of Potosí (Draft), May 11, 1825, in Bo-AN, MI, tomo 8, no. 63.

46. Videla to Sucre (Copy), May 10, 1825, in Lecuna (ed.), *Documentos*, I, 203; Sucre to Bolívar, May 12, 1825, in O'Leary (ed.), *Memorias del general O'Leary*, I, 257.

47. [Estenós] to Sucre (Copy), May 29, 1825, in Lecuna (ed.), *Documentos*, I, 482–83.

geography: "For my own part, I have no doubts of the result of a War, as we could easily embark our troops down the Marañón, and at once put an end to the Brazilian Empire."[48]

Only the rains averted a clash between Brazilians and Spanish Americans in Chiquitos. By the time Videla's troops managed to enter the province, the Brazilian forces had withdrawn to Mato Grosso, followed by Ramos and other royalist émigrés. Either the soldiers or the royalists, or both, plundered the missions of Chiquitos in their hurried retreat, and Videla's demands for the return of the stolen silverwork and cattle were not completely satisfied for almost a year. Nonetheless, authorities in Mato Grosso hastened to make appropriate expressions of regret over the incident and to restore the stolen goods, hoping to forestall retaliation. William Miller, the English-born general now serving as prefect of Potosí, wrote in late July, "The affair of the Brazilians has dissipated like smoke."[49]

The townspeople of Mato Grosso had clearly expected that the emperor would approve of the annexation of Chiquitos. In justifying its action, the provisional government stressed the military advantages accruing to the empire from the absorption of the neighboring province. The additional territory, it was asserted, could be easily defended and would serve as a buffer zone to protect the capital of Mato Grosso from attack. The municipal council, in a separate communication, mentioned not only improved defenses but also the addition of 60,000 subjects to the empire and the acquisition of natural resources needed in Mato Grosso, such as salt and copper.[50]

Gregorio Funes, the Argentine-born prelate who represented Gran Colombia in Buenos Aires, saw the Chiquitos affair within

48. "Extract of a letter from an officer on the personal staff of General Bolívar dated Arequipa June 7th, 1825" (MS in GB-PRO, FO 18/14, fls. 211–12). See also F[rancis] B[urdett] O'Connor to [Miller], June 7, 1825, in Ar-AGN, Sala VII, Carranza Ms, legajo 7-3-9.

49. Seckinger, "The Chiquitos Affair," 27–30; [Miller] to Las Heras (Draft), July 27, 1825, in Ar-AGN, Sala VII, Carranza Ms, legajo 7-4-2.

50. Mato Grosso provisional government to Pedro I, April 15, 1825, in Br-AHI, tomo 308/2/8; Mato Grosso town council to Pedro I, April 13, 1825, in Br-AN, SPE, pasta IJJ⁹ 527. The council exaggerated the population of Chiquitos, which stood at about 16,000. "Estado gral. que manifiesta el numero de Almas, q. tiene cada uno de los diez Pueblos, q. componen este Partido de Chiqˢ . . . ," December 12, 1825 (MS accompanying José Miguel de Velasco to [Sucre, No. 290], December 27, 1825, in Bo-AN, MI, tomo 4, no. 14).

the context of Luso-Brazilian expansionism. To Bolívar he related a conversation with Manuel José García, the Argentine minister of government and foreign relations:

> The ambitious projects of the Portuguese Brazilians and the means of containing them occupied us for a long while. We established, first of all, that extending the breadth of their Empire from the Amazon River to the banks of the Paraguay and Plata Rivers enters into their general plan, without renouncing their ancient pretensions with regard to the frontier of Peru, of which I spoke at length in my *Ensayo Histórico*, dealing with the dividing line [of 1494], always frustrated by their perfidy and their evil artifices.
>
> With these antecedents, it would not be strange to imagine that the invasion of Chiquitos was a consequence of the spirit that animates them. But on this point I agree with the Minister in that it was done without the Emperor's order and only with the presumed object of pleasing him. Perhaps the invader knew that the Emperor viewed with mortal disgust the war that Your Excellency waged on the Spaniards of Peru.[51]

To Funes, then, the annexation represented yet another example of Brazilians taking advantage of the opportunity to move their borders to the west. When news of the affair reached the Brazilian capital in early August, however, Dom Pedro immediately disavowed the actions of the Mato Grosso government as opposed to his "generous and liberal principles" and published the disavowal in the *Diário Fluminense*.[52] Chiquitos lacked the commercial and strategic value of the Banda Oriental, and the emperor had no interest in a quixotic scheme of aggrandizement in the west while his attempt to absorb the Cisplatine was being challenged in the south. The short-lived annexation of Chiquitos yielded no new lands to Brazil but rather enraged the authorities in the emerging nation of Bolivia and fanned Spanish-American suspicions of the emperor.

51. Funes to Bolívar, August 26, 1825, in O'Leary (ed.), *Memorias del general O'Leary*, XI, 139–40. See also Gregorio Funes, *Ensayo de la historia civil del Paraguay, Buenos-Ayres y Tucumán* (Buenos Aires, 1816–17), III, 371–73.
52. Decree of August 6, 1825, in *Diário Fluminense*, August 6, 1825, p. 121.

OTHER BOUNDARY QUESTIONS

The Banda Oriental and Chiquitos disputes were the most serious territorial issues faced by Pedro I, but they were not the only ones. Not one of Brazil's borders was definitively established at the time of independence. By 1834 most of the neighboring states had made some effort to negotiate boundary settlements. The first Peruvian minister to Rio, for example, broached the matter with the imperial government in 1827, but he was recalled before any serious discussions began. The Lima chancery considered the question of the Brazilian-Peruvian frontier an important one but did not press the matter. Duarte da Ponte Ribeiro, the Brazilian minister in Lima, reported in 1832: "This Government knows the difficulties of such a Treaty, and, every time a conversation has taken place on this matter, I have not found it difficult to persuade [the government] that it should be left for later."[53]

The first Colombian minister to Rio was authorized to negotiate a treaty of limits, but he professed to be unable to accomplish anything for lack of information about the border region. His replacement, Juan María Gómez, raised the issue with the Brazilian foreign minister in August, 1829, but found him unprepared to discuss it. The Colombian quickly assured the foreign minister that Bogotá was more interested in a treaty of friendship, trade, and navigation and was willing to put aside the boundary question for the moment. Gómez offered these reassurances "in order to dissipate any suspicion of sinister views on the part of Colombia with regard to extension of territory, etc., so that this fear not frustrate the celebration of the treaty of friendship."[54]

In January, 1830, however, the Colombian representative again brought up the matter. The Brazilian government pointed out that little was known of the topography and settlement patterns in the Upper Amazon but offered to insert in the treaty of friendship a clause stating that "there be recognized, for the time being, as limits those that are currently considered as such." As preparation

53. Cáceres to Marquês de Queluz, July 25, 1827, in Br-AHI, tomo 287/4/10; Duarte da Ponte Ribeiro, "Memoria sobre as Republicas do Pacifico," April 7, 1832 (MS in Br-AHI, Ponte Ribeiro Ms, lata 269, maço 3, pasta 1).
54. Revenga to Palacios, June 6, 1826, and Palacios to Colombian MRE (No. 28), March 2, 1828, in Co-ADC, tomo 158, fls. 6–8, 242–43; Juan María Gómez to Colombian MRE (No. 6), August 26, 1829, *ibid.*, tomo 159, fl. 90.

Pedro I, emperor of Brazil, 1822–1831

From Assis Cintra, *D. Pedro I e o Grito da Independência* (São Paulo, 1921).
Reprinted by permission of Companhia Melhoramentos de São Paulo.

Coronation of Pedro I, December 1, 1822

From Jean Baptiste Debret, *Voyage pittoresque et historique au Brésil*
(1834–39), III.

Simón Bolívar, president of Gran Colombia, 1819–1830;
dictator of Peru, 1824–1826; president of Bolivia, 1825.

From *Bolívar: Hombre del presente, nuncio del porvenir* (Lima, 1978), 92.
Reprinted by permission of Auge Editores S.A.

Antonio José de Sucre, president of Bolivia, 1825–1828
Courtesy William L. Lofstrom

Bernardino Rivadavia, Argentine minister of government and
foreign relations, 1821–1824; Argentine minister to Great
Britain, 1824–1825; president of the United Provinces of the
Río de la Plata, 1826–1827.

From Diego Abad de Santillán, *Historia Argentina*
(Buenos Aires, 1965), II, 133.
Reprinted by permission of Tipográfica Editora Argentina S.A.

José Gaspar de Francia, supreme dictator of Paraguay,
1814–1840
From J. P. Robertson and W. P. Robertson, *Letters on Paraguay* . . .
(London, 1838), I, frontispiece.

Francisco de Paula Santander, vice-president of Gran
Colombia, 1821–1828

From cover of *1840—Muerte de Santander* (Bogotá, 1940). Reprinted by
permission of the Academia Colombiana de Historia.

Manuel Dorrego, governor of Buenos Aires Province,
1827–1828

From Manuel Dorrego, *Dorrego, tribuno y periodista* (Buenos Aires, 1907),
frontispiece.

José Bonifácio

José Bonifácio de Andrada e Silva, Brazilian minister of the
empire and foreign affairs, 1822–1823
From José Maria Latino Coelho, *Elogio histórico de José Bonifácio* (Rio de
Janeiro, [1942]).

Manuel José García, Argentine minister of government and
foreign relations, 1825–1827; Argentine emissary
to Brazil, 1827.

From Diego Abad de Santillán, *Historia Argentina*
(Buenos Aires, 1965), II, 103.
Reprinted by permission of Tipográfica Editora Argentina S.A.

Pedro Gual, Colombian minister of foreign relations,
1821–1825; Colombian minister to the American Congress,
1825–1829.

From Rafael Caldera, *Pedro Gual: El Congreso de Panamá y la integración
latinoamericana* (Caracas, 1976), frontispiece. Reprinted by permission of
Presidencia de la República de Venezuela.

George Canning, British foreign secretary, 1822–1827
From George Canning, *Speeches* (Liverpool, 1825), frontispiece.

Gregorio Funes, Colombian minister to the United Provinces,
1823–1827; Bolivian minister to the United Provinces,
1827–1828.

From Mariano de Vedia y Mitre, *El Deán Funes en la historia argentina*
(2nd ed.; Buenos Aires, 1910), frontispiece.

Mariano Egaña, Chilean minister to Great Britain,
1825–1829
From Mariano Egaña, *Cartas de Mariano Egaña, 1824–1829*
(Santiago, 1948), frontispiece.

for a permanent settlement, the imperial government suggested a return to the expedient of the 1750 and 1777 treaties: each party should name a commission of engineers to explore the frontier region and determine the proper boundaries. Gómez judged this a reasonable suggestion and one at harmony with the interests of Gran Colombia. He recommended that the Bogotá chancery obtain a copy of a memorandum on the area written by Baron Alexander von Humboldt, the German naturalist who had explored much of Spanish America at the turn of the century.[55]

Officially, the negotiation of commercial and boundary treaties had been left to the Colombian government and the Brazilian minister in Bogotá. But Gómez, fearing that the antagonism of the Brazilian Chamber of Deputies toward the diplomatic corps would lead to the closing of many legations, including the mission to Gran Colombia, offered to take over the negotiations himself in Rio. A prompt settlement was urgent, he wrote the Colombian foreign minister, because the Brazilians were taking advantage of Colombia's internal troubles to occupy points along the border.[56]

The Brazilian minister did not even propose a treaty of limits to the Bogotá chancery, because he reasoned that Brazil soon might have to deal with an independent Venezuelan government. As Gran Colombia sank into domestic turmoil and Bolívar left in disgust for a voluntary exile, the Colombian government instructed Gómez to suspend any efforts to obtain treaties with Brazil until peace and unity were restored.[57] In 1831 the Brazilian legation in Bogotá was closed, followed by the Colombian legation in Rio de Janeiro the next year. The question of boundaries was left for a later generation to resolve.

With regard to common borders with Paraguay, the imperial government enjoyed a strong position, because the Portuguese crown had established fortifications on the Paraguay River dur-

55. [MNE] to J. M. Gómez (Draft), March 3, 1830, in Br-AHI, maço 282/3/16; J. M. Gómez to Colombian MRE (No. 5), March 4, 1830, in Co-ADC, tomo 159, fls. 92–93.

56. J. M. Gómez to Colombian MRE (No. 9), October 30, 1830, in Co-ADC, tomo 159, fl. 95.

57. Sousa Dias to Miguel Calmon du Pin e Almeida (No. 16, Copy), July 3, 1830, in Br-AHI, Arquivo II, tomo 403/2/3; Vicente Barrero to J. M. Gómez (No. 3), November 14, 1830, in Co-ADC, tomo 159, fl. 97; marginal note dated March 28, 1831, on dispatch from J. M. Gómez to Colombian MRE (No. 9), October 30, 1830, in Co-ADC, tomo 159, fl. 95. See also Zubieta, *Apuntaciones*, 532–49.

ing the eighteenth century. Dr. Francia, however, claimed all the lands north to the Río Blanco on the left bank of the Paraguay and to the Rio Jauru on the right bank. He insisted that Brazil evacuate Fort Coimbra and the settlement of Albuquerque in southern Mato Grosso. Francia was unable to push the Brazilians out, however, and the imperial government eventually imposed a settlement on defeated Paraguay following the war of 1864–1870.[58]

The creation of Uruguay did not eliminate the need to fix boundaries in the extreme south. The leaders of the emergent state feared that Brazil and Argentina—which, by the peace convention that had ended the war, were to examine and pass judgment on the Uruguayan constitution before withdrawing their troops and leaving the Orientals to themselves—would define borders to their own satisfaction. Thus, the Uruguayan observer at the Brazilian-Argentine talks in Rio de Janeiro received instructions to insist that his government's views be taken into consideration. "The question of limits," wrote Fructuoso Rivera, then minister of foreign relations in Montevideo, "which should be discussed and resolved in drafting and concluding the definitive treaty, is too grave and too much affects the principal interests of this State for it to be abandoned exclusively to the Ministers of His Majesty the Emperor and of the Argentine Republic."[59] The imperial government, however, made it clear to Buenos Aires that their common interest required they not consent to "the expansion of the territory that constitutes the new Oriental state of Uruguay beyond the limits currently recognized or that might be established by a subsequent treaty." In other words, the two powerful states should impose boundaries on Uruguay and, more specifically, never permit the incorporation of Entre Ríos or Rio Grande do Sul into the new nation.[60]

Montevideo later took the lead in challenging Brazil on the is-

58. Francia to [José León] Ramírez, June 8, 1829, in Pa-AN, SH, vol. 240; Ramos, *La política del Brasil*, 21–43; Harris G. Warren, "Brazil's Paraguayan Policy, 1869–1876," *The Americas*, XXVIII (1972), 388–406; John Hoyt Williams, "The Undrawn Line: Three Centuries of Strife on the Paraguayan-Mato Grosso Frontier," *Luso-Brazilian Review*, XVII (1980), 28–35.

59. Fructuoso Rivera to [Nicolás Herrera] (No. 3 bis), January 9, 1830, in Ur-AGN, FAA, Herrera Ms, caja 17, carpeta 3.

60. Guido to Argentine MRE (No. 16), June 22, 1830, in Ar-AGN, Sala X, legajo 1-7-6.

sue of borders. In mid-1834, the Uruguayan foreign minister proposed to his Bolivian counterpart that the Spanish-American nations form a bloc for the purpose of negotiating boundary settlements with Brazil from a position of strength. They should insist that frontiers be delimited according to the areas occupied by Spain and Portugal, determined whenever possible by the treaty of 1777 and subsequent operations of the binational boundary commissions. The Uruguayan foreign minister appealed to the solidarity and common interests of the republics:

> The Hispanic American States—members of a single family and heirs, by titles of birth and glory, of the soil their ancestors took possession of—have been able in good time to establish their reciprocal independence, without failing, however, to preserve those bonds that should guarantee the integrity of their common patrimony against the pretensions of outsiders. The documents that each of these States guards in its archives, the traditions of their inhabitants, [and] the indestructible monuments that testify to the ancient origin of the existence of sites are all necessarily connected pieces of a single, indivisible title that all of the sister Republics owe each other in the self-interest of each, but especially of those that have the immediate interest of not seeing their own territory dismembered.

Uruguay proposed that the republics pool their information about the frontier regions and prepare a common brief to establish their ownership. Each country would dispatch an accredited minister to Rio de Janeiro, carrying "instructions to proceed in absolute agreement [with the other Spanish-American representatives] in regard to everything concerning the true limits of each of the confederated Republics, without consenting that a single one be defrauded of its just pretensions."[61]

The Bolivian government agreed to the proposal, but the imperial cabinet easily turned aside the attempt to form a Spanish-American bloc.[62] Moreover, an independent Bolivian effort to fix

61. J. Obes to Bolivian MRE (Copy), July 13, 1834, in Bo-AMREC, tomo BRA-1-R-1, fls. 14–15.

62. Mariano Armaza to Uruguayan MRE (Copy), [n.d.], *ibid.*, fl. 15; Andrés Santa Cruz to Armaza, March 4, 1835, in Bo-UMSA, Biblioteca Central, Sección

the borders with Brazil came to naught. In 1835 the Brazilian cabinet declared itself unable to negotiate a boundary settlement, citing "the state of confusion in which the Empire was found, and with two provinces in open rebellion," the lack of urgency in determining permanent borders, and the delay in obtaining documents from Mato Grosso.[63]

In time, the wisdom of the Uruguayan proposal would become apparent. Individually, the Spanish-American nations were no match for Brazil in securing territorial claims, either by direct negotiation or by mediation. Rio de Janeiro successfully evaded definitive settlements in the early years of independence and eventually earned a well-deserved reputation for obtaining favorable decisions on boundary disputes, particularly under the Barão do Rio Branco. Independent Brazil upheld the Portuguese tradition of territorial expansion.

TRADE

Commercial questions also arose between the Brazilian monarchy and the republics. With the collapse of the monopolistic commercial systems of Spain and Portugal, the successor states of Latin America had the opportunity to expand trade among themselves as well as with the industrializing nations of the North Atlantic. Brazil's main commercial interests in South America lay, as always, in the Plata. In 1822 Brazil supplied 12.6 percent of the total imports that passed through the port of Buenos Aires, ranking second only to Britain, which accounted for 50.9 percent. The Brazilians furnished sugar, *yerba mate* (herbal tea), tobacco, rum, and a number of other products, receiving mostly specie and some tallow in return.[64] The Cisplatine War temporarily interrupted this profitable traffic, but the trade resumed with the return of peace in 1828. Commercial concerns were among the causes of the war;

de Manuscritos, tomo 617, fl. 105; Juan E. Pivel Devoto, "La misión de Francisco J. Muñoz a Bolivia: Contribución al estudio de nuestra historia diplomática (1831–1835)," *Revista del Instituto Histórico y Geográfico del Uruguay*, IX (1932), 213–98; [Álvaro] Teixeira Soares, *Diplomacia do império no Rio da Prata (até 1865)* (Rio de Janeiro, 1955), 75–85.

63. Armaza to Bolivian MRE (No. 35), December 21, 1835, in Bo-AMREC, tomo BRA-1-R-1, fl. 135.

64. R. Montgomery *et al.*, "Report on the Trade of the River Plate," July 29, 1824 (MS in GB-PRO, FO 6/4, fls. 174, 193–95).

one of the principal motives for the Luso-Brazilian attempt to absorb the Banda Oriental was the prospect of greater participation in the Platine trade, and the resistance of the United Provinces stemmed in part from the determination to deny the empire such an advantage.[65]

Brazil also maintained commercial relations with Paraguay. Dr. Francia permitted a strictly controlled trade through Itapúa (present-day Encarnación), on the Paraná River. To overtures for an exchange with Mato Grosso, however, the Paraguayan dictator turned a deaf ear. He wanted nothing to do with "the contemptible trade in bagatelles, which amounts to no more than some hammocks, a little bit of cotton, and some bolts of very ordinary, crude cotton cloth," and which he suspected would merely provide a pretext for spying.[66]

The authorities in Mato Grosso also attempted to develop commerce with Bolivia. Despite the reciprocal interest of the Bolivians, however, no realistic basis for a profitable exchange existed, and the trade never amounted to anything.[67]

The possibility of commercial interchange in the Amazon basin arose soon after Brazil became independent. In 1823 the Colombian minister in London recommended the establishment of relations with Brazil, citing as one advantage the opportunity to develop trade in the Amazon: "Even though disputes have arisen recently between Brazil and Buenos Aires over the future possession of Montevideo, they should not impede Colombia's hastening to make the banks of the Río Negro prosper, and even to attract the products of that Brazilian frontier toward the Orinoco, since Angostura [present-day Ciudad Bolívar, in Venezuela] offers them a better and more accessible market than [Belém do]

65. See, for example, the following: Forbes to Adams [No. 10], April 1, 1821, in Manning (ed.), *Diplomatic Correspondence,* I, 575; "Consideraciones politico-mercantiles sobre la incorporacion de Montevideo, Por I.S.V. Natural de Minas Gerais," 1822 (MS in Br-BN, SM, I-31, 22, 17); Hood to Canning, April 22, 1824, and Manuel de Sarratea to Canning, November 7, 1825, in Webster (ed.), *Britain and the Independence of Latin America,* I, 110, 135.

66. Francia to Ramírez, March 24, 1824, in Pa-AN, SH, vol. 237. For a subsequent attempt to open trade from Mato Grosso, see Saturnino to Visconde de Santo Amaro (No. 4), March 15, 1826, and Saturnino to Inhambupe (No. 9), June 14, 1826, in Br-AHI, tomo 308/2/8. On the Itapúa trade, see Williams, *The Rise and Fall of the Paraguayan Republic,* 67–71.

67. See the correspondence in Br-AHI, tomo 308/2/8, and in Bo-AN, MI, tomo 14, no. 18.

Para or Macapá."[68] Others made similar suggestions from time to time, but by 1830 both the Colombian minister in Rio and the Brazilian minister in Bogotá had realized that commerce between the two countries—whether by river, sea, or land—was unlikely for the immediate future. When the Colombian legation in the Brazilian capital was closed in 1831, the Bogotá chancery instructed the departing minister that any vice-consuls named by him should cease their functions.[69]

The notion of an Amazon trade also found currency in Peru,[70] but Ponte Ribeiro doubted its feasibility. "Commercial relations between this country and Brazil," he wrote from Lima in 1829, "are and will always be null because they produce the same products."[71] Chile, on the other hand, offered excellent possibilities to Brazilian merchants, in Ponte Ribeiro's view. He argued that Chile had not only better prospects than the other republics for consolidating internal order but also an economy complementing Brazil's. The empire, he suggested, could trade *yerba mate*, sugar, coffee, and tobacco for specie and wheat flour.[72]

By the 1830s the high hopes for a vigorous trade between Brazil and Spanish America had faded. In 1835 the imperial government maintained consular representatives only in Buenos Aires and Montevideo; of the South American republics, only Argentina, Uruguay, and Chile had consular officials in Brazil.[73]

Commercial questions were not of critical importance in intra-

68. Revenga to Colombian MRE (No. 46), May 27, 1823, Co-ADC, tomo 475, fl. 56. See also Rebelo to Carvalho e Melo (No. 25), June 25, 1825, in Br-AHI, tomo 233/2/19; and Estanislao Vergara to [Estenós] (Copy), May 11, 1829, in Co-AHN, H/AA, tomo 28, fls. 365–66.

69. Dias to Calmon (No. 16, Copy), July 3, 1830, in Br-AHI, Arquivo II, tomo 403/2/3; J. M. Gómez to Colombian MRE (No. 9), October 30, 1830, in Co-ADC, tomo 159, fl. 95; Félix Restrepo to J. M. Gómez (No. 16, Copy), August 7, 1831, in Co-ADC, tomo 50, fl. 123.

70. Ricketts to Canning (No. 26), December 27, 1826, in Humphreys (ed.), *British Consular Reports*, 181; Ponte Ribeiro to Aracati (Nos. 4 and 8), October 26 and December 16, 1829, in Br-AHI, tomo 212/2/4; Ponte Ribeiro, "Memoria," April 7, 1832 (MS in Br-AHI, Ponte Ribeiro Ms, lata 269, maço 3, pasta 1).

71. Ponte Ribeiro to [Gomes da Silva?], October 24, 1829, in Br-AHMI, I-POB 24.10.829 Rib.c.

72. Ponte Ribeiro to Aracati, September 14, 1829, to Calmon (No. 8), May 28, 1830, and to Francisco Carneiro de Campos, August 15, 1832, all in Br-AHI, tomo 212/2/4. For a Chilean appreciation of the Brazilian trade, see [Egaña to Chilean MRE] (No. 137, Copy), September 18, 1826, in Ch-AN, MinRE, vol. 13.

73. Brazil, Ministério das Relações Exteriores, *Relatório*, 1835, n. p.

South American relations unless they were tied up with territorial and strategic issues, as in the cases of the Banda Oriental and Guayaquil disputes. Likewise, the problem of boundaries became pivotal only when the contested territory offered immediate economic or strategic benefits. In the case of the Banda Oriental, the boundary question overshadowed all other considerations. The Buenos Aires government's casting of the quarrel in ideological terms was an attempt to obtain the support of the other republics by cloaking specific and direct advantages in lofty principles. Significantly, valuable territory was at stake in both of the international wars that took place in South America in the 1820s, and these two conflicts served as the foci of South American power politics during that period.

Four • Power Politics
Alliances and Illusions

 DURING THE 1820s the ground rules of international relations in South America were in flux. The leaders of the various South American states self-consciously looked to European models and frequently cited the desirability of maintaining "equilibrium" on the continent. These same leaders intuitively perceived threats to their own countries' security or hegemony in the actions of their neighbors, and they responded in ways calculated to preserve and further their own national interests. In short, South Americans participated in a system of power politics.

Robert N. Burr defines such a system in terms of efforts to maintain equilibrium, competition for relative advantage according to certain principles and techniques, primary concern with intrasystem relations, and relative freedom from external influences. Focusing on the development of a continental system, he divides the nineteenth century into two periods: the era of *regional* power politics, from independence to the late 1860s, and the era of *continental* power politics, from the late 1860s into the first quarter of the twentieth century.[1]

Practically all of the characteristics enumerated by Burr were already present in the 1820s: governments perceived and responded to threats to the equilibrium, competed in accordance with the principles of power politics, emphasized relations with the other nations of the continent rather than with outside powers, and enjoyed relative freedom from external pressures. But other elements were lacking. Technological limitations precluded

1. Robert N. Burr, *By Reason or Force: Chile and the Balancing of Power in South America, 1830–1905* (Berkeley, Calif., 1965), 3–10.

the ability to communicate intentions quickly and effectively at distant points. The precarious progress of state building, as reflected in weak national governments and chronic instability, also hampered the formation of a continental system.

The Brazilian empire was a key element in the power politics of the 1820s. Although the orientation of his foreign policy was decidedly European, Dom Pedro actively pursued territorial and commercial interests in the Plata and participated in one of the two major international conflicts of the period. As the largest and most populous country in South America, and as a monarchy linked to the ruling houses of Europe, Brazil provoked fear and jealousy in the republics. The empire thus figured prominently in the maneuvering among the Spanish-American nations.

BRAZIL AND PARAGUAY

In its efforts to maintain possession of the Banda Oriental, the imperial government turned to Paraguay as a possible ally. Antônio Manuel Corréia da Cámara had been commissioned to represent Brazil in Asunción as well as Buenos Aires in 1822, but he had returned directly from the Argentine capital without attempting to break down the diplomatic isolation of Paraguay, unbreached since 1813. In July, 1823, the former agent penned a long, rambling memorandum to the minister of foreign affairs, proposing a Paraguayan alliance as the cornerstone of Brazil's Platine policy. According to Corréia da Câmara's view of the world, the Continental Alliance was the only first-rate power, Britain but a fading star, the United States a "caricature of Power," Peru and Upper Peru "forever secured" for Spain, and the other American republics no more than contemptible and anarchic principalities. Only Paraguay, under the benign despotism of Dr. Francia, merited praise. "Allied to that Government," Corréia da Câmara declared, "we would easily dispose of the Province of Entre Ríos. Our Southern Provinces would then be impenetrable. Without this Alliance we will lose the Cisplatine State and leave Rio Grande do Sul and Mato Grosso exposed; we will be weak and little consistent anywhere else." In closing, he offered to undertake the mission to Asunción.[2]

2. Corréia da Câmara to [Francisco Carneiro de Campos], July 28, 1823, in Br-AHI, tomo 205/2/14.

The imperial government made no immediate response, perhaps from fear of offending Buenos Aires while Valentín Gómez attempted to negotiate a settlement of the Banda Oriental dispute. But in April, 1824, two months after Gómez had departed Rio, Corréia da Câmara was designated consul and commercial agent to Paraguay.[3] At the consul's urging, the foreign minister subsequently authorized him to assume the functions of political agent if Dr. Francia would accept him in that capacity. Luring the government of Paraguay, and those of other Platine provinces if possible, into some accommodation with Brazil formed the object of Corréia da Câmara's mission.[4]

The agent did not leave Rio de Janeiro until the last quarter of 1824. After spending some time in Montevideo, he at length arrived at the border in mid-1825 and secured permission to proceed to Asunción, the first foreign diplomat to do so in twelve years. In the last days of August, Corréia da Câmara entered the Paraguayan capital like some latter-day Marco Polo. His reports described a numerous and contented populace tending bountiful fields and thriving under the firm guidance of the benevolent Dr. Francia. The Brazilian emissary noted a general antipathy toward Buenos Aires, and, after conversations with the dictator, he confidently anticipated the forging of an alliance between the two countries. United with Paraguay, he wrote his superiors in Rio de Janeiro, Brazil need fear nothing in the Plata nor on the frontier with Upper Peru.[5]

During the three months he remained in Asunción, Corréia da Câmara courted the strange, ascetic Dr. Francia, who was nearing his fiftieth birthday. In losing no opportunity to demonstrate the good intentions of the imperial government, the Brazilian agent conceded every point raised by the dictator. Corréia da Câmara promised that subsequent communications would address Dr. Francia as chief of an independent republic and not as governor of the province of Paraguay; that borders would be adjusted to Paraguay's satisfaction; and that the imperial government would prevent further Indian attacks from Mato Grosso, which, accord-

3. Corréia da Câmara to [Carvalho e Melo], April 28, 1824, *ibid.*, tomo 201/1/5. The formal decree was dated May 31, 1824; *ADI*, V, 245–47.

4. Ramos, *La política del Brasil*, 81–84.

5. Corréia da Câmara to Carvalho e Melo (No. 1, Secret), September 4, 1825, in Br-AHI, tomo 201/1/5.

ing to Francia, took place with the encouragement of the Brazilian authorities on the frontier. In addition to these sweeping pledges, Corréia da Câmara promised that Brazil would furnish certain munitions to Paraguay. Lacking authorization to negotiate a treaty embodying these points, he departed for Rio de Janeiro to obtain new credentials. In the closing days of 1825 the imperial government, now officially at war with the United Provinces, instructed him to conclude a treaty of defensive alliance with Paraguay or, at the very least, to secure Francia's neutrality. But Corréia da Câmara was already en route to the Brazilian capital.[6]

The Brazilian agent apparently had not posted his correspondence, no doubt because of his oft-expressed fear of spies, and his auspicious reception in Asunción was revealed only on his arrival in Rio in early February, 1826. The imperial government followed up with a direct communication to Dr. Francia, bestowing de facto recognition on his regime. The Brazilian foreign ministry promised to halt the Indian depredations from Mato Grosso and to give careful consideration to Paraguay's territorial claims. Dr. Francia was told that a duly authorized diplomatic agent would soon depart for Asunción to take up matters of mutual interest. In the meantime, the foreign minister ordered the government of Mato Grosso to discourage the Indian forays into Paraguay and facilitate the negotiations of the Brazilian representative in Asunción.[7]

Not surprisingly, the post of chargé d'affaires to Paraguay went to Corréia da Câmara. Named in April, 1826, the agent remained in Rio until late November, during which time he bombarded the foreign minister, the Marquês de Inhambupe, with a steady stream of recommendations. In his eagerness to obtain a Paraguayan al-

6. Ramos, *La política del Brasil*, 107–27. See also [Corréia da Câmara to Carvalho e Melo?], November 4 and 15, 1825, in Br-BN, SM, Rio-Branco Ms, I-29, 26, 10, docs. 41 and 43.

7. *Diário Fluminense*, February 10, 1826, pp. 125–26; Luís Moutinho Lima Álvares e Silva to José Gabriel Benítez (Copy), March 17, 1826, in Br-AHI, maço 318/4/6; [Inhambupe to Saturnino] (Drafts), March 20 and June 2, 1826, in Br-AHI, maço 308/2/15. Halting the Indian attacks remained a preoccupation of the Brazilian government for years. Saturnino to Inhambupe (No. 21), December 4, 1826, and Saturnino to Queluz (No. 6), April 5, 1827, in Br-AHI, tomo 308/2/8; Jerônimo Joaquim Nunes to José Antonio Sosa, January 15, 1827, in Pa-AN, SH, vol. 232; Calmon to Conde do Pardo, March 6, 1830, in Br-AN, SPE, pasta IG¹ 321. For a study of this long-standing problem, mainly from the Paraguayan point of view, see Williams, "The Undrawn Line," 17–40.

liance, Corréia da Câmara urged that Brazil meet all of Francia's demands and ingratiate him in any way, to the point of replacing Brazilian personnel on the borders. He also advocated that the imperial government send the dictator, as a sign of good faith, twelve artillery pieces and 100 horses in addition to the munitions Francia had requested.[8]

Inhambupe did not heed all of these suggestions, which would have made good Corréia da Câmara's unauthorized promises to the Paraguayan chief. The foreign minister did empower his representative to negotiate a treaty, but only regarding peace, friendship, and trade. The treaty was to provide for the exchange of diplomatic, consular, and commercial agents; for unrestricted trade between the two countries; and for the creation of a mixed commission to delineate the borders. Corréia da Câmara objected that Francia would never agree to unrestricted commerce and argued that he himself should be authorized to conclude a border settlement without the expedient of a mixed commission.[9] Inhambupe accepted the notion of a regulated trade but declined to place sweeping powers in the hands of his representative.

In February, 1827, Corréia da Câmara arrived in the Missions territory and notified Dr. Francia of his new credentials. Although permitted to cross the Paraná River to Itapúa in September, the Brazilian agent waited in vain for authorization to proceed to Asunción. By this time, the Paraguayan dictator had received the communication from the imperial government and correctly surmised that Corréia da Câmara's promises would not be honored in their entirety. Moreover, the chargé kept announcing the imminent arrival of the munitions, while in reality the ship bearing them could not ascend the Paraná due to the naval war in the Plata estuary. Such broken pledges reinforced Francia's growing paranoia. Threatened by conquest from Buenos Aires and intrigue from the Argentine littoral provinces, the dictator also had uncovered a massive smuggling ring and subversive unrest, both involving foreigners. His response was to restrict even tighter Paraguay's contacts with the outside world, and he wanted to hear no more of Corréia da Câmara's talk of alliances.[10]

8. [Corréia da Câmara], "Apontamentos," April 11, 1826 (MS in Br-AHI, tomo 201/1/5).

9. Inhambupe to Corréia da Câmara, October 20, 1826, in Br-AHI, maço 318/4/6; Corréia da Câmara to Inhambupe, October 26, 1826, *ibid.*, tomo 201/1/5.

10. Williams, *The Rise and Fall of the Paraguayan Republic*, 54–56, 72–79.

Francia left the Brazilian in suspense, neither inviting him to Asunción nor sending him away. After having supped at Francia's table, Corréia da Câmara now found himself languishing in a squalid hut on the frontier. For two years he remained there—nostalgic, no doubt, for those halcyon months of 1825 when he had the dictator's ear—begging for readmission to Paraguay and pleading with the imperial government to satisfy Dr. Francia's conditions so that the treaty might be concluded.[11]

Instead, the Rio chancery recalled its agent in April, 1828. When he received this message eleven months later, Corréia da Câmara notified Francia and requested his passports. The dictator, however, instructed his delegate at the border:

> Tell the Envoy Corréia that no Passport is remitted because his legation is considered inopportune and unnecessary under the circumstances, and that he may thus withdraw again. His own role uncovers and makes clear the little faith and uselessness of his coming, which is not directed at fulfilling effectively those dispositions, in which the Sovereign of Brazil is said to find himself, of ordering that complete satisfaction be given to the Republic of Paraguay with regard to all of its reclamations, but rather solely to delay and waste time (perhaps years) with futile pretexts of vain, frivolous, and fruitless measures, surely with the idea of trying in this manner to obstruct and frustrate our just demands.[12]

Despite his bitter experiences, Corréia da Câmara never lost his admiration for Dr. Francia nor his conviction that a Paraguayan alliance offered Brazil the only chance to avoid internal dissolution or conquest by its many enemies. The Paraguayan connection, he wrote, "is advantageous to us, and will be in the future more than ever, for the security of Our Southern Provinces and in order to preserve an indispensable equilibrium with the Argentine Federation."[13] Dom Pedro and his advisors, it appears, had greater interest in fomenting commercial relations and in neutralizing Paraguay than in pursuing a military alliance, at least by the time the agent had returned to Paraguay in 1827.

11. See Corréia da Câmara's dispatches, in Br-AHI, tomo 201/1/5.
12. Francia to Ramírez, June 8, 1829, in Pa-AN, SH, vol. 240.
13. Corréia da Câmara to Aracati, January 17, 1829, in Br-AHI, tomo 201/1/5.

Corréia da Câmara's mission served the long-range Luso-Brazilian strategy that aimed at preventing the unification of the old viceroyalty of the Río de la Plata in a single state. Dr. Francia would not likely have entered the Cisplatine War on the side of Buenos Aires, but the imperial government could not be sure of that. Moreover, the dictator might have sought territorial gains in Corrientes or the Missions territory, or he might have attempted to organize a confederation of smaller Platine states. Either action could have complicated the Brazilian effort to retain the Banda Oriental, and the erection of a strong state in the Plata would have threatened Brazil's southern frontier. Despite Corréia da Câmara's plaintive correspondence, the overture to Asunción may be seen as a successful effort to foster divisions among the republics of the Plata while the imperial government fought for possession of the Cisplatine.[14]

BUENOS AIRES AND BOLIVAR

As the second belligerent in the struggle for the Banda Oriental, the United Provinces of the Río de la Plata also took an interest in the attitudes of the other South American states. Argentine efforts to obtain diplomatic and military support first focused on Simón Bolívar, head of Gran Colombia and Peru. In 1823 and 1824 the Buenos Aires government offered the post of minister to Bogotá twice to Manuel Dorrego and twice to Carlos de Alvear, but both men rejected the assignment.[15] During 1825 the search for an understanding with Bolívar became increasingly important to Buenos Aires.

After the Battle of Ayacucho in December, 1824, and the elimination of a small royalist contingent in Upper Peru in April, 1825, only the Peruvian port of Callao and the island of Chiloé, off the

14. On Corréia da Câmara's mission, see Ramos, *La política del Brasil*, 78–178; Hann, "Brazil and the Río de la Plata," 397–405; and Williams, *The Rise and Fall of the Paraguayan Republic*, 68–69. Much of Corréia da Câmara's correspondence is published in *Annaes do Itamaraty*, III–IV.
15. M. J. García to Alvear, March 23, 1823, in Ar-AGN, Sala VII, Alvear Ms, legajo 1-1-5, doc. 2; Forbes to Adams [No. 8], August 13, 1824, in Manning (ed.), *Diplomatic Correspondence*, I, 641–42; Las Heras, "Instrucciones que regirán al Snr Gral de las Provincias del Rio de la Plata, Dⁿ Carlos de Alvear . . ." September 22, 1824 (MS in Ar-AGN, Sala X, legajo 1-5-2); Alvear to Argentine MRE (No. 15), January 1, 1825, in Ar-AGN, Sala X, legajo 1-5-2.

coast of Chile, remained in royalist hands. The destruction of
Spanish power radically altered the international situation in South
America. Ayacucho established Bolívar's preeminence and raised
the possibility of his personal hegemony over the continent. To
Bolívar belonged the credit for the liberation of the northern half
of South America. As president of Gran Colombia, dictator of
Peru, and arbiter of Upper Peru's future, he was the most powerful and prestigious of the Latin American leaders. Gran Colombia was already one of the strongest of the new nations, as
well as the most respected in Europe and North America, and had
seized the initiative in Spanish-American international affairs by
promoting the idea of an American congress. If Bolívar's new
project—the union of Gran Colombia, Peru, and Bolivia in an
"Andean Federation"—came to fruition, he might dominate all
of South America. This prospect was especially troubling to the
leaders of Buenos Aires.

During the first weeks of 1825 rumors of a Spanish victory in
Peru dismayed the Argentines. But, on January 21, news of the
royalist defeat at Ayacucho arrived in Buenos Aires, touching off
three days and nights of delirious celebrations. For the next five
weeks, the Argentines rejoiced over the final triumph of the independence movement.[16]

While members of the Buenos Aires government participated
publicly in the festivities, in private they found Ayacucho a mixed
blessing. First of all, the demise of Spain eliminated the best ex-
cuse for avoiding a showdown with Brazil over the Banda Oriental; the public demand for war now would prove irresistible.
Second, Buenos Aires hoped to establish its authority over Upper
Peru, which had formed part of the viceroyalty of the Río de la
Plata since its creation in 1776. Third, Bolívar's enormous popularity seemed to threaten the leadership of the centralist administration in Buenos Aires. For all of these reasons, the Argentine
government viewed the Liberator's preeminence with some trepi-
dation.[17]

16. Gabriel René-Moreno, *Ayacucho en Buenos Aires y prevaricación de Rivadavia* (Madrid, n.d.), 29–60.
17. *Ibid.*, 82–263; Carlos S. A. Segreti, "El nacimiento de Bolivia," *Revista de
la Universidad Nacional de Córdoba*, IX (1968), 55–98; Forbes to Adams [No.
13], January 23, 1825, in Manning (ed.), *Diplomatic Correspondence*, I, 646; *El
Argos de Buenos Aires*, February 23 and 26, and March 2, 1825, all p. 1; Forbes
to U.S. secretary of state (No. 18), April 22, 1825, in Forbes, *Once años*, 356–57.

Nonetheless, the leaders of the United Provinces attempted to obtain Bolívar's support in the dispute with Brazil. In early May, 1825, Governor Juan Gregorio de Las Heras and Minister of Government and Foreign Affairs Manuel José García persuaded Carlos de Alvear—recently returned from his mission to London and Washington—to accept a new assignment as special emissary to the Liberator. José Miguel Díaz Vélez was named co-minister, with the responsibility of inviting the Upper Peruvian assembly to opt for union with the United Provinces. Alvear's duties were to impress on Bolívar Buenos Aires' desire for good relations with the other republics and point out the danger Brazil posed to all. In particular, Alvear's instructions called for encouraging the formulation of a common policy by Gran Colombia, Peru, Chile, and the United Provinces to force Dom Pedro to evacuate the Banda Oriental. If Bolívar were agreeable, the Buenos Aires government proposed to send a minister to Rio de Janeiro to present the joint demands of the republics. Supplementary instructions authorized the emissaries to negotiate a special treaty of alliance for the purpose of a combined attack on Brazil in the event the emperor refused to comply. The United Provinces and Peru would contribute 4,000 men each, and Buenos Aires would defray most of the expenses of naval and land operations.[18]

The Alvear-Díaz Vélez mission seemingly had excellent prospects, for in early 1825 Bolívar had become convinced that Brazil intended to aid the Continental Alliance in suppressing the republican regimes of Spanish America. Moreover, the Chiquitos affair constituted a serious affront to Bolívar, who could use the incident to force Dom Pedro's hand in the Plata. About two weeks after learning of the annexation of Chiquitos by the Mato Grosso government, Sucre wrote William Miller that he would await Bolívar's arrival "to think about a more formal Expedition to threaten Brazilian territory in a positive manner, to see if we can oblige the Emperor to quit the Banda Oriental."[19] Independently, Miller notified Las Heras of recent events and made a similar observation: "Those sons of Portuguese have chosen a bad time to

18. Instructions accompanying M. J. García to Alvear and Díaz Vélez, June 10, 1825, in Restelli (comp.), *La gestión diplomática*, 7–11; García to Alvear and Díaz Vélez, June 16, 1825, *ibid.*, 15–18.

19. Sucre to Miller, [May] 19, 1825, in Ar-AGN, Sala VII, Carranza Ms, legajo 7-3-5. This letter is dated April 19, but internal evidence shows that it actually was written in May.

declare war on us. Perhaps the diversion that we are going to make will be opportune for the aims that Buenos Aires has in Montevideo."[20] Sucre also informed Las Heras of the Brazilian incursion and broached the possibility of a joint campaign. Using only troops from Peru, Sucre wrote, he could invade the empire by way of Mato Grosso, occupy a large portion of the country, and "carry the banners of the revolution" into Brazil. Then the emperor could be compelled to restore the Banda Oriental to the United Provinces in return for the lands seized by Upper Peru. Sucre suggested that the Buenos Aires government seek an understanding to this end with Bolívar, who could authorize the use of Colombian and Peruvian troops in the operation.[21]

Sucre's message arrived before Alvear and Díaz Vélez had departed for Upper Peru. The Chiquitos affair presented Buenos Aires with the perfect opportunity to reach an agreement with Bolívar. Las Heras drafted new instructions for Alvear and Díaz Vélez, since the invasion of Chiquitos and Sucre's message "have modified circumstances to a large extent and enable us to adopt a less uncertain line of conduct." Before the incident on the Upper Peruvian frontier, reasoned the Argentine chief, Bolívar might not have committed himself to a war against Brazil. Now, however, "the conduct of the Emperor forces the Republics to make common cause with the Río de la Plata, because it is evident that the security of all is threatened by this voracious power that arises in the heart of the Continent." Las Heras instructed his agents to paint the Chiquitos affair as proof of Dom Pedro's support for legitimacy and sufficient motive for Bolívar to attack the empire "by sea and by land," thereby giving Buenos Aires more time to prepare for war in the Banda Oriental. The Argentine leader again authorized Alvear and Díaz Vélez to negotiate a secret treaty and offered to finance the operations of a Peruvian division advancing into Mato Grosso. A promise of Argentine participation in the Panama Congress was to be offered as a tacit quid pro quo.[22]

During the months preceding his meeting with the Argentine

20. Miller to Las Heras, May 20, 1825, in Ar-AGN, Sala VII, Carranza Ms, legajo 7-4-2. In using "sons of Portuguese," Miller made an intentional play on words; *hijos de portugueses* implied *hijos de puta*, or "sons of bitches." He used the same expression in a letter to Sucre (Draft), May 28, 1825, *ibid.*

21. Sucre to president of United Provinces (Secret, No. 1, Copy), May 20, 1825, in Lecuna (ed.), *Documentos*, I, 223–25.

22. Las Heras, "Adición a las instrucciones . . ." June 25, 1825, in Restelli (comp.), *La gestión diplomática*, 21–23.

emissaries in October, Bolívar tried to fathom the significance of the Chiquitos episode and to decide whether further military action was necessary. From the beginning, he had taken the incursion into Chiquitos as an isolated incident, but he accepted the possibility that it formed part of a worldwide plot by the enemies of republicanism. In late May the Liberator, in a letter to Santander, outlined an appropriate strategy in case this fear proved to be well founded: "I think the first thing we should do, if the Holy Alliance mixes in our affairs, is that Peru and Buenos Aires immediately should occupy Brazil; Chile [should occupy] Chiloé; Colombia, Guatemala, and Mexico should see to their own defense; and all America should form a single cause, all united to defend the places attacked or threatened."[23] If the Argentine government were agreeable, Bolívar proposed to invade Paraguay and overthrow Dr. Francia, remaining afterwards in a position to menace Brazil. But the Liberator wished to sound out the British government before embarking on a Brazilian campaign, convinced that the support of Great Britain was essential to the survival of the republics. He therefore asked others to approach British agents and find out how Canning might react to an anti-Brazilian coalition.[24]

Informed of the objective of the Argentine mission, Bolívar promised Santander: "Since this matter is *very grave*, I will not let myself be dragged along precipitously either by glory or by flattery." But the Liberator could not shake his fear of intervention by the European monarchies or his concern over the conduct of the "young, hare-brained, legitimate, and Bourbon" emperor of Brazil: "Tomorrow the Holy Alliance may commission him to make war against us as heir of all the lost rights of all the Bourbons."[25]

In early September, Bolívar seemed ready to undertake a new

---

23. Bolívar to Santander, May 30, 1825, in [Bolívar], *Cartas del Libertador*, IV, 337–38. See also Bolívar to Unánue, May 30, 1825, *ibid.*, 345.

24. Bolívar to Funes, May 28, 1825, and Bolívar to Mariano Sarratea, May 29, 1825, in [Bolívar], *Cartas del Libertador*, IV, 334–35, 337. The Liberator's hostility toward Francia was due to the dictator's archconservatism and imprisonment of Aimé Bonpland, the famous French naturalist whom Bolívar had invited to America.

25. Bolívar to Santander, August 6, 1825, in [Bolívar], *Cartas del Libertador*, IV, 411. See also Bolívar to Tomás de Heres, July 29 and August 6, 1825, *ibid.*, 406–409. Dom Pedro was a Bourbon through his mother, Carlota Joaquina—the daughter of Charles IV and the sister of Ferdinand VII of Spain.

campaign. "Everything is going badly in Buenos Aires," he wrote Santander, "because the Portuguese squeeze them tighter every day. It seems to me that we'll have to help those cursed ingrates. The demon of glory should carry us to Tierra del Fuego, and in truth what do we risk? This army is not needed there [in Gran Colombia], and the nations of the South need some of the victors of Ayacucho for their peace and liberty." He went on to ask his vice-president: "I beg you to ask congress in my name to let me follow my destiny and go where America's danger and Colombia's glory call us." A few days earlier, the Liberator had instructed Sucre to order the exploration of the Pilcomayo and Bermejo rivers to determine the feasibility of sending 4,000 to 6,000 men to invade western Brazil by way of the Paraguay River.[26]

By the time the Argentine representatives met Bolívar in Potosí, the new Bolivian state was taking shape. The constituent assembly called by Sucre met in Chuquisaca from July 10 till early October. On August 6 the delegates opted for independence rather than union with Peru or the United Provinces; they christened Upper Peru the Bolívar Republic, soon to be changed to the Republic of Bolivia. In addition to honoring the Liberator by bestowing his name on the country, the assembly also invested him with the title of President for Life and asked him to draft a constitution. Bolívar exercised the executive power in Bolivia when he consulted with Alvear and Díaz Vélez, but he would resign the lifetime presidency in favor of Sucre at the end of 1825, before returning to Lima.[27]

The Argentine ministers arrived in Potosí on October 7. Bolívar put off receiving them officially but agreed to a private conference on the following day. For the next three months, the Venezuelan and the Argentines discussed a variety of issues affecting the South American nations—most important, the possibility of collaboration in recovering the Banda Oriental—while Bolívar circulated among the highland cities, organizing the new state and basking in the well-deserved acclaim of a grateful population. Though well tanned and still vigorous, he appeared older than his forty-two years and had begun to wear his curly hair cropped short since it started turning gray a few years earlier. His reputation,

26. Bolívar to Santander, September 8, 1825, *ibid.*, 437; Sucre to prefect of Chuquisaca (Draft), September 4, 1825, in Bo-AN, MI, tomo 8, no. 63.
27. Lofstrom, *The Promise and Problem of Reform*, 33–42.

military bearing, and penetrating eyes made him an imposing figure.

Alvear was an excellent choice for dealing with this living legend. Like the Liberator, he was a wealthy, socially prominent creole who had achieved military distinction during the wars of independence. Six years Bolívar's junior, Alvear briefly had headed the Buenos Aires government in 1815 and later served as Argentina's first minister to the United States. His charm and deferential manner proved effective in winning the Liberator's ear.

From the first interviews on October 8 and 9, Bolívar showed a contradictory and vacillating attitude toward Alvear's proposal that Gran Colombia, Peru, Chile, and the United Provinces form an anti-Brazilian alliance. On the one hand, he seemed anxious to go to war, against Brazil or Paraguay or both. On the other, he held back, showing fears of the Continental Alliance, concern for the views of the British and Colombian governments, and suspicion of Buenos Aires. Bolívar professed to have no authority to engage in diplomatic discussions on behalf of Gran Colombia and Peru, and later he said that the governments of both countries had agreed not to enter into any new treaties, instead assigning this prerogative to the Congress of Panama. His coyness clearly emanated from his distrust of the Buenos Aires administration. He complained several times about the attacks on himself published in *El Argos de Buenos Aires*, which, despite the denials of the two ministers, he considered the official newspaper of the Argentine government. Bolívar also felt that Gregorio Funes, the Argentine-born prelate who represented Gran Colombia in Buenos Aires, had been treated in cavalier fashion by Las Heras and García.[28]

Nonetheless, the Liberator was not inalterably opposed to all collaboration with Buenos Aires. He admitted that his personal opinion of the Brazilian emperor and the usurpation of the Banda Oriental coincided with theirs. He claimed to be convinced that his participation in the coming war with Brazil was necessary, but

28. The major sources for the conferences of October 8 and 9 are Alvear and Díaz Vélez's notes, published in Restelli (comp.), *La gestión diplomática*, 121–32. All quotes are from these notes. Bolívar's secretary left a memorandum describing a conference that allegedly took place on October 10, but the document seems to be a resumé of the meetings on the two previous days. Lecuna (ed.), *Documentos*, I, 517–21. The Liberator wrote that he had only two interviews with the Argentines at this time. Bolívar to Funes, October 12, 1825, in [Bolívar], *Cartas del Libertador*, IV, 463.

he worried that Great Britain might object. Alvear suggested that Bolívar appoint a representative to accompany an Argentine minister to Rio de Janeiro, where the two would present a joint protest of the emperor's violation of Chiquitos and his attempt to absorb the Banda Oriental. The Liberator readily agreed; earlier he had commissioned his adjutant, Daniel Florence O'Leary, to make Dom Pedro aware of his displeasure over the Chiquitos affair but had postponed the mission until he could consult with the Argentine emissaries.[29] Bolívar preferred that O'Leary not broach the matter of the Banda Oriental, however, and even wanted his adjutant to state "that the Liberator will take no part in this matter, so as not to alarm the Emperor."

When Alvear objected that such a statement would not help Buenos Aires, Bolívar offered to overthrow Dr. Francia and restore Paraguay to the United Provinces. In Paraguay, "he would be able to augment his army, and under any pretext, which in those cases is never lacking, [he would be able] to aid the Government of the United Provinces if it were involved in a war with the Brazilians." Alvear expressed his doubt that the Argentine congress would approve such an undertaking.[30] Shortly thereafter, Bolívar mentioned his anxiety about the future of the new state founded in Upper Peru and abruptly proposed: "Recognize the Bolívar Republic, stipulating as a condition that it take part with 4,000 or 5,000 men in the war with Brazil, and I will see that the proposition is accepted."

The Liberator had three means of championing the cause of Buenos Aires, two of them short of armed conflict. The first—public expressions of support for the Argentines—he gave freely. By prior agreement with Alvear, he censured the actions of "an American prince" in Chiquitos and the Banda Oriental in a speech

29. O'Leary to [Miller], August 29 and September 14, 1825, in Ar-AGN, Sala VII, Carranza Ms, legajo 7-3-9.

30. Bolívar and his secretary claimed that the Argentine ministers initiated the proposal to invade Paraguay. Bolívar to Santander, October 10 (October 11 postscript), 1825, in [Bolívar], *Cartas del Libertador*, IV, 459; Estenós' notes of October 10 conference, in Lecuna (ed.), *Documentos*, I, 520. In view of his earlier expressions of interest in overthrowing Francia, however, and considering his order to investigate possible routes for such an invasion, it appears more likely that the idea was Bolívar's. Sucre also attributed the proposal to the Liberator. Sucre to Santander, October 11, 1825, in Lecuna (ed.), *Documentos*, I, 380. Alvear was correct in thinking that the Argentine government preferred that Bolívar stay away

that was widely reported in the press of various countries.[31] A second possibility was the dispatch of a representative to Rio to deliver a protest to the emperor. Although Bolívar temporarily reneged on his promise to designate O'Leary his personal emissary, he did encourage the Argentine ministers to approach the Peruvian government to this end, and he himself recommended the idea to the caretaker administration in Lima.[32]

The third option—Bolívar's active participation in the war—remained the critical question. The Liberator could not help but be tempted by the prospect of a Brazilian campaign. The destruction of the last monarchy in the New World would embellish his military career, and an invasion of Brazil from Bolivia would afford an opportunity to overthrow Francia, whom Bolívar detested. More important, the grand coalition proposed by Buenos Aires offered a means of restoring unity to Spanish America, for a war against Brazil as a representative of monarchical reaction would, in effect, extend the movement for independence from Europe. And finally, the presumed fragmentation of Brazil into several autonomous republics would virtually guarantee the hegemony of Gran Colombia—or of the Andean Federation that the Liberator now favored.

Although he would not pledge Colombian or Peruvian troops against the empire, Bolívar dangled the possibility of Bolivian military aid from the time of his first conversations with Alvear and Díaz Vélez. The Liberator informed the Bolivian constituent assembly in Chuquisaca that he wanted to rescue the Argentines, and he found the assembly agreeable. In a letter to Santander, Bolívar stressed his intention to leave Gran Colombia out of any commitment to Buenos Aires: "I have in no way compromised Colombia, nor will I ever compromise her in the least. Now I command only Peruvian peoples, and I do not represent a grain of Colombian sand. If the Brazilians seek more quarrels with us,

---

from Paraguay. M. J. García to [Alvear and Díaz Vélez], November 19, 1825, in Restelli (comp.), *La gestión diplomática*, 118–19.

31. Bolívar's speech of October 16, 1825, in [Bolívar], *Cartas del Libertador*, IV, 471–72.

32. Estenós to Peruvian MRE, October 24, 1825, Alvear and Díaz Vélez to García (No. 21), October 27, 1825, Alvear and Díaz Vélez to [Ignacio Álvarez Thomas], October 27, 1825, all in Restelli (comp.), *La gestión diplomática*, 139, 141, 221–22.

I will fight them as a Bolivian, a name that has belonged to me since before my birth."[33]

About two weeks after arriving in Potosí, Alvear reported to García: "The Liberator ardently wishes to take part in the war, but he wants to do it with the agreement of Colombia and Lima. He says [to tell] you that, if these refuse, he will do it alone with this State." Alvear suggested that the Buenos Aires government instruct its representatives to the Panama Congress to bring up the question of Brazil before that body. He added: "Bolívar maintains that he is not authorized to discuss [this matter]; nevertheless, he has written [about it] and he will make every possible effort. I'll tell you more: in any case we have him for certain, even if it is only as chief of this State."[34] In November the Argentine ministers returned to Bolívar's earlier suggestion that Buenos Aires demand an alliance against Brazil as the quid pro quo for Argentine recognition of Bolivian independence, and the Liberator agreed to submit such a project to the assembly. Soon thereafter, Bolívar named Mariano Serrano to the post of Bolivian minister in Buenos Aires and authorized him to negotiate a treaty along the lines proposed by Alvear and Díaz Vélez.[35]

Bolívar clearly had a personal antipathy for Dom Pedro and still worried that the "Holy Alliance" might intervene in America. But his principal motive for longing to do battle in Brazil seems to have been a thirst for military glory and for uniting Spanish America under his personal rule. Alvear constantly played on Bolívar's vanity with outright flattery as well as proposals that went far beyond his instructions. In one of their earliest conferences, the Argentine ministers told the Liberator that he should establish a protectorate over all of Spanish America "as the only means of saving it from the evils that threaten it."[36]

33. Olañeta to Bolívar, October 19, 1825, in O'Leary (ed.), *Memorias del general O'Leary*, XI, 24; Bolívar to Santander, October 21, 1825, in [Bolívar], *Cartas del Libertador*, IV, 486.

34. Alvear to M. J. García, October 23, 1825, in Gregorio F. Rodríguez [comp.], *Contribución histórica y documental* (Buenos Aires, 1921), II, 140–141.

35. Alvear and Díaz Vélez to Bolívar, November 10, 1825, Estenós to [Alvear and Díaz Vélez], November 14, 1825, Alvear and Díaz Vélez to Argentine MRE (No. 35), December 3, 1825, all in Restelli (comp.), *La gestión diplomática*, 167–69, 184–85.

36. Bolívar to Santander, October 10 (October 11 postscript), 1825, in [Bolívar], *Cartas del Libertador*, IV, 458.

By November, Bolívar and Alvear had become intimate friends, and the Argentine general secretly proposed the union of Bolivia and the United Provinces under the Liberator's rule. Alvear's arts of persuasion were such that Bolívar was convinced that "with the exception of four members of the government, all the people [of Buenos Aires] want me like a guardian angel." The Liberator again asked Santander to obtain congressional authorization for his remaining absent from Colombia, in order that he could pursue his dream of continental unity: "[Y]ou should make the greatest efforts so that Colombia's glory does not remain incomplete and so that I may be the regulator of all South America. Understand that Chiloé and Chile will be lost forever without me; understand also that by remaining in the South I can succor Colombia with 20,000 hand-picked and incorruptible men. In a word, all will be lost if I go [back to Bogotá]. Therefore, ask congress for permission for me to stay two years *in the lands to the South of Peru*. Using this phrase embraces everything that I want." He went on to compare himself to Julius Caesar in a passage that reveals both the scope of his ambitions and the depth of his need for personal distinction: "Caesar in Gaul threatened Rome, I in Bolivia threaten all the conspirators of America, and consequently I will save all the republics. If I lose my positions in the South, the Congress of Panama will count for nothing and the emperor of Brazil will devour the Río de la Plata and Bolivia."[37]

Some Spanish Americans felt that Bolívar should attack Brazil, either as punishment for the violation of Chiquitos, or to forestall the emperor's aiding some reactionary plot of the European monarchies, or to rescue Buenos Aires. Manuel Vidaurre, one of the Peruvian delegates to the Panama Congress, waxed poetic in urging the Liberator to take a hand: "New triumphs await Your Excellency in Rio de Janeiro and Brazil. There they will erect a column with this inscription: *With the point of Bolívar's sword, the word King was erased from all the Americas*."[38] Others who ap-

37. Bolívar to Santander, November 11, 1825, *ibid.*, 517–19. On the Liberator's desire for glory, see Masur, *Simon Bolivar*, 398–407.

38. Manuel Vidaurre to Bolívar, November 16, 1825, in O'Leary (ed.), *Memorias del general O'Leary*, X, 383. Vidaurre planned to ignore any Brazilian representative who might arrive in Panama, unless the Peruvian government ordered otherwise. M. V[idaurre] to José de la Mar, December 24, 1825, in Raúl Porras Barrenechea (comp.), *El Congreso de Panamá (1826)* (Lima, 1930), 467.

proved of Bolívar's participation in a war against the empire included Bernardo O'Higgins, formerly supreme director of Chile, now exiled in Peru; the Bolivian Andrés Santa Cruz; and the Chilean Manuel de Salazar.[39]

Some, however, opposed the idea of a punitive expedition against Brazil. Hipólito Unánue and Tomás de Heres, members of the triumvirate that the Liberator had left in charge of the Peruvian government, emphasized the risk of such an undertaking. Heres wrote the Liberator: "I do not know what this business of Brazil has for me, that no matter how hard I try to persuade myself that a war with the Emperor is just, necessary, and expedient, I cannot do it."[40] Joaquín Mosquera y Arboleda, formerly Colombian minister to Buenos Aires, and Pedro Briceño Méndez, one of the two Colombian delegates to the Panama Congress, expressed to Santander their hope that Gran Colombia would not get involved. Sucre likewise preferred that the northern republics stay out of Buenos Aires' quarrel if possible. Although he believed that the recovery of the Banda Oriental by force could be accomplished easily enough, he feared that an assault on Brazil would alarm both the Continental Alliance and Great Britain.[41]

The most vociferous opponent of a general war was Santander. Perceiving Bolívar's sharp interest in the coming conferences with Alvear and Díaz Vélez, the Colombian vice-president urged Bolívar not to take part in a war against the empire. Like Sucre, Santander could not believe that Great Britain and the Continental Alliance would stand by while the republics overthrew Dom Pedro. "The Brazilian government," he wrote, "may be considered the reserve of the Holy Alliance, the Bourbons, and the enemies of our independence, and considering this it is our duty to do everything possible to avoid their using this reserve and put-

---

39. Bernardo O'Higgins to Heres, July 22, 1825, in Ernesto de la Cruz (ed.), *Epistolario de D. Bernardo O'Higgins* (Madrid, 1920), II, 53; Santa Cruz to Miller, September 5 and 20, 1825, in Ar-AGN, Sala VII, Carranza Ms, legajo 7-3-5; Manuel de Salazar to O'Leary, December 8, 1825, in O'Leary (ed.), *Memorias del general O'Leary*, XI, 90.

40. Heres to Bolívar, September 4, 1825, in O'Leary (ed.), *Memorias del general O'Leary*, V, 132–33.

41. Joaquín Mosquera y Arboleda to Santander, January 20, 1826, and Briceño to Santander, January 30, 1826, in *Archivo Santander* (Bogotá, [1913]–32), XIV, 26, 45; Sucre to Santander, September 27, 1825, *ibid.*, XIII, 186; Sucre to Santander, October 11, 1825, in Lecuna (ed.), *Documentos*, I, 379–380; Sucre to Miller, December 22, 1825, in Ar-AGN, Sala VII, Carranza Ms, legajo 7-3-5.

ting it in motion." Santander proposed that Buenos Aires raise an army with the collaboration of Peru, Bolivia, and Chile; meanwhile, the Argentine government should use this gathering force to intimidate Dom Pedro while seeking to persuade Great Britain to pressure the emperor. "It seems to me," he continued, "that Colombia should not get involved in the question at all, so that we not, by going in as saviors, be crucified by the Holy Alliance before the others due to our geographical position."[42] Now that Spain had been defeated, Santander was more interested in promoting the political and economic development of his own country than in pursuing Spanish-American unity at the cost of a new war. Despite his own suspicions of Dom Pedro, he remained opposed to the involvement of the Liberator or Gran Colombia in any conflict with Brazil.

Like Santander, George Canning also hoped to avoid a general war. "The maintenance of Monarchy in Brazil is an object of anxious solicitude to your Gov[ernmen]t," he had recently reminded Sir Charles Stuart, the British minister in Rio, just before the repercussions of the Chiquitos affair enhanced the possibility of an anti-Brazilian coalition.[43] Canning intended that Great Britain remain neutral in the dispute between Brazil and the United Provinces, and he actively sought to limit the conflict, should it come to that, to the two original parties. He instructed his representative in Bogotá to convey to the Colombian government his expectation that Brazil "will be looked upon with a friendly eye by the other New States of America, with whom G[rea]t Britain has entered into relations of amity. Having respected in them the forms of Gov[ernmen]ts which they have thought proper to establish, we feel that we have a just right to require in return a similar consideration and respect for the independent monarchy of Brazil."[44]

42. Santander to Bolívar, November 6, 1825, in Roberto Cortázar (comp.), *Cartas y mensajes de Santander* (Bogotá, 1953–56), V, 374–76. See also Santander to Bolívar, May 6, September 6, October 6 and 20, November 21, December 6, 1825, January 6 and 21, February 6, 1826, *ibid.*, 273–77, 337–38, 364, 367, 383, 396, VI, 36–37, 79–80, 114–15.
43. Canning to Stuart (No. 10, Draft), April 30, 1825, in GB-PRO, FO 13/1, fl. 155.
44. Canning to Stuart (No. 23, Secret, Draft), June 16, 1825, *ibid.*, FO 13/2, fls. 44–49; Rivadavia to Argentine MRE (No. 6), June 22, 1825, in Ar-AGN, Sala X, legajo 1-1-8; Canning to Patrick Campbell (No. 14, Draft), November 3, 1825, in GB-PRO, FO 18/11, fls. 133–34.

In deciding whether to accept the Argentine proposal, Bolívar also had to contend with his own deep suspicions of Buenos Aires. Like many of the prominent leaders of the northern part of the continent, the Liberator mistrusted the *Porteños*. Since Ayacucho, the vehement attacks of the Argentine press had angered Bolívar and his comrades. In commenting on a series of articles in *El Argos de Buenos Aires*, Sucre said to Bolívar: "They are afraid that you will go to conquer them, and they are the rabble that most deserves punishment for their imbecility and uselessness in our war [against Spain], their miserable pride, and their nullity for anything other than mouthing banalities and being ungrateful. Not for nothing are they abhorred in these provinces [*i.e.*, Upper Peru] as much as the Spaniards." Santander's opinion was similar: "I distrust the Argentines, including General Alvear; I discover in them a font of duplicity, and I consider them very conceited, proud, and ambitious." O'Leary expressed this sentiment more succinctly: "Buenos Aires is the center of intrigue and evil."[45]

Reports from Gregorio Funes deepened Bolívar's mistrust. The seventy-six-year-old cleric, who nursed a passionate hatred of the Brazilians and longed for a war to liberate the Banda Oriental, believed that Buenos Aires would neither take decisive action against Brazil nor allow the Liberator to invade Paraguay. By late October, 1825, Funes's dispatches, with their accounts of *Porteño* deceit and reluctance to aid the Orientals, had persuaded Bolívar that he should not credit the assurances of the Argentine ministers.[46]

The Liberator also had to consider the financial and logistical problems that an invasion posed. Fifteen years of warfare had shattered the local economies of Spanish America through outright destruction, disruption of trade, migration of the labor force, and the enormous expense of supporting both royalist and republican armies. Even though the Buenos Aires government had offered to underwrite the costs of Bolívar's campaign, the immediate financing of the expedition would fall on Upper Peru.

45. Sucre to Bolívar, June 6, 1825, in O'Leary (ed.), *Memorias del general O'Leary*, I, 265; Santander to Bolívar, March 6, 1826, in Cortázar (comp.), *Cartas y mensajes*, VI, 190; O'Leary to Santander, January 23, 1826, in *Archivo Santander*, XIV, 41.

46. Bolívar to Heres, October 27, 1825, and Bolívar to Santander, October 27, 1825, in [Bolívar], *Cartas del Libertador*, IV, 495, 500–501. See Funes to Bolívar, August 14 and 26, September 28, October 18, November 26, December 10 and 26, 1825, in O'Leary (ed.), *Memorias del general O'Leary*, XI, 138–56, 159–160.

Moreover, if the Liberator heeded the wishes of the Argentine government, his troops would not march south to the Banda Oriental, presumably supported en route by the inhabitants of the Argentine provinces, but instead would strike through the western lowlands of Bolivia into Mato Grosso and on to the Brazilian coast. Such a route posed serious problems of logistics—not necessarily superior to those overcome by Bolívar during his campaigns in Venezuela and New Granada, but certainly not to be taken lightly. Travel from the Mato Grosso–Bolivian border to Rio de Janeiro required four to five months along a trail unfit for wheeled vehicles. Since few settlers lived along the route, packmule drovers had to carry supplies to feed themselves and their animals.[47] Moving an army across this inhospitable terrain entailed obvious difficulties.

Sucre perceived the situation clearly. He described the problematical nature of this route to Santander and at the same time divined the reason that the Buenos Aires administration wanted Bolívar to attack western Brazil rather than proceed directly to the Banda Oriental: "General Miller writes me that he has heard that the [Argentine] Government is trying to ask the Liberator to send auxiliaries by way of Mato Grosso, etc., which is the same as saying by way of the Orinoco or the Rio Negro, etc., since it is all uninhabited wilderness, etc. [Miller also writes] that they distrust our liberalism too much to want us to go via Salta and Córdoba. This pretension is very funny; not one of our soldiers would get there by way of Mato Grosso."[48]

Bolívar and Sucre had at least three sources of information about the frontier region. A Spanish engineer who had served on one of the joint commissions that had tried to plot the boundaries between Spanish and Portuguese America, and an Italian recently

---

47. Luiz de Alincourt, "Rezultado dos trabalhos e indagações statisticas da Provincia de Matto-Grosso . . . (Cuyabá 1828)," *Anais da Biblioteca Nacional do Rio de Janeiro*, VIII (1880–1881), 85–86. For a detailed description of the hazards of overland travel through Mato Grosso and Chiquitos, see Fernando Cacho, "Ytinerario de un viaje por tierra desde el Río Janeyro hasta Lima (Perú) por Don Fernando Cacho Teniente Coronel al servicio de España Año 1818," in Félix Denegri Luna, *En torno a Ramón Castilla* (Lima, 1969), 35–139.

48. Sucre to Santander, February 28, 1826, in *Archivo Santander*, XIV, 106. Miller himself minimized the geographical obstacles in the belief that Brazilian republicans would have supported the invaders. John Miller, *Memoirs of General Miller, in the Service of the Republica of Peru* (2nd ed.; London, 1829), II, 300.

arrived from Mato Grosso, reportedly drew up, at the Liberator's request, an itinerary for an invasion.[49] A third person familiar with Mato Grosso was Facundo Infante, a Spanish officer who had traveled overland from Rio de Janeiro to Upper Peru in 1824–1825 but had arrived too late to aid the royalists. Joining the victorious republicans, Infante soon became chief of staff of the United Liberating Army and the intimate counselor of both Sucre and Bolívar. A Brazilian trader who was in Bolivia in November, 1825, credited Infante with dissuading the Liberator from accepting the alliance proposed by the Argentine emissaries.[50] This report no doubt reflected the gossip circulating in Chiquisaca and may not be reliable. It did not specify Infante's reasons for opposing a Brazilian campaign; but, given the Spaniard's firsthand knowledge of the terrain between the Bolivian highlands and Rio de Janeiro, logistical considerations certainly might have played a part.

With all of these concerns weighing on him, Bolívar showed less enthusiasm about joining the fray when the Argentine emissaries renewed their overtures in early December. He continued to sympathize with the United Provinces but expressed doubt that Peru and Gran Colombia would sign a treaty with Buenos Aires, since they had agreed to delegate such powers to the Panama Congress. As for himself, he professed an eagerness to help, but "now I have no authority to dispose of a single soldier against the emperor of Brazil."[51]

The Liberator's waning interest in a Brazilian campaign appeared clearly in a letter to Santander. Dom Pedro's conciliatory gestures had persuaded Bolívar that the Chiquitos affair had been no more than an unfortunate incident and did not presage a pol-

49. Ponte Ribeiro, "Memoria sobre as republicas do Pacifico," April 7, 1832 (MS in Br-AHI, Ponte Ribeiro Ms, lata 269, maço 3, pasta 1). This document identifies the Spaniard as a certain Soto Mayor. The Italian was certainly Giuseppe Angelini, a merchant who returned to Mato Grosso in July, 1826. See the sources listed in the following note.

50. João Nepomoceno Pires de Miranda, "Estado actual del Peru," July 20, 1826 (MS accompanying Saturnino to Inhambupe [No. 15], August 9, 1826, in Br-AHI, tomo 308/2/8). This document is published with introduction and explanatory notes: Ron L. Seckinger, "A projetada aliança grã-colombiana-rioplatense contra o Brasil: Um documento inédito," *Mensário do Arquivo Nacional*, Vol. V, No. 1 (1974), 33–40.

51. Bolívar to Alvear, December 5, 1825, in [Bolívar], *Cartas del Libertador*, IV, 534–36.

icy of territorial aggrandizement: "By the Brazilians' correspondence you will see that they are afraid of us and do not want to get into a dispute with us. This makes me infinitely happy, because there has been enough war and now it is time to await death in repose." He anticipated that the emperor would finally agree to a negotiated settlement of the Banda Oriental question.[52]

Bolívar continued to encourage Buenos Aires to recover the Banda Oriental, and he attempted to use the conflict as a means of securing Argentine recognition of an independent Bolivia. He pointed out that the Bolivian government could sign no treaty with the United Provinces until its independence had been acknowledged by the latter; as bait, he suggested that Buenos Aires ask for Bolivian participation in the war as compensation for Argentine efforts to liberate Upper Peru from Spanish rule. In the last days of December, when he announced his imminent departure to resume the direction of the government in Lima, Bolívar promised Alvear and Díaz Vélez, "on his word of honor and in the most expressive manner," that his first concern would be to dispatch O'Leary in the company of a Peruvian representative to demand satisfaction from Dom Pedro.[53]

A few weeks earlier the Buenos Aires administration had decided to fight alone rather than risk the extension of Bolívar's influence to the Plata. No doubt the early victories of the Orientals had fanned hopes that Colombian or Bolivian aid was unnecesary. García ordered the emissaries in Chuquisaca to tell the Liberator that the Argentine government did not agree with him "concerning the necessity of forming a federal body of the American nations" and would by itself "satisfy what national honor demands." Having delivered this message, and having reiterated the friendly sentiments of the United Provinces toward the northern republics, Alvear and Díaz Vélez were to bid farewell to the Liberator and return home.[54]

The Argentine ministers earlier had judged it "prudent" not to inform the Colombian president that Las Heras and García had rejected, in no uncertain terms, his proposal to invade Paraguay.

52. Bolívar to Santander, December 12, 1825, in [Bolívar], *Cartas del Libertador*, IV, 539–540.

53. Alvear and Díaz Vélez to Argentine MRE (Nos. 38 and 51), December 13 and 30, 1825, in Restelli (comp.), *La gestión diplomática*, 192–93, 223–24.

54. M. J. García to [Alvear and Díaz Vélez], December 3, 1825, *ibid.*, 149.

With similar prudence, they declined to follow García's new orders to the letter, for fear of prompting the Liberator to cancel O'Leary's trip to Rio de Janeiro. Rather than close down the legation, they decided that Díaz Vélez would remain in Bolivia while Alvear returned to Buenos Aires and reported on their mission. A subsequent dispatch from García, instructing the ministers to accept Bolívar's suggestion of an Argentine-Bolivian alliance and a Bolivian advance into Mato Grosso, arrived after the Liberator's departure.[55]

On January 1, 1826, the Colombian president took leave of Alvear and Díaz Vélez in Chuquisaca. In his final toast to the Argentine agents, he wished them success in their differences with Brazil, "because justice should triumph in the end."[56] With that, the Liberator turned toward Lima. Although talk of a republican coalition persisted throughout the coming year, the critical moment had passed. When Bolívar descended the Andes, he rode west, not east, and with him went all likelihood of a coordinated attack on the empire. Behind him, he left Brazil still intact and still monarchical.

THE ANDEAN REPUBLICS AND THE CISPLATINE WAR

Although the Alvear–Díaz Vélez mission had failed to obtain a military commitment from the Liberator, other possibilities were open to the United Provinces. In August, 1825, the Chilean foreign minister notified García that the government of Supreme Director Ramón Freire recognized the "imperious necessity" of a common effort against Brazil, for the empire threatened the in-

55. Alvear to M. J. García, December 21, 1825, in Rodríguez [comp.], *Contribución*, II, 143; Alvear and Díaz Vélez to Argentine MRE (Nos. 58 and 59), January 8 and 18, 1826, and García to Alvear and Díaz Vélez, January 12, 1826, all in Restelli (comp.), *La gestión diplomática*, 233–34, 150–152, 173–74.

56. Alvear and Díaz Vélez to Argentine MRE (No. 55), January 1, 1826, in Restelli (comp.), *La gestión diplomática*, 229–30. See also *El Cóndor de Bolivia*, January 5, 1826, p. 1–2. On the mission of Alvear and Díaz Vélez, see the following: [Daniel F. O'Leary], *Narración*, II, 422–41, Vol. XXVIII of *Memorias del general O'Leary*; Arnaldo Vieira de Mello, *Bolívar, o Brasil e os nossos vizinhos do Prata: Da questão de Chiquitos à guerra da Cisplatina* (Rio de Janeiro, 1963), 183–216; Humberto Vásquez-Machicado, "La invasión brasilera a Chiquitos y la diplomacia argentina de 1825," *Segundo Congreso Internacional de Historia de América*, IV, 371–400; and Davis, *Carlos de Alvear*, 62–83.

dependence of all the republics. The Chilean implied that military aid would be authorized once the legislature convened. García did not follow up this opening immediately. But, on October 25, 1825, the day the Argentine congress voted to seat the Oriental delegates and thereby ensured the outbreak of hostilities with Brazil, the foreign minister ordered his representative in Lima, Ignacio Álvarez Thomas, to leave for Santiago and seek a Chilean commitment to furnish assistance in the event of war.[57]

The Argentine approach to Chile was erratic and indecisive. Instructions to Álvarez alternated between pressing for a formal agreement and breaking off negotiations, depending on how the war in the Banda Oriental proceeded at a given moment.[58] Despite the contradictory instructions, however, Álvarez eventually managed to obtain a satisfactory pact. On arriving in Santiago in March, 1826, he first proposed that Chile lend assistance in three ways: (1) appoint a representative to carry a protest to Rio in union with representatives from the United Provinces, Peru, and Bolivia; (2) send a corps of troops across the Andes to be stationed in the United Provinces; and (3) loan several warships to help raise the blockade of the Plata. In May, on the orders of the Buenos Aires government—again directed by Rivadavia, with his foreign minister, Francisco de la Cruz—Álvarez broached the idea of a mutual guarantee of borders against third parties, only to abandon the effort in June after receiving new instructions.[59]

The Freire regime, Álvarez discovered, was not eager to take part in the war against Brazil, despite its repeated affirmations of support. Mariano Egaña, the Chilean minister in London, had advised his government in January, 1826, to avoid involvement in Buenos Aires' quarrel with Brazil. Although Egaña considered Dom Pedro a dangerous neighbor and the enemy of republican governments, he, like Santander, was not inclined to see his na-

57. Vidal del Río to Argentine MRE (Secret), August 17, 1825, in Ar-AGN, Sala X, legajo 1-8-2; M. J. García to Álvarez Thomas (No. 2), October 25, 1825, *ibid.*, legajo 1-8-10.

58. M. J. García to Álvarez Thomas (No. 7), December 9, 1825, in Ar-AGN, Sala X, legajo 1-8-10; Rivadavia to Álvarez Thomas (Copy), May 1, 1826, *ibid.*, tomo 1-10-12, fls. 31–37; Rivadavia, "Instrucciones que deberán regir al Sor Gral. D. Ignacio Alvarez y Tomás . . ." (Copy), May 8, 1826 (MS in Ar-AGN, Sala X, tomo 1-10-12, fls. 38–39).

59. Álvarez Thomas to Blanco Encalada, March 18 and June 22, 1826, in Ch-AMRE, Argentina, tomo 7, fls. 47, 65.

tion fight Argentine battles: "[W]hile considering that to violate the territorial integrity of our neighbors is to threaten our own, you will not forget that the Government of Buenos Aires today offers no guarantees on which a formal compromise may be supported, and that—for great enterprises that can decide the fate of Nations—the most appropriate Cabinet is not one that has never shown a broad perspective and whose principal force consists of journalists and Clubs, which are not important aids in a war." Whether or not this advice carried weight in the Freire administration, Álvarez' efforts to negotiate a treaty encountered resistance due to domestic political unrest and reluctance to become involved in the war.[60]

The Argentine government tried to assuage the fears of the Santiago chancery by explaining that, in signing the treaty, Chile would merely give a "moral example that would benefit all the Continent"; whether the treaty should apply to the current conflict was a separate matter that could be settled later. Eventually this formula provided a basis for Chile's agreeing to the proposed alliance. By the pact signed on November 20, the two nations agreed to defend each other's borders from aggression by other countries. Although the Argentine congress ratified the treaty in January, 1827, the Chilean government procrastinated throughout that year and never formally sanctioned the document.[61]

The Freire administration did, however, sell munitions and warships to the United Provinces. In early 1826 Buenos Aires dispatched Colonel Juan Ventura Vásquez to Santiago to purchase a part of the Chilean naval squadron. Ventura obtained three warships and 30,000 *pesos* worth of arms, but the enterprise was ill-fated. Off Cape Horn, a storm sent the largest ship to the bottom of the sea, along with Ventura and the entire crew. One of the other ships returned to Valparaíso, where it was sold at a loss. The third made it into the South Atlantic but was never used

60. [Egaña to Chilean MRE] (No. 104, Copy), January 14, 1826, in Ch-AN, MinRE, tomo 13; Álvarez Thomas to Francisco de la Cruz, July 1, 1826, and Álvarez Thomas to Cruz (Nos. 26 and 32), September 24 and October 15, 1826, in Ar-AGN, Sala X, legajo 1-8-10.

61. Rivadavia to Álvarez Thomas, August 8, 1826, in Rodríguez [comp.], *Contribución*, II, 186–87; Manuel José Gandarillas to Argentine MRE, March 28, 1827, and Juan Francisco de Zegers to Argentine MRE (No. 1), June 27, 1827, in Ar-AGMREC, Misiones, caja 15; Zegers to Argentine MRE (Copy), September 10, 1827, in Ch-AMRE, Argentina, tomo 6, fl. 7.

against the Brazilians.[62] Neither by means of the treaty nor by the sale of arms did Chile contribute significantly to the cause of the United Provinces.

The Colombian, Peruvian, and Bolivian governments did even less. The Bogotá chancery openly sympathized with Buenos Aires but remained neutral, arguing that the conflict in the Plata did not require that Gran Colombia furnish military assistance as stipulated in the *casus foederis* clause of the 1823 treaty with the United Provinces. What is more, Gran Colombia in 1826 became the first of the Spanish-American republics to name a regular diplomatic agent—discounting Valentín Gómez, who represented Buenos Aires on a special mission—to Dom Pedro's court, and at a time when that court was at war with the Argentines.[63] Throughout the Cisplatine conflict, the Colombian government consistently encouraged the other republics to look on the Brazilian monarchy as an American state and not as a tool of reactionary Europe.

Peruvian officials continued to fear that Dom Pedro would help the Continental Alliance to stifle the republican regimes in the Americas.[64] Nonetheless, Bolívar's government in Lima named a consul general to Rio in June, 1826, and authorized him to assume the functions of chargé d'affaires if the imperial cabinet would recognize him in that capacity. Peruvian suspicions were evident in the agent's instructions, for his "most important task" was to investigate reports of the emperor's complicity in reactionary plots against the republics. But, by the mission, Peru—like Gran Colombia—served notice that it would not take the side of Buenos Aires solely out of republican solidarity. Bolívar notified

62. "Memorandum" (MS accompanying Miguel Maria Lisboa to Januário da Cunha Barbosa, May 26, 1841, in Br-BN, SM, I–3, 12, 43); Benjamín Villegas Basavilbaso, "La adquisición de armamentos navales en Chile durante la guerra del Brasil," *Boletín de la Academia Nacional de la Historia*, IV (1927), 133–47.

63. *Gaceta de Colombia*, January 1 and November 12, 1826; Revenga to Gual and Briceño, April 8, 1826, in Co-ADC, tomo 606, fls. 100–103; Revenga to Hurtado (No. 94, Copy), April 9, 1826, in Co-ADC, tomo 488, fls. 29–30; Revenga to Palacios, March 29, 1826, in Co-ADC, tomo 158, fl. 1.

64. Doc. quoting Pando, accompanying Pando to Unánue and Larrea y Loredo, June 29, 1826, in O'Leary (ed.), *Memorias del general O'Leary*, XXIV, 8. Belaúnde, in *Bolívar and the Political Thought of the Spanish American Revolution*, 276–77, attributes the document to Pando and emphasizes his perception of a Brazilian threat. The Liberator fretted that a Brazilian victory might endanger the security of the other republics. Bolívar to Santander, April 7, 1826, and Bolívar to Funes, July 1, 1826, in [Bolívar], *Cartas del Libertador*, V, 79–82, 186.

the British ministers in Lima and Bogotá that he had no intention of entering the war.[65]

Sucre intended to stay out of the quarrel, too. When the Bolivian government appointed a minister to the United Provinces in February, 1826, he was warned that Buenos Aires probably would request aid or a formal alliance. Since Sucre would not commit himself without the approval of the Bolivian legislature and the Panama Congress, the minister was instructed to confine himself to securing Argentine recognition of Bolivia and to leave the matter of a treaty for later. The *Porteño* leaders actually had little interest in a Bolivian alliance at that moment; they were more concerned with frustrating the Bolivian absorption of Tarija and with trying to reestablish Buenos Aires' authority over all of Upper Peru. As a consequence, the Argentine foreign minister insisted that Díaz Vélez return from Chuquisaca and declined to accept the credentials of Sucre's emissary. The Bolivian government summoned the latter home and demanded an explanation from Buenos Aires. Relations between the two countries dropped from chilly to arctic. Casimiro Olañeta, a Bolivian official, wrote Bolívar that "if an angel descends from the sky and says he is Argentine, one must beware of him."[66]

The governments of Chile, Gran Colombia, Peru, and Bolivia all sympathized with Buenos Aires, but none perceived the Brazilian threat to be so great as to warrant going to the aid of the United Provinces. Moreover, internal problems and suspicions of the Argentines militated against such collaboration.

Until 1827, relationships among the new states of South America derived directly from the circumstances of the independence

65. Decree of June 22, 1826, in Porras Barrenechea (comp.), *El Congreso de Panamá*, 74; Pando to Cáceres, August 10, 1826, *ibid.*, 86–88; Ricketts to Canning (Secret), June 1, 1826, in GB-PRO, FO 61/8, fl. 5; P. Campbell to Canning (Private and Confidential), July 9, 1826, in GB-PRO, FO 18/27, fls. 149–50.

66. [Infante?] to Serrano, February 6, 1826, in Lecuna (ed.), *Documentos*, II, 31–32; Cruz to Díaz Vélez, April 26 and May 18, 1826, in Restelli (comp.), *La gestión diplomática*, 248–49, 259–60; Manuel Toro to Infante (No. 9), August 3, 1826, in Bo-AN, MinRE, Bolivia-Argentina, tomo 1, no. 4; Cruz to [Infante], November 10, 1826, in Bo-AN, MinRE, Bolivia-Argentina, tomo 1, no. 5; Olañeta to Bolívar, September 20, 1826, in O'Leary (ed.), *Memorias del general O'Leary*, XI, 26. Anti-Argentine sentiment may also be seen in the following issues of *El Cóndor de Bolivia*: November 6, 1826, supplement, 1–4; January 4, 1827, pp. 1–2; January 11, 1827, pp. 1–3; January 18, 1827, p. 2; January 25, 1827, pp. 1–2.

movement. The Cisplatine question arose soon after the movement began in Buenos Aires, and Portuguese military involvement in the Banda Oriental dated from 1811. Long-standing hostility between the independent regimes of Buenos Aires and Paraguay provided an opportunity for Dom Pedro to seek an alliance with Dr. Francia; the Luso-Brazilian interest in detaching Paraguay—as well as the Banda Oriental and the Argentine littoral provinces—from loyalty to Buenos Aires had begun when the Portuguese court arrived in 1808. The close association of Gran Colombia, Peru, and Bolivia, as well as the limited collaboration between the United Provinces and Chile, stemmed from the wars of independence. The Argentine call for a republican coalition in 1825 also hearkened back to Spanish-American cooperation in the struggle against Ferdinand. Intra-South American relations between 1825 and 1827, then, may be seen as a continuation of patterns established since 1808.

Beginning in 1827, these patterns shifted radically. Realignments ruptured bonds of friendship and brought together nations formerly hostile toward each other. These changes were precipitated by a bitter enmity between Peru on the one hand and Gran Colombia and Bolivia on the other. As a consequence of this conflict, the northern republics again were drawn into the Cisplatine question and again considered the place of the Brazilian monarchy in the international order. As the Banda Oriental dispute had shaped Argentine and Brazilian diplomacy with regard to the other South American countries, so now the international tensions in the north shaped Peruvian, Bolivian, and Colombian diplomacy with regard to Argentina and Brazil.

Five • Power Politics
Toward a New Order

WHEN Gran Colombia appointed a new minister to Rio de Janeiro in mid-1828, Bolívar wrote him: "[W]e should always be grateful to the Brazilian emperor, who has always shown himself rather favorably disposed toward us."[1] This represented a startling reassessment of Dom Pedro, whom Bolívar three years earlier had considered a "hare-brained" reactionary intent on subverting the republics. As Gran Colombia's relations with Peru declined, the Liberator had no choice but to take another look at an international order he previously had taken for granted.

For the most part, Brazil remained a passive spectator to the realignment that took place beginning in 1827, but the other South American states seldom failed to take the empire into consideration as they maneuvered for advantage. As Gran Colombia and Peru moved toward the war of 1828–1829—the second major international conflict of the 1820s—Lima broke with Rio de Janeiro as a means of seeking the support of Buenos Aires; Bogotá, on the other hand, looked to Brazil as a potential ally.

Meanwhile, the attention of the imperial government remained fixed on the Plata. After more than two years of armed conflict, both Brazil and Argentina realized the dispute over the Banda Oriental could not be settled by force of arms and accepted British mediation as a way out of the impasse. The negotiations resulted in the creation of the buffer state of Uruguay. Although

1. Bolívar to Francisco Carabaño (Copy), July 9, 1828, in [Bolívar], *Cartas del Libertador*, VI, 369–370.

this solution did not end Brazilian and Argentine competition in the Plata, it did provide a basis for terminating the war.

Dom Pedro's effort to absorb the Cisplatine contributed to Spanish-American fears of Brazilian dominance. Those who speculated on the "equilibrium" of the continent almost invariably assigned a key role to Brazil. Although one government or another sometimes perceived a threat to the equilibrium, no league ever emerged to meet such a challenge. South Americans might cite the European "balance of power" model, but they lacked the developed state system that made such a model feasible. Under the conditions of the 1820s, no regime was likely to imperil its fragile authority by going to war for such a tenuous principle. Competition for relative advantage, however, was constant.

BRAZIL AND THE
PERUVIAN-COLOMBIAN-BOLIVIAN CONFLICT

The origins of the clash between Peru and Gran Colombia lay partly in a territorial dispute; both nations claimed debatable lands along the border, and Peru coveted the port of Guayaquil, which Gran Colombia had annexed in 1822. Peruvian dissatisfaction with Bolívar, which burgeoned after his return to Bogotá, also contributed to the conflict. In December, 1826, Peru dutifully adopted the Liberator's Bolivian constitution and appeared ready to join Gran Colombia and Bolivia in an Andean Federation. But, late in the following month, Bolívar's enemies seized power in Lima and overturned the constitution. The new government rejected Bolívar's personal leadership, his authoritarian political model, and his championship of Colombian hegemony. Relations between Peru and Gran Colombia worsened steadily during 1827 and 1828.[2]

The Peruvian break with Bolívar also made conflict with Bolivia more likely. In addition to the usual disagreement over common borders, the two countries now were separated by differing ideologies and attitudes toward the Liberator. Sucre, Bolívar's most loyal partisan and a fellow Venezuelan, presided over the Bolivian state, an authoritarian political system designed by Bo-

2. Basadre, *Historia de la república del Perú*, I, 157–95, 295–97; Zubieta, *Apuntaciones*, 162–75.

lívar himself. Moreover, a Colombian army remained in Bolivia to support Sucre's regime. The Peruvian leaders saw themselves flanked by a Colombian satellite and feared Bolivia would aid Gran Colombia in the event of war. By mid-1827, Lima was searching for diplomatic support to check the perceived threat from Bolívar and Sucre.

One ploy used by the Peruvian government was a claim that the Liberator was in league with Dom Pedro. Immediately after the coup of January, 1827, the Peruvian Manuel Vidaurre charged that Bolívar and the Brazilian emperor intended to divide South America between them, forming "two empires."[3] The Lima chancery, in keeping with this view, stifled the recent rapprochement with Brazil and began to court the United Provinces. The new government in Lima ordered José Domingo Cáceres, sent to Rio as consul general the previous year, to undertake a new mission in Buenos Aires; even though the emperor had recognized Peru and readily accepted Cáceres at the rank of chargé, Lima broke relations by withdrawing its representative. Apprehensive that Cáceres might remain loyal to Bolívar, however, the Peruvian government recalled him almost immediately from the Argentine capital.[4]

In August, 1827, Estanislao Lynch, the Argentine consul in Lima, reported Peruvian President José de La Mar's "intimate conviction that our struggle is not only for the Banda Oriental but also for the principles of the American system, and that its outcome will be transcendental for the American States." Nonetheless, La Mar was less interested in Peruvian participation in the

3. Vidaurre to Santander, January 29, 1827, in *El Peruano* (Lima), February 21, 1827, p. 2. For other speculations about such an understanding between Bolívar and Dom Pedro, see the following: Sarratea to Argentine MRE (Secret, No. 26), July 18, 1826, in Ar-AGN, Sala X, legajo 1-1-8; Robert Gordon to [John] Lord Ponsonby (Copy), December 4, 1826, in GB-PRO, FO 13/26, fls. 225–26; Tudor to Clay (Confidential), February 3, 1827, in Manning (ed.), *Diplomatic Correspondence*, II, 1818; Ricketts to Canning (No. 6), March 3, 1827, in GB-PRO, FO 61/11, fls. 117–120; Campino to Chilean MRE (No. 9), September 3, 1828, in Ch-AMRE, Perú, tomo 9.

4. Cáceres to Pando, February 20, 1827, and Cáceres to Vidaurre, July 22, 1827, in Pe-AMRE, 1827, carpeta 5-2; Francisco Javier Mariátegui to Cáceres (Copy), August 20, 1827, *ibid.*, tomo 461–C, fl. 4; João Batista Moreira to João Carlos de Saldanha Oliveira e Daun (No. 3), September 17, 1827, in Po-ANTT, MinNE, caixa "Legação de Portugal no Brasil, 1826–1830"; Estanislao Lynch to Argentine MRE (No. 61), September 14, 1827, in Ar-AGMREC, Misiones, caja 15.

Cisplatine War than in joint action with regard to Bolivia. As long as Sucre and his Colombian troops remained in the latter country, the anti-Bolivarist regime in Lima would not be secure. Likewise, the United Provinces could not expect aid from Sucre, in view of Bolívar's antipathy toward Buenos Aires. Lynch therefore suggested to his government that the ouster of Sucre would permit Bolivia to join the war against Brazil and simultaneously eliminate a threat to Peruvian security. To obtain this collaboration, La Mar was prepared to negotiate a treaty of alliance with the United Provinces, although Peruvian assistance would be limited to diplomatic support for the time being.[5]

No such negotiation took place, possibly because of Lynch's replacement by another agent. Moreover, despite repeated promises to name a representative in Buenos Aires, the Lima chancery did not do so until February, 1828. By this time, a change in the Argentine government had compromised the Peruvian strategy. Manuel José García had negotiated a peace treaty with Brazil in the early months of 1827, but, since the pact left the Banda Oriental in Brazilian possession, it was rejected by the Argentine congress. In the ensuing political crisis, Bernardino Rivadavia abandoned the presidency in July and was replaced by Vicente López. With the dissolution of the congress in August the United Provinces reverted to a loose confederation, and Manuel Dorrego assumed the governorship of Buenos Aires province.[6]

Although Dorrego's warm friendship with Bolívar and Sucre cast doubt on the viability of a Lima-Buenos Aires axis, the Peruvian government overcame its misgivings and appointed Andrés Santa Cruz minister to the Argentine capital. The Peruvian foreign minister instructed Santa Cruz to cultivate good relations with the Dorrego administration but to resist requests for military assistance against Brazil, for "now more than ever we should avoid attracting such a powerful enemy." Considering the precarious state of the public treasury, not to mention the hostility of Gran Colombia and Bolivia, the foreign minister affirmed that "we must

5. Lynch to Cruz (No. 59), August 23, 1827, and Lynch to Argentine MRE (Nos. 60 and 61), September 1 and 14, 1827, in Ar-AGMREC, Misiones, caja 15; Lynch to Argentine MRE (No. 68), September 30, 1827, in Ar-AGN, Sala X, legajo 1-9-2.
6. Hugo R. Galmarini, *Del fracaso unitario al triunfo federal, 1824–1830* (Buenos Aires, [1974]), 69–77.

first save our own country before succoring our neighbor." Santa Cruz never fulfilled his mission. He arrived in Santiago, his secondary post, but early snows blocked the Andean passes, and he was unable to proceed. Elected president of Bolivia in August, 1828, Santa Cruz returned directly to assume his duties.[7]

The realignment that came in the wake of the anti-Bolivarist coup in Lima also involved Chile. Before the end of 1826 the Chilean government had come to suspect that Bolívar might try to extend his power over the rest of the continent, and news of the overthrow of his regime in Lima touched off spirited celebrations in Chile.[8] In April, 1827, the Santiago chancery commissioned Pedro Trujillo to negotiate with Peru a treaty providing for reciprocal commercial advantages and a defensive alliance, the latter inspired largely by fears of the Liberator.[9] When the Peruvian regime sought to purchase ships and munitions from Chile in November, the Chilean foreign minister expressed his government's conviction that "should the war in question unfortunately transpire, Chile would see itself threatened by the same evils that Peru would suffer, and its independence would become illusory." He suggested that, as a means of formulating a common policy toward the Bolívar and Sucre regimes, the Lima chancery discuss a treaty of alliance with the Chilean agent sent earlier in the year.[10]

Trujillo, however, departed from his instructions and omitted the article calling for military assistance in time of war. Such action seemed necessary, he explained to his government, to avoid compromising Chile in Peru's impending clash with Gran Colombia and Bolivia. The minister feared that Bolívar would triumph and reestablish his control over Peru, in which case the Liberator would abrogate the treaty and close Peru to Chilean

---

7. Mariátegui to [Santa Cruz] (Copy), February 14, 1828, in Pe-AMRE, 1828, carpeta 5-2; M. de Salazar to Chilean MRE, Lima, September 21, 1828, in Ch-AMRE, Perú, tomo 8.

8. Mariano Álvarez to Gandarillas, November 20, 1826, in Ch-AMRE, Perú, tomo 8; Gandarillas to [M. Álvarez] (Copy), November 24, 1826, *ibid.*, Argentina, tomo 9, fl. 9; Allen to Clay, March 12, 1827, in Manning (ed.), *Diplomatic Correspondence*, II, 1116.

9. Gandarillas to Pedro Trujillo (Copy), April 1, 1827, in Ch-AN, MinRE, tomo 21, fls. 3–5; Zegers to Egaña (Nos. 249 and 250, Copies), May 22 and June 5, 1827, in Ch-AMRE, Argentina, tomo 10, fls. 6–8.

10. Mariátegui to Chilean MRE, November 5, 1827, in Ch-AMRE, Perú, tomo 8; Zegers to Peruvian MRE (Copy), December 10, 1827, *ibid.*, Perú, tomo 12, fls. 5–6.

commerce.[11] Trujillo therefore confined the treaty to commercial aspects, and once again an attempt to forge a military alliance came to naught.

Meanwhile, Peru's independent foreign policy had repercussions in Bolivia, where Sucre already was contemplating a rapprochement with the United Provinces as a means of checking Brazil's power. In February, 1827, an anonymous letter published in *El Cóndor de Bolivia* advocated the union of Argentina, Chile, and Bolivia as a counterweight to the empire. The author invoked the European example of equilibrium-maintenance and argued that the American nations should do likewise.

> Brazil is a strong power that in the long run will bend the politics of all America in its favor. Its extension, natural resources, geographical position, [and] form of government give it a threatening power over the other States. We see that since its birth it has submerged one of our sister Republics in misfortune, and it is certain that it will reduce [Buenos Aires] to a humiliating and onerous peace. Brazil probably will progress more rapidly than the peoples that surround it, and the success of its struggle with Buenos Aires will encourage the Emperor to other enterprises. We should, then, take precautions against the blows of a giant, for it may be called that in comparison with us.

The proposed solution was a federation of Argentina, Chile, and Bolivia, with its capital at a central point in the Argentine interior. "Certainly America will repose with greater surety of peace if this project is realized; because, if the power of Brazil is contained— which is the object that should have the greatest attention—the equilibrium will remain very well protected."[12]

Observing that the suggestion was received favorably by the Bolivian elite, Sucre quickly adopted it as an alternative to Bolívar's Andean Federation, which he considered unfeasible because

11. Trujillo to Chilean MRE (No. 48, Secret), January 21, 1828, in Ch-AMRE, Perú, tomo 7, fls. 235–36. After the war with Gran Colombia had begun, the Lima chancery again pressed for an offensive-defensive alliance, but Trujillo refused to commit Chile in the struggle. Trujillo to Chilean MRE (No. 75), January 10, 1829, *ibid.*, fls. 277–78.

12. *El Cóndor de Bolivia*, February 1, 1827, p. 3.

of Peruvian hostility and lack of public support in Bolivia. Soon, however, he discarded the original rationale. Instead of pointing to the Brazilian danger, he justified the federation in terms of the interests of Bolivia, Gran Colombia, and America in general. By November he had come to view the federation as a means of strengthening his regime against the growing pressures from Peru.[13]

In June, 1827, Sucre named the aged Gregorio Funes, still serving as the Colombian minister in Buenos Aires, to represent Bolivia in the same capital and to present his proposal for a federation to the Argentine government.[14] Before receiving these instructions, Funes, apparently in response to earlier correspondence with Bolívar or Sucre, already had set out to effect a rapprochement. Anticipating the election of Vicente López, Funes and Manuel Dorrego sounded him out on the possibility of an understanding with Gran Colombia and Bolivia, and they found him receptive. After López replaced Rivadavia in July, Funes and Dorrego visited his foreign minister, Marcos Balcarce, and assured him that both the Colombian and Bolivian governments wanted to renew their friendship with Buenos Aires. Funes also said that Sucre would be willing to sign a treaty providing for Bolivian participation in the war against Brazil.[15]

The new Argentine regime responded eagerly. The emperor's usurpation of the Banda Oriental, Balcarce wrote the Bolivian foreign minister, should make it obvious to the American states, "that the peace and security of all will constantly be threatened by that voracious Power that is rising in the heart of the Continent." On behalf of the Argentine government, Balcarce proposed an offensive-defensive alliance; in the meantime, he suggested that Bolivia prepare "all the forces necessary to attack Brazil

13. Sucre to Bolívar, March 11, June 4, and November 12, 1827, in O'Leary (ed.), *Memorias del general O'Leary*, I, 424, 432–33, 467.
14. Sucre's first letters to Funes have not been located but are mentioned in subsequent correspondence. For a copy of the project of federation, dated April 4, 1827, see GB-PRO, FO 61/11, fl. 323. The Colombian government had exonerated Funes of his diplomatic post in November, 1826, but he did not receive word until August, 1827. Funes to Marcos Balcarce, August 11, 1827, in Ar-AGN, Sala X, legajo 1-9-11.
15. Funes to [Sucre], July 10 and 18, 1827, in O'Leary (ed.), *Memorias del general O'Leary*, XI, 227, 229–32; Manuel Dorrego to [Sucre], July 18, 1827, *ibid.*, 290–293.

on the Mato Grosso border, so as to carry war and insurrection to the heart of the Empire and to combine with the forces of the Argentine Republic to menace the Emperor in his very capital."[16]

After Dorrego assumed command of the Buenos Aires government in late August, he continued to pursue an understanding with Sucre. In November he appointed Francisco Ignacio Bustos envoy to Bolivia. By this time Dorrego had received Sucre's proposal for a federation, yet he took no notice of it. Instead, he instructed Bustos to seek a treaty along the lines suggested earlier by Balcarce: a bilateral, "defensive" alliance aimed at Brazil, and a Bolivian commitment to occupy Mato Grosso until the emperor evacuated the Banda Oriental.[17]

Funes apparently had misrepresented Sucre's ideas, for the latter's conception of the rapprochement differed substantially from Dorrego's. Late in 1827 the Bolivian president still talked of a federation of Bolivia, Argentina, and Chile rather than a bilateral alliance against Brazil. He did not rule out an attack on the empire, but first he wanted to see the treaty of federation signed. From Sucre's point of view, Peru rather than Brazil constituted the greater peril. Although he did not specifically request Argentine support in his differences with the maverick Peruvian government, his correspondence clearly reveals his hope that closer relations with Buenos Aires would provide a counterweight to Lima. From Santiago, Andrés Santa Cruz interpreted Sucre's overtures to Argentina as an attempt to form "an anti-popular and very particularly an anti-Peruvian pact."[18]

Even as he tried to improve relations with Buenos Aires, Sucre sought to establish a direct connection with Brazil for the first time. In September, 1827, he asked Leandro Palacios, the Colombian minister in Rio de Janeiro, to solicit the emperor's recognition of Bolivia; afterwards, the two countries would exchange ministers

16. M. Balcarce to Bolivian MRE, July [16?], 1827, in Bo-AN, MinRE, Bolivia-Argentina, tomo 1, no. 9.

17. Dorrego to [Sucre], September 3, October 26, and November 4, 1827, *ibid.*, no. 8; Funes to [Sucre], September 26, 1827, in O'Leary (ed.), *Memorias del general O'Leary*, XI, 238–41; "Instrucciones que deberá observar al Enviado extraordinario D^{or} D^n Francisco Ignacio Bustos . . ." November 3, 1827 (MS in Ar-AGN, Sala X, legajo 1-9-5).

18. Sucre to Funes, November 22, December 7 and 22, 1827, in Ar-AGN, Sala VII, Guido Ms, legajo 16-1-8; Santa Cruz to Peruvian MRE (No. 8), May 12, 1828, in Pe-AMRE, 1828, carpeta 5-4.

and negotiate a treaty of friendship and commerce. Dom Pedro readily agreed, recognizing the Bolivian government in January, 1828. Rather than attack Brazil, then, Sucre planned to send a diplomatic agent to Rio.[19]

In late January, Bustos arrived in Chuquisaca to seek a military alliance. Like Bolívar on the eve of the Alvear–Díaz Vélez mission more than two years earlier, Sucre intended to avoid entanglement in the Argentine war against Brazil. Bustos actively conspired with Sucre's enemies, who on April 18 launched a rebellion in which the president was wounded. At the end of the month, after the uprising had been put down, the administration severed relations with the Argentine minister and lodged a complaint with his government. By this time, Buenos Aires, having decided that peace with Brazil was imminent, had ordered Bustos to withdraw the proposal for a Bolivian strike into Mato Grosso.[20] For the second time, an Argentine mission to Upper Peru produced no alliance.

In early 1828 Sucre counted on the support of Gran Colombia to deter Peru from invading Bolivia.[21] But awe of the Liberator proved an inadequate deterrent, and, when the anticipated invasion occurred, no one came to Sucre's aid. Taking advantage of the April rebellion in Chuquisaca, General Agustín Gamarra led the Peruvian army across the border on May 1, 1828; the intervention, he claimed, sprang solely from a desire to save the life of the Bolivian president and to restore order in a troubled country—a rationale vehemently contested by Sucre. The Bolivian army offered little resistance and capitulated in early July. The victors imposed a peace treaty requiring the abrogation of the Bolivian

---

19. Sucre to Bolívar, September 19, 1827, in O'Leary (ed.), *Memorias del general O'Leary*, I, 456; Infante to Palacios, October 23, 1827, in Co-ADC, tomo 158, fl. 125; Aracati to Palacios, January 2, 1828, in Co-ADC, tomo 158, fl. 202; *El Cóndor de Bolivia*, April 5, 1828, p. 1; [Infante] to Aracati (No. 1, Copy), April 5, 1828, in Bo-AN, MinRE, Bolivia-Brasil, tomo 1, no. 2. Two years later, the Bolivian government was still trying to get Brazil to agree to an exchange of ministers. [Bolivian MRE] to MNE (Copy), June 26, 1830, in Bo-AN, MinRE, Bolivia-Brasil, tomo 1, no. 2.

20. Sucre to Bolívar, January 27, 1828, in O'Leary (ed.), *Memorias del general O'Leary*, I, 488; Juan Ramón Balcarce to Francisco Ignacio Bustos (No. 3, Copy), March 26, 1828, in Ar-AGN, Sala X, tomo 44-5-40, fl. 173.

21. Sucre to Juan José Flores, January 26 and February 3, 1828, in O'Leary (ed.), *Memorias del general O'Leary*, I, 623–25; Sucre to Bolívar, January 27 and April 12, 1828, *ibid.*, 493–95.

constitution and the departure of Sucre and most foreign-born troops.[22]

The Peruvian invasion was motivated principally by the conviction that Sucre would attack Peru in support of his mentor, Bolívar. The Peruvians saw their action as a preemptive strike to eliminate an enemy in the south before facing a more dangerous enemy in the north. Ideological differences, evidenced by frequent Peruvian diatribes against the lifetime presidency of the Bolivian constitution, also played a part.[23]

Several facts suggest that the intervention in Bolivia was prompted by fears of Gran Colombia. For one thing, Peruvian leaders justified the invasion in terms of strategic considerations and of ending the "Colombian domination" and "foreign tutelage" of Bolivia.[24] Second, as soon as Sucre had been removed from the presidency, Lima began negotiations to secure the use of Bolivian troops in the coming war with Gran Colombia.[25] And third, Peru used the peace treaty to court Buenos Aires, still seen as a potential ally in the dispute with Bolívar. The treaty stated, "The

22. Gamarra to Chuquisaca provisional government, April 30, 1828, in Bo-AN, MinRE, Bolivia-Perú, tomo 1, no. 2; Lofstrom, *The Promise and Problem of Reform*, 553–57.

23. Trujillo to Chilean MRE (Secret), May 28, 1827, in Ch-AMRE, Perú, tomo 7, fl. 170; Lynch to Cruz (Nos. 47, 58, and 59), June 6, August 19 and 23, 1827, in Ar-AGMREC, Misiones, caja 15; Willimott to Canning (No. 7), September 24, 1827, and Willimott to Viscount Dudley (No. 3), November 16, 1827, in GB-PRO, FO 61/13, fls. 254, 298–302; Mariátegui to British foreign secretary, November 16, 1827, in GB-PRO, FO 61/13, fls. 340–41; La Mar to Gamarra, January 12, 1828, in Ar-AGN, Sala VII, García Ms, legajo 1-6-2; La Mar to Guido, September 17, 1828, Ar-AGN, Sala VII, Guido Ms, legajo 16-1-9.

24. Gamarra to León Galindo, May 3, 1828, in *El Cóndor de Bolivia*, May 22, 1828, p. 1; La Mar to Gamarra, May 19, 1828, in Ar-AGN, Sala VII, García Ms, legajo 1-6-2; José María Galdiano to [Santa Cruz] (Copy), May 30, 1828, in Pe-AMRE, tomo 461-C, fls. 7–8; *Boletín del Ejército del Sud del Perú Ausiliar de Bolivia* [Potosí?], July 14, 1828; Gamarra to [Sucre], July 17, 1828, in Bo-BN, Rück Ms, no. 440; Manuel Salazar y Baquíjano to Velasco, September 28, 1828, in Bo-AN, MinRE, Bolivia-Perú, tomo 1, no. 16; M. Álvarez to Bolivian MRE (No. 5), March 23, 1830, in Bo-AN, MinRE, Bolivia-Perú, tomo 1, no. 10; Peru, *Manifiesto del gobierno del Perú, en contestación al que ha dado el General Bolívar, sobre los motivos que tiene para hacerle la guerra* (Lima, 1828), 10–11, 19. Lofstrom, in *The Promise and Problem of Reform*, 582, rejects these arguments as mere rationalizations and emphasizes Peruvian internal politics as the principal motive for the invasion.

25. Riglos to Argentine MRE, August 10 and November 24, 1828, in Ar-AGN, Sala X, legajo 1-9-3; Olañeta to Ángel Moscoso, October 29, 1828, in Bo-BN, Rück Ms, no. 441; Justo Figuerola to Pando, December 6, 1828, in Pe-AMRE, 1828, carpeta 5-7.

Peruvian and Bolivian Republics will not enter into relations with the Empire of Brazil until the latter makes peace with the Argentine Republic."[26]

The Peruvian invasion of Bolivia provoked another realignment, for the Colombian government turned to Brazil as a possible ally. As pointed out earlier, the Bogotá chancery had treated the empire warmly since 1825 and had been the first of the Spanish-American republics to regularize diplomatic relations. Informed of the Argentine overture to Sucre, Bolívar's government discouraged Bolivian participation in the war against Brazil. The Colombian foreign minister argued, in brief, that the Argentines had made their bed and must lie in it. Buenos Aires had refused to send delegates to the Panama Congress, where, the Colombians reasoned, the Banda Oriental dispute might have been resolved peacefully, and therefore none of the other republics were obliged to come to the aid of the Argentines.[27]

Soon after learning of the Peruvian invasion of Bolivia, the Bogotá chancery countermanded earlier orders to close the legation in Rio, but the new directions arrived after the Colombian minister had departed. A new appointee apparently declined the post but, in September, 1828, Bogotá finally found a willing agent in Juan María Gómez, formerly secretary of the legation under Palacios.[28]

Two motives appear to have inspired the approach to Brazil: the desire for an ally to balance an increasingly hostile Peru, and Bolívar's growing preference for more authoritarian political solutions to the problem of "anarchy." The British minister in Bogotá highlighted this second motive: "General Bolívar seems to be already convinced that the Republican forms of government are chimeras and he is on that account the more desirous to maintain relations of intimate friendship with the Emperor of Brazil. Conceiving no doubt that Brazil and Colombia will ultimately give the tone to the political institutions of the New States, whose

26. Article 12 of Treaty of Piquiza, July 6, 1828, in Peru, MinRE, *Colección de los tratados . . .*, II, 174.
27. Revenga to Bolivian MRE, January 8, 1828, in Bo-AMREC, tomo CAV-5-R-1.
28. Palacios to Aracati, October 30, 1828, in Br-AHI, maço 282/3/12; Bolívar to Carabaño (Copy), July 9, 1828, in [Bolívar], *Cartas del Libertador*, VI, 369–70; Vergara to J. M. Gómez (Copy), September 10, 1828, in Co-ADC, tomo 50, fl. 43.

prosperity appears to depend on the adoption of more vigorous and permanent Systems of Government."[29] Whether or not he had become a monarchist, as some allege, Bolívar clearly admired the stability of the Brazilian monarchy in contrast to the unruly—and, from his point of view, ungrateful—politics of the republics.

A more elaborate rationale appeared in the instructions issued to Gómez in November, calling for the negotiation of a treaty of friendship, commerce, and navigation with Brazil. On the one hand, the Liberator anticipated that a rapprochement with the empire would help Gran Colombia obtain the recognition of Spain and the other European monarchies. On the other hand, he saw in Brazil a formidable ally. As the foreign minister wrote Gómez, "Colombia can no longer count on the other states of America for anything, because some show disdain [and] others an outright aversion; only from Brazil can it hope for something." The Colombian government had attempted to develop its foreign policy in concert with the other republics, the minister asserted, but their obstructionism had at last induced Bolívar to recall the Colombian representative to the Panama Congress; "having considered the perfidy of some, the indifference of others, and one may say the repugnance of all to handle their affairs in common, the Liberator has thought it proper that Colombia concentrate on itself and promote its [own] happiness without heeding the interests of the others." A Brazilian alliance, the foreign minister continued, would serve as the keystone of Gran Colombia's independent foreign policy: "There is no doubt that these two states are the strongest in America, nor that they are more stable and have more resources for their defense; united in friendship, at least in opinion, the strength of each will be augmented by that of the other. It is true that [the alliance] may engender some jealousy and mistrust among the other states: but they would restrain themselves for fear of a league between Brazil and Colombia, which would take place if they for some reason began a war." Gómez was instructed to remind the imperial government that Gran Colombia for years had shown its desire for peace, whereas Peru had for-

29. James Henderson to John Bidwell, September 14, 1828, in GB-PRO, FO 18/56, fl. 174. See also Vergara to José Fernández Madrid (No. 222), July 8, 1828, in Co-ADC, tomo 489, fl. 308; and Sousa Dias to Aracati (No. 6, Copy), April 5, 1830, in Br-AHI, Arquivo II, tomo 403/2/3.

bidden Bolivia, by the Treaty of Piquiza, to establish relations with Brazil.[30]

In searching for support in the dispute with Peru, Bolívar had totally rejected the internationalism of the Panama Congress. Now he favored collaboration between the two largest and most powerful states on the continent, by which each could pursue its own interests without fear of harassment by troublesome neighbors.

But this project was as fruitless as those to establish an American league and an Andean Federation. When Gómez arrived in Rio in August, 1829, he discovered that Dom Pedro preferred the negotiations take place in Bogotá. The imperial cabinet did not intend to authorize its minister, Luís de Sousa Dias, to conclude any treaty until he had reported on the Liberator's attitude toward Brazil. Sousa Dias did not reach Bogotá until March, 1830, long after the end of the war between Gran Colombia and Peru (August, 1828 to July, 1829). He found the government very well disposed toward the empire but saw no reason for Rio to send him credentials for the negotiation of a treaty. "In view . . . of the vacillating state in which this [government] finds itself, as well as the spirit of provincialism and discord that prevails in diverse Departments of the Republic," the Brazilian minister wrote in April, "I not only remain convinced of the absolute uselessness of the Full Powers in question, of which I certainly will dare not make use, but I also fear that many years will yet pass before the Government or Governments of the Country that presently embraces the unsettled Republic of Colombia will offer the requisite guarantees so that we can establish fixed and stable relations with them by means of Treaties."[31]

In November, 1830, after both Venezuela and Ecuador had separated from Gran Colombia and Bolívar had left Bogotá for exile, Sousa Dias decided that the situation had stabilized adequately to warrant pursuing a treaty, and he asked for the necessary credentials. On the very same day, however, the Colombian foreign minister notified his agent in Rio that neither a treaty

---

30. Vergara to J. M. Gómez, November 24, 1828, in Co-ADC, tomo 159, fls. 168–72.

31. J. M. Gómez to Colombian MRE (No. 6), August 26, 1829, in Co-ADC, tomo 159, fls. 89–92; [MNE] to Sousa Dias (Draft), October 26, 1829, in Br-AHI, maço 204/2/16; Sousa Dias to Aracati (No. 10, Copy), April 22, 1830, in Br-AHI, Arquivo II, tomo 403/2/3.

of friendship nor one of limits could be concluded "until the Republic is tranquil and the national [territorial] integrity is reestablished." Furthermore, the imperial government had already sent Sousa Dias a letter of recall in August, ordering that his secretary remain as interim chargé and consul general. Since the secretary had died, the legation was closed when Sousa Dias departed Bogotá in early 1831. The Colombian government summoned Gómez home in August of that year, and he left Rio early in 1832.[32]

Relations between the two countries were severed without the stabilizing alliance Bolívar wanted and without so much as a treaty of friendship. In mid-1832, the Colombian foreign minister, in repeating Gómez' recall, affirmed his government's interest in cultivating relations with Brazil as soon as the three sections of the country had settled their differences. "This longed-for day is not far off," he added, perhaps with more hope than conviction.[33] But the disintegration of Gran Colombia was irreversible, and relations between Brazil and the truncated state of New Granada remained broken for many years.

Neither the Peruvian approach to Buenos Aires nor the Colombian approach to Brazil bore fruit. As in the case of the Banda Oriental dispute, the rivalries among the northern republics spurred efforts to obtain diplomatic and military support across the continent. But, again like the Platine case, attempts to secure alliances derived from the immediacy of local conflicts; in the absence of more permanent bases of association, such overtures invariably came to nothing.

THE CREATION OF URUGUAY

Without allies, the Brazilians and Argentines fought to a draw in the Banda Oriental. Neither side managed to make good its claim by force of arms, and in a state of exhaustion the belligerents finally agreed to the creation of an independent nation as the only

32. Sousa Dias to Calmon (No. 22, Copy), November 14, 1830, in Br-AHI, Arquivo II, tomo 403/2/3; Barrero to J. M. Gómez (No. 3), November 14, 1830, in Co-ADC, tomo 159, fls. 231–32; Sousa Dias to Calmon (No. 4, Copy), January 31, 1831, in Br-AHI, Arquivo II, tomo 403/2/3; F. Restrepo to J. M. Gómez (No. 16, Copy), August 7, 1831, in Co-ADC, tomo 50, fls. 122–23; Gómez to Carneiro de Campos, January 27, 1832, in Br-AHI, maço 282/3/12.

33. Alejandro Vélez to J. M. Gómez (No. 17, Copy), May 21, 1832, in Co-ADC, tomo 50, fls. 123–24.

means of resolving the dispute. At this point, the British government at last succeeded in mediating the settlement after three frustrating years.

London had attempted to avert war during the early 1820s, because the prospect of a conflict in the Plata threatened British interests in two ways. In the first place, the outbreak of war would seriously damage British commerce by hindering production, diverting wealth to warfare, and interfering with maritime traffic through blockades and privateering. Second, war might undermine the stability of the Brazilian monarchy. Great Britain intended that Brazil be a client state, as Portugal had been since the mid-seventeenth century, and demanded commercial privileges as well as the abolition of the slave trade as the price of recognition; thus, the British had a direct stake in perpetuating the Bragança dynasty in Brazil. Moreover, Canning wanted to preserve the monarchy to avoid an ideological split between Europe and America.

In 1824 some members of the Oriental elite had proposed that the disputed territory become a colony of Great Britain. The British rejected the overture, no doubt recalling the abortive attempts to conquer Buenos Aires and Montevideo in 1806 and 1807.[34] But many persons continued to believe that Great Britain harbored designs on the Banda Oriental. Canning attempted to dispel such suspicions by maintaining a strict impartiality between the contending parties, even though he considered the Argentine claim superior. Both the Brazilian and Argentine governments asked him to intercede—each anticipating his support—but he declined. When Sir Charles Stuart sailed to Rio in mid-1825 to negotiate the treaty between Portugal and Brazil, Canning instructed him not to become involved in the question and not to give Dom Pedro the impression that Britain recognized any Brazilian right to the Banda Oriental.[35]

On arriving in the Brazilian capital amid rumors of Bolívar's going to the aid of Buenos Aires, Stuart urged Canning to reconsider. Direct action was essential, he asserted, if Britain intended

34. Hood to Canning, April 22, 1824, in Webster (ed.), *Britain and the Independence of Latin America*, I, 109–110; Francis Lord Conyngham to Hood, August 6, 1824, *ibid.*, 113–14.

35. Canning to Stuart (No. 23, Secret, Draft), June 16, 1825, in GB-PRO, FO 13/2, fls. 39–49.

to avert the fall of the Brazilian monarchy. The British minister characterized the negotiations between Brazil and Portugal as of secondary importance in comparison with the Banda Oriental controversy. Stuart was a persistent Cassandra, predicting the formation of an anti-Brazilian coalition and conjuring up apocalyptic visions of the destruction of the monarchy and the fragmentation of Brazil into a number of republics.[36] By the end of September, Canning—pressed by both parties to intervene and seeing war as almost certain—agreed to try to head off the conflict.[37] Failing to do so, he adopted a two-pronged approach to restoring peace, discouraging the Colombian government from aiding Buenos Aires while promoting the idea of a negotiated settlement through British mediation.

In early 1826, when John Lord Ponsonby was preparing to assume the post of minister to Buenos Aires, Canning ordered him to touch at Rio de Janeiro en route and sound out the emperor. The British foreign secretary suggested two possible solutions: the return of the Banda Oriental to the United Provinces, in return for a pecuniary compensation to cover the expenses of occupation since 1816, or the creation of an independent state. The third option, retention by Brazil, did not enter into British thinking at all. Since the imperial government considered possession of the Cisplatine the sine qua non of any negotiation, Ponsonby's prospects for success were dim.[38]

On arriving in Rio in May, 1826, the British minister presented an Argentine proposal to pay compensation in exchange for the return of the Banda Oriental. Distressed by their failure to crush the Oriental resistance quickly, the emperor's advisors seemed amenable, but Dom Pedro himself would brook no suggestion of surrender. He painted the issue as a question of his honor

36. Stuart to Canning (Private, No. 7), August 11, 1825, in GB-PRO, FO 13/20, fls. 39–41; Stuart to Canning (Nos. 57 and 59), August 16 and 18, 1825, *ibid.*, FO 13/4, fls. 98–103, 109–112; Stuart to Canning (No. 93), November 18, 1825, in GB-PRO, FO 13/6, fls. 212–13; Stuart to Canning (No. 23), April 16, 1826, in GB-PRO, FO 13/18, fls. 158–59.
37. Canning to Parish (Nos. 11 and 13, Drafts), September 26 and October [19], 1825, in GB-PRO, FO 6/7, fls. 52–55, 68–71.
38. Canning to Ponsonby (Nos. 2 and 3, Drafts), February 28 and March 18, 1826, *ibid.*, FO 6/12, fls. 8–14, 16–44; Inhambupe to Itabaiana (No. 151, Copy), May 6, 1826, in BR-AHI, tomo 268/1/14, fls. 172–73; Inhambupe to Marquês de Resende (No. 49), May 4, 1826, in Br-AHI, Arquivo II, tomo 427/1/1.

and Brazil's, and vowed to continue the fight. Ponsonby's efforts to frighten the emperor by raising the possibility of an invasion headed by Bolívar had no effect. The Brazilian government offered to extend recognition to Buenos Aires—actually, Dom João already had done so years earlier—and to make Montevideo a free port, but no more. Ponsonby had to depart for Buenos Aires without a serious counterproposal to lay before the Argentine government.[39]

In the Argentine capital, Ponsonby continued to seek adequate bases for an understanding, maintaining contact with the Brazilian government through the chargé in Rio, Robert Gordon. Neither Rio nor Buenos Aires paid heed, and the war continued. Canning's refusal to offer a British guarantee of an independent Cisplatine state inadvertently discouraged this option, but, before the close of 1826, the Argentine government accepted the principle of independence. Even though Dom Pedro rejected this possibility when Gordon proposed it in February, 1827, Buenos Aires commissioned Manuel José García two months later to undertake direct negotiations in Rio. García was authorized to conclude a peace treaty that either returned the Banda Oriental to the United Provinces or provided for its erection as an independent nation. If the imperial government proved obstinate, his instructions required García to return home.[40]

In his conversations with the Brazilian foreign minister in May, the Argentine emissary found that Dom Pedro remained inflexible in his determination to retain the disputed territory, all the more so following humiliating reverses suffered by the Brazilian forces on land and sea. Rather than depart with no agreement at all, García exceeded his instructions and signed a treaty recognizing Brazilian ownership of the Banda Oriental in exchange for the emperor's promise to provide for the well-being of the Orientals.

39. Ponsonby to Canning (Nos. 2 and 6), May 26, 1826, in GB-PRO, FO 6/12, fls. 145–56, 199–202; Ponsonby to Inhambupe (Private), June 4 and 12, 1826, and Ponsonby to Inhambupe (Secret and Confidential), July 25, 1826, in Br-AHI, lata 223, maço 2, pasta 17; Delavat y Rincón to Infantado (No. 161), May 30, 1826, in Sp-AHN, Estado, legajo 5852.

40. Queluz to [Gordon], February 19, 1827, in GB-PRO, FO 13/36, fls. 153–57; Gordon to Canning (No. 12), February 21, 1827, *ibid.*, fls. 136–41; "Instrucciones que deberán regir al Sor D. Manuel José García en el desempeño de la comision que se le ha conferido á la Corte del Janeiro," April 19, 1827 (MS in Ar-AGN, Sala VII, Guido Ms, legajo 16-1-8).

García justified his conduct by saying he feared the disintegration of the United Provinces if the war continued, but this argument carried little weight in Buenos Aires. President Rivadavia and the congress repudiated the treaty, and neither the interim government of Vicente López nor the subsequent administration of Manuel Dorrego differed from Rivadavia on this point.[41]

The Argentine rejection cut short the contentment of the Brazilian government. According to the Portuguese minister in Rio, Dom Pedro received the news while attending the theater and declared: "Since they do not want to accept Peace, I will continue to make War."[42] The emperor spurned a later Argentine proposal calling for an evacuation of the Banda Oriental by both parties and permitting the Orientals to choose their own fate.[43]

In October, 1827, before the Brazilian response to this most recent suggestion, the Argentine foreign minister, Manuel Moreno, took another tack by asking the Colombian minister in Rio to attempt a mediation. Leandro Palacios' original instructions from his own government had authorized him to seek a peaceful settlement, so the Colombian agent readily brought the Argentine initiative to the attention of the imperial cabinet. Dom Pedro affirmed his willingness to pursue this line and asked Palacios to obtain a new proposal from Buenos Aires recommending, in the Colombian's words, "that I take care that nothing be confided to or done through Lord Ponsonby, because [the emperor] does not desire the always self-serving intervention of Europe in a purely American affair."[44]

Palacios considered the possibility that Dom Pedro's assent masked "some hidden, sinister aim on the part of Brazil, either to assure the success of the Campaign or to distract Colombia and the other American States from coming to an understanding with the Provinces of the Río de la Plata, and thereby gain time for its

41. M. J. García to Argentine MRE (Secret), June 21, 1827, [Rivadavia] to Argentine congress, June 25, 1827, and José María Rojas and Juan C. Varela to [Rivadavia, ca. June 25, 1827], in Ar-AGN, Sala X, legajo 1-7-5.

42. Moreira to Francisco de Almeida (No. 3), July 27, 1827, in Po-ANTT, MinNE, caixa "Legação de Portugal no Brazil, 1826–1830."

43. P[onsonby] to Gordon, September 18, 1827, in GB-PRO, FO 13/40, fl. 52; Gordon to Dudley (No. 36), November 10, 1827, *ibid.*, FO 13/39, fls. 134–37.

44. Moreno to Palacios, October 16, 1827, in Co-ADC, paquete "Consulados de la Argentina en Colombia . . ."; Palacios to Colombian MRE (No. 18), November 6 (November 10 postscript), 1827, *ibid.*, tomo 158, fls. 81–88.

operations," but ultimately he was convinced of the emperor's sincerity. The Colombian's correspondence with Buenos Aires encountered extraordinary delays, however, and, by the time he received a reply from the Argentine foreign minister in March, 1828, Palacios had been recalled by his government. Suspecting that the British had interfered with his correspondence, he attributed the failure of his peace efforts to Argentine jealousy and British intrigue. On learning of Palacios' role in the negotiations, the Bogotá chancery rescinded his recall, but by then he already had departed the Brazilian capital.[45]

Meanwhile, as the third year of the war began, the Brazilian emperor showed himself willing, at last, to contemplate a compromise. His single-minded prosecution of the conflict had eroded support for his regime, and Dom Pedro had little choice but to accept the independence of the Cisplatine, the minimal demand of the Argentines. Just as he earlier had ignored the counsels of those who had questioned the wisdom of going to war over that region, so now he rode roughshod over the objections of most members of the Council of State to its surrender. "Lassitude, exhaustion, internal added to external differences, a growing conviction on both sides of the impossibility of a complete triumph on either," summarized Viscount Dudley, who had succeeded Canning as foreign secretary, finally had brought the belligerents together for serious negotiations.[46]

During 1828 the details were worked out through British mediation. On August 27 Argentine and Brazilian representatives signed a preliminary convention in Rio de Janeiro, providing for the independence of the Banda Oriental, which was to be guaranteed by the two contracting parties. The Orientals themselves were to choose their own form of government, although the constitution of the new state would need the approval of both Brazil and Argentina before going into effect. The negotiation of a definitive peace treaty was left for later.[47]

45. Palacios to Colombian MRE (No. 19), November 14, 1827, [Palacios] to Revenga, March 4, 1828, and Vergara to Palacios, April 21, 1828, in Co-ADC, tomo 158, fls. 85–86, 89–90a, 94–95.

46. José Feliciano Fernandes Pinheiro, "Memorias do Visconde de S. Leopoldo," *RIHGB*, XXXVIII, No. 2 (1875), 18–20, 44–46; Dudley to Gordon (No. 18, Draft), April 7, 1828, in GB-PRO, FO 13/46, fls. 79–80.

47. The convention appeared in *Diário Fluminense*, October 27, 1828, pp. 395–97. Much of the FO correspondence is published in Luís Alberto de Herrera, *La*

The Spanish agent in Rio considered the convention merely "a truce, or suspension of hostilities," and, indeed, both the Brazilian and Argentine governments looked on it as but a temporary solution. Argentine compliance was immediately cast into doubt by the overthrow and execution of Dorrego in December, 1828, but the new regime signaled its intention to observe the peace agreement in its entirety. In mid-1830 Brazil and Argentina bestowed their blessing on the constitution establishing the Oriental Republic of Uruguay.[48] No permanent peace treaty was ever negotiated, however, mainly because of the political instability reigning in Argentina and Uruguay, and soon to afflict Brazil as well.

The Banda Oriental conflict was crucial in defining respective spheres of influence and the limits of competition in the Plata. Neither party accepted this lesson immediately, for both Rio and Buenos Aires continued to keep a hand in Uruguayan affairs. Even before the preliminary convention was signed, Dom Pedro began trying to persuade the Vatican to create a separate bishopric in Montevideo, heretofore subordinate to that of Buenos Aires; although expressed in terms of the Church's interests, the request clearly aimed at reducing Argentine influence. In 1830 the Brazilian foreign minister repeated the appeal to the newly arrived papal nuncio, commenting that Uruguay probably would not survive as an independent state and would have to be incorporated into Brazil or Argentina.[49]

Following the abdication of Pedro I in 1831, the regency rec-

---

misión Ponsonby ([Montevideo], 1930), II. On the resolution of the conflict, see Herrera, *La misión Ponsonby*, I; and Hann, "Brazil and the Río de la Plata," 405–35.

48. Delavat y Rincón to González Salmón (No. 268), September 3, 1828, in Sp-AHN, Estado, legajo 5854; [Guido] to Aracati (Draft), December 16, 1828, in Ar-AGN, Sala VII, Guido Ms, legajo 16-1-9; Juan E. Pivel Devoto, *La misión de Nicolás Herrera a Río de Janeiro (1829–1830): Contribución al estudio de nuestra historia diplomática* (Montevideo, 1932); Ariosto D. González, *La misión de Santiago Vázquez a Buenos Aires, 1829–1830* (Montevideo, 1950).

49. Gómez Labrador to Cardinal Bernetti, September 25, 1828, and Bernetti to Gómez, September 28, 1828, in Va-ASV, ASS, rubrica 249, busto 437, fasciolo 2; Pedro Alcântara Ximenes to Leo XII, [November, 1828], and Bernetti to secretary of the Sacred Congregation of the Consistory (Very Secret), November 14, 1828, *ibid.*, rubrica 279, busto 592, fasciolo 4; [Ostini] to Albani (No. 56), June 12, 1830, *ibid.*, rubrica 251, busto 448, fasciolo 3.

onciled itself to Uruguayan independence, but Argentine ambitions to recover the area persisted until the fall of Juan Manuel de Rosas in 1852. Eventually, Rio and Buenos Aires recognized the limits of their power and forswore efforts to absorb the buffer state of Uruguay. Their competition for hegemony continued, however, and the old Banda Oriental continued to serve as the cockpit of Brazilian and Argentine rivalries in the Plata.

MAINTAINING THE EQUILIBRIUM, PURSUING THE ADVANTAGE

As seen in the Cisplatine conflict, South American leaders frequently showed concern that one nation or another might attain a relative advantage over the others, thereby upsetting a theoretical balance among them. Many of the events described in this and the preceding chapters reveal a preoccupation with maintaining the equilibrium and gaining an edge over other countries. After 1808, for example, Luso-Brazilian strategy aimed at frustrating the emergence of a unified state in the Plata by encouraging the fragmentation of the viceroyalty. Both the Portuguese court and the independent Brazilian monarchy sought to absorb the Cisplatine and to prevent Buenos Aires from establishing control over that area as well as Paraguay. If successful, this policy would give Brazil a favorable equilibrium—that is, a competitive advantage—in the Plata. Corréia da Câmara's mission to Asunción fit into this broad strategy, attempting to neutralize Dr. Francia in the Banda Oriental dispute and to draw Paraguay into the orbit of Rio de Janeiro.

Fear of Colombian power was evident in the cautiousness of the Argentine approach to Bolívar in 1825, in Peruvian strategy following the coup of January, 1827, and in the Chilean attempt to secure a treaty with Peru in 1827–1828. Likewise, the specter of Brazilian hegemony frightened many. Alvear and Díaz Vélez couched their appeal to the Liberator not only in terms of Brazil's monarchical and presumably reactionary government, but also in terms of the danger that Dom Pedro might dominate the entire continent; both arguments carried weight with Bolívar. Sucre's projected federation of Bolivia, Argentina, and Chile originally found its rationale in the threat of Brazilian preeminence. In all of these cases, the desirability of maintaining the equilibrium was a palpable concern.

In assessing the relative power of the South American states, contemporaries considered territory, population, natural resources, political consolidation, and government revenues the most important elements. On the basis of such criteria, observers rated Gran Colombia, Brazil, Chile, and Bolivia the preeminent nations of the 1820s. Perceptions of Gran Colombia's role tended to be phrased in terms of Bolívar's personal power. But the other three inspired explicit analyses.

In early 1826 Pedro Gual, then representing Gran Colombia at the Panama Congress, rejoiced in the Oriental victories over the Brazilians and expressed hope that Argentina might be able to check Brazil in the Plata: "Whatever the past conduct of Buenos Aires may have been, I will always be cheered by any event that tends to give that State its lost importance. To live in peace in a hemisphere, it is indispensable to establish over the long run a power equilibrium as well balanced as possible and boundaries as definite as our present topographical knowledge permits."[50] José Rafael Revenga, the Colombian foreign minister, referred to the Cisplatine War in similar terms. He held that "this struggle may eventually prejudice the equilibrium that is desirable among all the continental States"; he argued that the conclusion of the conflict would therefore serve the interests of all, and that the republics should pressure Dom Pedro to surrender the disputed territory.[51]

From this point of view, the creation of Uruguay—"a cotton ball between two crystals," in the memorable words attributed to Lord Ponsonby—helped to stabilize the equilibrium in the Plata. From Brussels, José de San Martín applauded the event: "[A]lthough the Independence of the Banda Oriental is a painful loss for the Provinces of the Union, a great advantage results from our withdrawing from contact with the Brazilians, a contact that left a permanent seed of war."[52]

Chile also attracted attention as a future power. The Austrian

50. Gual to Santander, February 10, 1826, in *Archivo Santander*, XIV, 77.

51. Revenga to Bolívar's secretary (Copy), April 21, 1826, in Co-ADC, tomo 4, fls. 115–16.

52. José de San Martín to Guido, July 20, 1828, in Felipe Barreda Laos, *General Tomás Guido, vida, diplomacia, revelaciones y confidencias* (Buenos Aires, 1942), 360–361.

representative in Rio asserted that Chile showed more promise than any of the other states of Spanish South America. "It is still impossible to foresee," wrote Baron von Mareschal, "what will be the nature, strength, and respective boundaries of the Governments that are perforce being formed from Chile to Colombia. But the State that seemingly should profit most immediately from the expulsion of the Spaniards is that of Chile, having a homogeneous though limited population, no slavery, and excellent ports healthy during all the seasons of the year—advantages that are denied the coasts of Mexico and Peru." When Duarte da Ponte Ribeiro initiated Brazilian diplomacy on the Pacific coast in 1829, he echoed the Austrian's favorable assessment: "According to what I am told, none of the new Governments is in the circumstances of the Chilean to achieve consolidation, and it is the one that has more resources and fewer needs." Indeed, it was precisely the early consolidation of the Chilean state that permitted the Santiago chancery to pursue an aggressive and eminently successful foreign policy aimed at maintaining an advantage among the Pacific coast nations after 1830.[53]

A British agent who prepared a detailed report on Bolivia in 1827 pointed to that country as a military force to be reckoned with in South America. Owing to its restricted territory and concentrated population, he suggested, Bolivia could maintain troops in garrison and deploy them quickly to any border; Peru and Argentina, on the other hand, could place armies on the Bolivian frontier only after considerable time and at considerable expense.[54]

As the future would demonstrate, the British agent's assessment was overly optimistic. Geography may have offered military advantages, but it also carried serious liabilities. Access to external markets was available only through Cobija, Bolivia's sole seaport, which lacked adequate facilities and was separated from the highland population centers by vast reaches of difficult terrain. Moreover, inability to revive the mining industry left the national government with few sources of revenue save the traditional ap-

53. Mareschal to Metternich (No. 9–C, Copy), March 17, 1825, in Br-AIHGB, lata 349, doc. 8; Ponte Ribeiro to Aracati, Lima, September 14, 1829, in Br-AHI, tomo 212/2/4; Burr, *By Reason or Force, passim.*

54. W. Pentland to Ricketts, December 2, 1827, in GB-PRO, FO 61/12, fls. 242–43.

propriation of the surplus production of the Indian communities. In the absence of a strong state apparatus, Bolivia remained vulnerable to more powerful neighbors and eventually lost portions of the national territory to Chile, Brazil, and Paraguay, and suffered constant interference from Peru.[55]

The significance of the creation of Bolivia lay not in the erection of a major power in the heart of the continent, for that never transpired, but rather in denying possession of the highland region to Peru and Argentina. During the colonial period, first Lima and then Buenos Aires had enjoyed administrative jurisdiction over Upper Peru and, as capitals of successor states, both aspired to reestablish that jurisdiction. If either Peru or Argentina managed to absorb Upper Peru, the resulting nation would have an enormous territorial extent and population, and would become one of the dominant forces of South America.

Leaders of other states feared this possibility and were relieved by the creation of Bolivia. The Barão de Itabaiana, for example, wrote the Brazilian foreign minister from London in 1826: "By what I have gathered from [the Colombian minister] and the other Ministers of the Spanish-American States, there is not the least doubt about the dismemberment of the Provinces of Upper Peru and their erection in an independent and separate State. And since this event is, in my opinion, extraordinarily gratifying for Brazil, I beg Your Excellency to convey to His Imperial Majesty my humble congratulations for such an important event."[56]

A few months earlier, Mariano Egaña had also taken notice of Upper Peru from his vantage point as Chilean minister in London. His dispatch is worth quoting at length, for it is a keenly perceptive analysis of the issues at stake and a forceful argument on behalf of an aggressive, farsighted foreign policy in South America. Egaña began by pointing out that the ultimate disposition of Upper Peru, to be determined by the assembly summoned by Sucre, might compromise the interests of Chile. Under such circum-

55. On the geographical problems facing Bolivia, see J. Valerie Fifer, *Bolivia: Land, Location, and Politics Since 1825* (Cambridge, England, 1972), 1–31; and William Lofstrom, "Cobija, Bolivia's First Outlet to the Sea," *The Americas*, XXXI (1974), 185–205. For an interpretation of Bolivia's geopolitical role, see Lewis A. Tambs, "Geopolitical Factors in Latin America," in Norman A. Bailey (ed.), *Latin America: Politics, Economics, and Hemispheric Security* (New York, 1965), 31–49.

56. Itabaiana to Visconde de Paranaguá (No. 71), January 11, 1826, in Br-AHI, tomo 216/1/3.

stances, he lamented the earlier recall from Peru of the Chilean army,

> which at so much cost had been sent and afterwards rein-
> forced, not with the single objective of bestowing liberty
> on that country, but also with the principal [objective] of
> maintaining there until its total pacification and final dis-
> position a useful influence in favor of the interests and
> prosperity of the Fatherland, which no Government can or
> should abandon.
>
> I already have told Your Lordship on another occasion
> that the time has arrived in which, withdrawing from the
> narrow circle of our internal affairs, we should think on a
> larger scale and, extending our sight toward the States
> that surround us, fix the bases of our future policy in or-
> der to leave secure for our grandchildren the gift of inde-
> pendence and happiness, which we are only now begin-
> ning to acquire. Neither the Andes nor the Atacama
> Desert is an adequate barrier to contain the ambitious
> projects of peoples whose population and resources
> should grow at an uncontrolled rate, and who with the
> passing of the years might acquire a chief who, uniting the
> force of his genius with the resources of his country, may
> endanger the independence or liberty of his neighbors. It
> would be the saddest error, the origin of misfortunes and
> tears, to direct our policy according to what our bounda-
> ries are today without considering what they may be in
> the years to come. If a philosopher, meditating on the situ-
> ation of Peru and Buenos Aires . . . were to assure us that
> Buenos Aires will remain with a republican Government, I
> do not think he would hit the mark predicting the same of
> Peru; and we should not let our security depend on cir-
> cumstances that may change each day or on institutions
> that may be altered in time, but rather on the immutable
> and permanent nature of things.[57]

Having discoursed on the principles of international relations, Egaña returned to the matter of Upper Peru and its relationship to Chilean interests:

57. [Egaña] to Chilean MRE (No. 87, Secret, Copy), October 18, 1825, in Ch-AN, MinRE, tomo 16.

It is considering this that the separation of Upper Peru, both from the Provinces of the Río de la Plata and the old Viceroyalty of Lima, is absolutely propitious to the security and prosperity of Chile. Forming an independent State, [Upper Peru] offers us these two advantages: first, it diminishes the preponderance of each of those two States; second, it remains in the center, balancing the forces of both, serving as a counterweight to that which particular circumstances make weaker, and by this conduct containing all ambitious pretension. With the independence of Upper Peru established, Chile need fear nothing of its neighbors. None of them is then powerful enough to attack it with impunity; on the contrary, it will always be respected, because its influence will then be of great weight in the mutual disagreements of these neighbors. The Provinces of the Río de la Plata, with a vast territory but largely incapable of prospering or populating themselves; Upper Peru, without commercial opportunities; and the ancient Viceroyalty [of Peru], without sufficient expanse and with fewer products and elements of prosperity than Chile. Never can any one of them separately make itself formidable to us. Their advancements will always be in proportion to our own, our enjoying the advantage by the more fortunate disposition of our country; and even if those States vary their form of Government, they would still not be fearful to us if they remain independent of each other. But the union of Upper Peru with the ancient Viceroyalty of Lima or with the Provinces of the Río de la Plata is a calamity for Chile, an evil that must be avoided at all costs, because it does not leave us the least confidence of our future security.[58]

Egaña described the role that Chile should fulfill in the South American international order:

Chile should establish a System of perpetual neutrality. It cannot be a conqueror, for its limits are ordained by nature. If the fire of war should at any time break out between its neighbors, it should assume the character of con-

58. *Ibid.*

ciliator. But it should never forget that there exist two peoples who by their geographical position must be its natural allies and friends: Colombia and Brazil. These two great states happily have no [territorial] contact with us; they cannot harm us without first passing through the other Republics of the South. But their friendship is useful to us against the enterprises of said neighbors.[59]

This analysis is a nonpareil application of the principles of power politics. It also constituted a blueprint for Chilean policy in South America. Once a measure of political stability had been attained under Diego Portales, the Chilean government would follow Egaña's advice and look beyond its own borders to maintain a favorable equilibrium. The peril of a Peruvian-Bolivian fusion continued to preoccupy the Santiago chancery and, when Andrés Santa Cruz effected this union in 1836, Chile went to war to keep both neighbors divided and weak.[60]

Egaña correctly predicted bonds of friendship between Chile and Brazil. Lacking common borders, the two countries were spared the usual territorial disputes; moreover, their strategic interests fell in different spheres, Chile's on the Pacific coast and Brazil's in the Plata. Throughout the nineteenth century, Rio and Santiago maintained harmonious relations. Contacts between Chile and New Granada were somewhat less amicable, for both competed for influence in the Pacific.[61]

The concept of equilibrium, already widely invoked during the 1820s, was borrowed from the historical experience of Europe, where the rise of one state typically provoked a coalition of others to check the power of the first. Only slowly did it become clear that the European model was not entirely appropriate for South America. Geography posed far more serious obstacles to military campaigns in South America than in Europe. Moreover, the weakness of the new states in the former colonial regions of Spain and Portugal inhibited the formulation of stable foreign policies

59. *Ibid.*
60. Burr, *By Reason or Force*, 12–57.
61. On Brazil, see Juan J. Fernández, *La república de Chile y el imperio del Brasil: Historia de sus relaciones diplomáticas* ([Santiago], 1959); and Alfredo Valladão, *Brasil e Chile na época do império: Amizade sem exemplo* (Rio de Janeiro, 1959). On New Granada, see Kitchens, "Colombian-Chilean Relations," 331–92; and Burr, *By Reason or Force*, 79–83.

and a strong state system. Finally, technological limitations of a government's ability to communicate its intentions and deploy troops compounded the difficulties. As in many other cases, the European model had to be adapted to South American conditions. The unilateral pursuit of relative advantage came easier than combined efforts to preserve the equilibrium.

The following figure summarizes intra–South American relations during the 1820s. The only consummated alliances were the three negotiated by Gran Colombia between 1821 and 1823 with Peru, Chile, and Argentina. These bilateral treaties aimed at ensuring cooperation during the final phase of the struggle against Spain. The Brazilian overture to Argentina in 1822 likewise represented a search for support while challenging Portuguese rule.

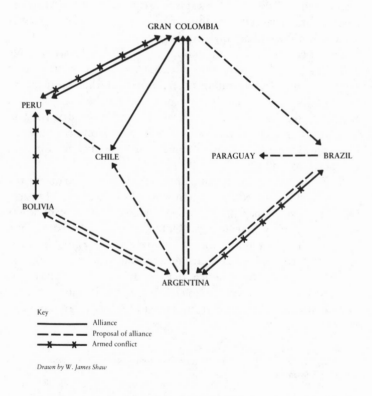

Drawn by W. James Shaw

International Relations in South America, 1821–1830

Almost all of the other proposals of alliances occurred at moments when the supplicant was embroiled in conflict, or on the verge of being so involved, with a neighbor. This was the case in the Brazilian approach to Paraguay, the Argentine appeals to Gran Colombia, Chile, and Bolivia, the later stage of the Bolivian proposal of confederation with Argentina, and the Colombian overture to Brazil. Only two instances were inspired by strategic considerations divorced from ongoing or impending conflicts. The Chilean approach to Peru in 1827 stemmed from Chilean fears of Bolívar and his supposedly Napoleonic ambitions. The first stage of the Bolivian overture to Argentina in the same year found its justification in the need to provide a counterweight to Brazilian power. In general, then, immediate, local considerations prevailed over broader strategic issues.

Epilogue

LIKE SATURN, the revolution devoured its children. By the end of the 1820s, the liberators were fading from the scene. A dispatch from the Chilean agent in Lima in January, 1829, poignantly captured the uncertainty of political life: "In a single day (the twenty-eighth of this month), the unpleasant news of the shooting of the President of Buenos Aires [Manuel Dorrego], and the beheading of the President of Bolivia, General [Pedro] Blanco, was received in this capital."[1]

In Argentina, Juan Manuel de Rosas established his personalist dictatorship, with Dorrego dead and San Martín and Rivadavia in exile. Chile witnessed the beginnings of political consolidation under Diego Portales, while Bernardo O'Higgins and Ramón Freire watched events from abroad. In 1830 Sucre fell victim to an assassin's bullets. In December of the same year a broken and bitterly disillusioned Bolívar, headed for a self-imposed exile, died on the Colombian coast. A few months later, in April, 1831, Dom Pedro—unwilling to accept popular demands that he dismiss his cabinet—abdicated the Brazilian crown in favor of his five-year-old son. Leaders who had risen to prominence during the wars of independence continued to rule in Venezuela, Ecuador, Peru, and Paraguay, but utopian projects were no longer in evidence. Only in Bolivia, where Andrés Santa Cruz pursued a program of authoritarian reform similar to Bolívar's, did a measure of optimism and a commitment to change persevere for a few years more.

The revolutionaries of 1810 had believed that independence

1. Trujillo to Chilean MRE (No. 79), January 31, 1829, in Ch-AMRE, Perú, vol. 7, fl. 285.

from Spain would mark the dawn of a new era of representative government, judicial equality, and economic opportunity. Twenty years later, such hopes had dissipated like smoke from the fields of battle, and the revolutionary generation beheld its brave new world with despair. Bolívar's celebrated lament—"He who follows a revolution plows the sea. America, for us, is ungovernable"—was the best known, but not the only, expression of this disillusionment. Sucre wrote, "We Americans have all built our political edifices on sand, and any audacious man can topple them with a push." After the American congress broke up, Pedro Gual complained: "The ills of my country and of all America have battered my spirit and sickened my body beyond all exaggeration."[2]

Throughout South America, governments turned to the Herculean task of consolidating political authority. The times were not propitious for great international projects like the Panama Congress; indeed, even normal diplomatic exchange lessened as the new states turned inward. Gual, who after Bolívar was the principal architect of Gran Colombia's internationalist foreign policy, indicated retrenchment as one option early in 1828. In the face of Peru's withdrawal from the American congress, and considering the fragile nature of the other states of Spanish South America, Gual asked for new instructions and presented his own assessment: "It seems to me that the Government of Colombia has no recourse but to embrace one of these two extremes: Either abandon, for the time being, the project of the American confederation, suspend all diplomatic relations with these Republics, concentrate on Colombia itself until it is completely reorganized, and then renew its efforts with hopes of greater success. Or tenaciously persevere in formulating a common policy with Mexico, which surely will give us Central America and very probably the other Republics, the comparative importance of which must sooner or later succumb to this power mass."[3]

The first of Gual's options pointed the way for the new states of South America. After 1830 diplomatic retrenchment was the

2. Bolívar to Flores, November 9, 1830, in [Bolívar], *Cartas del Libertador,* VII, 587; Sucre to Bolívar, December 20, 1827, in O'Leary (ed.), *Memorias del general O'Leary,* I, 476; Gual to Colombian MRE (No. 49, Copy), January 21, 1828, in Co-ADC, tomo 608.

3. Gual to Colombian MRE (No. 49, Copy), January 21, 1828, in Co-ADC, tomo 608.

order of the day. The truncated republic of New Granada cut back its diplomatic corps, particularly within Latin America. The Regency government in Brazil also closed a number of legations abroad and reduced the rank of others, responding to pressure from the Chamber of Deputies to balance the budget.[4] Whereas during the 1820s the new states eagerly had sought to establish relations with many nations, inadequate resources and internal problems now required a more modest exchange.

Retrenchment and less ambitious foreign-policy goals stemmed from the precarious nature of state organization. The limitations of foreign markets and the dominance of British merchants, combined with the devastation of local economies during the wars of independence, restricted the sources of revenue available to the new regimes. Lacking the means of building an effective state apparatus and the basis of achieving elite consensus, the South American governments could not mitigate the dispersion of political and military power, and so they remained the prey of centrifugal forces. Brazil and Chile made considerable progress in consolidating political authority before 1850, because of their early incorporation into the world economy, and Paraguay did the same under a series of strong-willed dictators while remaining, in large measure, economically isolated. But the other nations of the continent remained paragons of instability and fractiousness until increasing trade with the North Atlantic basin fostered national consolidation during the second half of the century. During the 1820s the fragility of the new states militated against grandiose projects like the American congress, the Andean Federation, the union of Bolivia, Chile, and Argentina, and the alliance of Gran Colombia and Brazil. Restrictions on each government's ability to mobilize its resources hindered the prosecution of war; neither Brazil nor Argentina could make good its claim to the Banda Oriental, and Peru was unable to detach the southern provinces of Gran Colombia.

Among these weak states, Great Britain appeared all powerful. Owing to its maritime and commercial dominance and its control over capital markets, Britain seemingly could have its way in South America. Its actual influence, however, is difficult to assess. The

4. Kitchens, "Colombian-Chilean Relations," 302–305; Brazil, Ministério das Relações Exteriores, *Relatório*, 1831, pp. 2–4, and 1832, pp. 8–11.

new governments of the continent undoubtedly catered to British wishes in many ways, particularly with regard to matters of trade and navigation. The largest and most important legation of each of the new states was almost invariably located in London, reflecting the desire for information about, and participation in, the London capital market and British trade in general. South American leaders frequently expressed concern over probable British reaction when considering policy options. All of London's broadest goals were realized: the protection of the rebellious colonies from the territorial ambitions of non-Iberian powers, the acquisition of advantageous trading rights, and the survival of the Brazilian monarchy.

But the possibilities of direct manipulation of South American governments by Britain were limited. In the Banda Oriental dispute, for example, the British cabinet failed to head off an armed conflict, suffered severe commercial losses because of the Brazilian blockade of the Plata, and could not mediate a settlement until both sides had come to realize that a military solution was not feasible. The slave-trade treaty with Brazil offers another example. Forced to abolish the traffic in Africans as part of the price of British recognition, the Brazilian government suffered the trade to continue more or less openly after the 1831 deadline. Not until 1850 did the imperial government outlaw the importation of slaves—responding to British pressures as well as other considerations—and effectively enforce the prohibition. The 1827 treaty was thus the classic *lei para inglês ver*—literally, a "law for Englishmen to see," that is, a law promulgated to please the British government and not observed in reality.[5]

Not even Great Britain could control the decision-making processes of the South American governments in the first decades after independence.[6] The inability of national elites to create viable nation-states meant that foreign powers had no way of applying leverage to shape policies. External influences were stronger during the second half of the nineteenth century, when national oligarchies consolidated political power and ruled in close alliance with

5. Bethell, *The Abolition of the Brazilian Slave Trade*, passim.
6. Joseph Smith, "New World Diplomacy: A Reappraisal of British Policy Toward Latin America, 1823–1850," *Inter-American Economic Affairs*, XXXII (1978), 3–24.

foreign governments and businessmen. During the period of this study, the might of Great Britain was deceiving, in that its capacity for directly influencing decision-making was less awesome than it might appear.

Despite disillusionment, diplomatic retrenchment, and the failure of every great international project, the decade of the 1820s established the main characteristics of South American diplomacy. The wars for independence had raised two potential bases for association among the new states. First, the struggle against Spain and the threat of intervention by the Continental Alliance unified the nascent governments of Spanish America in a common effort. When Brazil broke with Portugal, Dom Pedro showed his interest in joining the other Latin American nations in presenting a united front to Europe. One possibility, then, was Latin American internationalism built on a suspicion of, and a hostility toward, Europe. Second, ideology might have provided a basis for alignment since all of the new states of Spanish America ultimately chose republican forms of government and feared the European monarchies. Buenos Aires played on such fears in trying to organize a republican coalition against Brazil. Bolívar's original conception of the American congress postulated a league of Spanish-American republics; his use of the term *amphictyony*, invoking an ancient Greek confederation of states established around a religious center, suggests that he envisaged an alliance based on common ideology, language, and historical experience. Subsequent invitations to Brazil, Great Britain, the United States, and the Netherlands destroyed the homogeneity of the group and, by including monarchies, ruled out the formation of an ideological bloc.

Neither internationalism nor ideology was an insignificant force in foreign policy. Governments collaborated under certain circumstances, such as the struggle for independence, and often fretted over the form of government in neighboring countries. But national self-interest ultimately determined a state's actions. Abstract issues always remained secondary to territorial and strategic considerations. Colombian promotion of an American congress and Argentine efforts to forge a republican coalition failed because more immediate concerns prevailed within other governments. Even these projects were inspired at least in part by self-serving motives; Buenos Aires emphasized Brazil's monarchical form of government as a means of rallying the other republics, and Bolívar intended that the Panama Congress serve to guarantee Colombian leadership in Latin America.

The flexibility of alignments reveals the preeminence of national self-interest. Discrete, proximate causes determined relations among the South American nations, and thus combinations were always in flux. Competition for relative advantage formed the main preoccupation of each government with regard to its neighbors. Concern over the stability of the international equilibrium surfaced frequently, but no state seriously threatened to establish hegemony over the others, and no league ever materialized to check a menacing power.

By 1830 the territorial organization of South America had been roughly sketched. After the creation of Uruguay in 1828 and the secession of Ecuador and Venezuela from Gran Colombia over the next two years, no new states would appear until the separation of Panama from Colombia in 1903. All boundaries remained in dispute, however, and would continue to be the major source of friction among the South American nations.

Although the republics came to accept the Brazilian monarchy, the fear of Brazilian hegemony survived the transition to republican government in 1889 and has remained a major preoccupation until the present. In recent years, the governments and press of Spanish South America have shown a growing uneasiness at the prospect of subordination to Brazil. References to Brazil as a "giant" or a "voracious power," so common in the time of Pedro I, find echoes today. Having survived independence without fragmenting into several states, and having largely succeeded in defining its territorial extent in the face of competing claims, Brazil today is a nation in full pursuit of Great Power status. The outcome of this effort is uncertain, but it seems unquestionable that Brazil will long remain the pivot of South American international relations.

Select Bibliography

ARCHIVES

Argentina

Archivo General de la Nación, Buenos Aires
    Sala VII.
        Archivo de Ángel Justiniano Carranza.
        Archivo del Gral. Tomás Guido.
        Colección Carlos de Alvear.
        Colección Dr. Juan A. Farini.
        Colección Jacinto S. García.
        Colección T. Avellán Moncayo.
    Sala X.
        Correspondencia Oficial.
Archivo General del Ministerio de Relaciones Exteriores y Culto, Buenos
Aires
    Misiones, cajas 14, 15, 18.

Bolivia

Archivo del Ministerio de Relaciones Exteriores y Culto, La Paz
    Volumes: BRA-1-R-1; CAV-5-R-1; LIM-1-180; Sección de Sud-
    America, 1-A.
Archivo Nacional, Sucre
    Ministerio del Interior.
        1825: tomo 1, no. 3; tomo 2, no. 9; tomo 3, nos. 11–12; tomo
            4, no. 14; tomo 8, nos. 63, 65.
        1826: tomo 14, no. 18.
        1832: tomo 41, no. 33.
    Ministerio de Relaciones Exteriores.
        Bolivia-Argentina, tomo 1, nos. 2–5, 8–9.
        Bolivia-Brasil, tomo 1, no. 2.
        Bolivia-Perú, tomo 1, nos. 1b, 2, 10, 14.
        Copiadores, 1830–44.
Biblioteca Nacional, Sucre
    Colección Ernesto O. Rück, items 440–41, 446–47.

Bibliography

Universidad Mayor de San Andrés, La Paz
Philip T. Parkerson furnished abstracts of several documents from
tomo 617 in the Biblioteca Central, Sección de Manuscritos.

Brazil

Arquivo do Instituto Histórico e Geográfico Brasileiro, Rio de Janeiro
Copies of correspondence of Baron von Mareschal.
Arquivo Histórico do Itamarati, Rio de Janeiro
This is the single most valuable source for the present study. The
number of bundles and bound volumes of documents consulted is
too extensive to list here. Material was drawn from the following
sections:
Missões Diplomáticas Brasileiras.
Missões Especiais.
Govêrnos Estrangeiros.
Representações Diplomáticas Estrangeiras no Brasil.
Govêrnos, Repartições e Autoridades Regionais e Locais.
Correspondência Especial.
Correspondência de Personalidades da Época.
Correspondência Interna.
Arquivos das Missões Diplomáticas Brasileiras (Arquivo II).
Arquivo Particular de Duarte da Ponte Ribeiro.
Arquivo Histórico do Museu Imperial, Petrópolis
Scattered correspondence.
Arquivo Nacional, Rio de Janeiro
Seção do Poder Executivo, pastas IJJ⁹ 527, IG¹ 321.
Biblioteca Nacional, Rio de Janeiro
Seção de Manuscritos.
Coleção Rio-Branco.
Miscellaneous documents.

Chile

Archivo del Ministerio de Relaciones Exteriores, Santiago
Argentina, tomos 6–7, 9–10.
Bolivia, tomo 1.
Perú, tomos 7–9, 12.
Archivo Nacional, Santiago
Ministerio de Relaciones Exteriores, tomos 13, 16, 19, 21.

Colombia

Archivo Diplomático y Consular, Ministerio de Relaciones Exteriores,
Bogotá

Tomos 4, 8, 11, 50, 158–59, 257, 259, 267, 312, 475–77, 481, 488–
   89, 494, 606–608, 614.
Paquete: "Consulados de la Argentina en Colombia . . ."
Archivo Histórico Nacional, Bogotá
   Historia/Archivo Anexo, tomo 28.
   Miscelánea General/La República, tomos 24, 152.
   Secretaría de Guerra y Marina, tomos 374, 783, 1047, 1507, 1561.

Great Britain

Public Record Office, London
   The following runs of the Foreign Office General Correspondence
   files were consulted on microfilm:
       FO 6, Argentina, vols. 1–31.
       FO 13, Brazil, vols. 1–79.
       FO 16, Chile, vols. 1–10.
       FO 18, Colombia, vols. 1–81.
       FO 51, Monte Video, vols. 1–6.
       FO 61, Peru, vols. 1–18.

Paraguay

Archivo Nacional, Asunción
   Sección "Historia," tomos 232, 235, 237, 239–40, 430.

Peru

Archivo del Ministerio de Relaciones Exteriores, Lima
       1823: carpeta 5-17.
       1824: carpeta 5-17.
       1825: carpetas 5-8, 6-1.
       1826: carpetas 5-17, 6-1.
       1827: carpetas 5-2, 5-7, 5-17.
       1828: carpeta 5-2.
       Tomos 6-A, 7-A, 8-A, 15-A, 461-C, 464-C.

Portugal

Arquivo Nacional da Torre do Tombo, Lisbon
   Ministério dos Negócios Estrangeiros.
       Caixa "Legação de Portugal no Brasil, 1826–1830."
       Caixas "Legação de Portugal em Hespanha," 1824, 1825.
       Maço 160.
   Ministério do Reino.
       Intendência Geral da Policia, livros 21–22, 223, and maços 47,
       49–50, 226.

Bibliography

Spain

Archivo General de Indias, Sevilla
  Papeles de Estado, América en general.
    Legajo 17, doc. 60.
    Legajo 76, doc. 76.
    Legajo 78, doc. 34.
    Legajo 96, docs. 67–68.
    Legajo 97, docs. 20, 121, 124.
    Legajo 104, docs. 84, 94.
Archivo Histórico Nacional, Madrid
  Sección de Estado, legajos 219, 3772, 3781, 3790, 4525, 4528–29, 5388, 5838, 5849–54, 5856, 5888.

Uruguay

Archivo General de la Nación, Montevideo
  Fondo ex Archivo Administrativo.
    Archivo de Nicolás Herrera, caja 17, carpeta 3.
  Fondo ex Museo y Archivo Histórico Nacional, libro 61.

Vatican City

Archivio Segreto Vaticano
  Archivio del Segretario di Stato.
    Rubrica 249, busta 436, fasciolo 2.
    Rubrica 249, busta 437, fasciolo 2.
    Rubrica 251, busta 448, fasciolo 3.
    Rubrica 279, busta 592, fascioli 3–5.

Archival Guides

Brazil. Ministério das Relações Exteriores. Departamento de Administração. *Arquivo Histórico do Itamaraty: Parte I—Correspondência.* [Rio de Janeiro], 1952.
——. ——. ——. *Arquivo Histórico do Itamaraty: Parte III— 34—Arquivos Particulares. Barão de Ponte Ribeiro (Duarte da Ponte Ribeiro).* [Rio de Janeiro], 1965.
——. ——. ——. *Arquivo Histórico do Itamaraty: Parte III— 35—Pareceres do Conselho de Estado. 36—Documentos Históricos, Primeira Série (Volumes 1822–1930). 37—Documentos Históricos, Segunda Série (Avulsos 1822–1930).* [Rio de Janeiro], 1960.
Hahner, June E. "The Archivo Nacional in Asunción, Paraguay: Addendum." *Latin American Research Review,* VI (1971), 131–32.
Maior, Pedro Souto, comp. "Nos archivos de Hispanha: Relação dos manuscriptos que interessam ao Brasil." *Revista do Instituto Histórico e Geográfico Brasileiro,* LXXXI (1917), 5–288.

Bibliography

Pásztor, Lajos. *Guida delle fonti per la storia dell'America Latina negli archivi della Santa Sede e negli archivi ecclesiastici d'Italia.* Città del Vaticano, 1970.

Pescatello, Ann. "*Relatório* from Portugal: The Archives and Libraries of Portugal and Their Significance for the Study of Brazilian History." *Latin American Research Review,* V (1970), 17–52.

Seckinger, Ron L. "A Guide to Selected Diplomatic Archives of South America." *Latin American Research Review,* X (1975), 127–53.

Williams, John Hoyt. "The Archivo Nacional in Asunción, Paraguay." *Latin American Research Review,* VI (1971), 101–18.

PUBLISHED PRIMARY SOURCES

Government Documents

Argentine Republic. *Tratados, convenciones, protocolos, actos y acuerdos internacionales.* 11 vols. Buenos Aires, 1911–12.

Brazil. *Collecção das Decisões do Governo do Imperio do Brazil, 1831.* Rio de Janeiro, 1876.

———. *Manifiesto o exposición fundada, y justificativa del procedimiento de la Corte del Brasil con respecto al gobierno de las Provincias Unidas del Río de la Plata; y de los motivos que le obligan a declarar la guerra al referido gobierno.* Rio de Janeiro, 1825.

———. Câmara dos Deputados. *Annaes do Parlamento Brazileiro: Assembléa Constituinte, 1823.* 6 vols. Rio de Janeiro, 1876–84.

———. ———. *Annaes do Parlamento Brazileiro: Camara dos Srs. Deputados, 1826–31.* 22 vols. Rio de Janeiro, 1874–78.

———. Ministério das Relações Exteriores. *Relatório.* Rio de Janeiro, 1831, 1832, 1835. Title and publisher vary.

———. Senado Federal. *Atas do Conselho de Estado.* 3 vols. Brasília, 1973.

Peru. *Manifiesto del gobierno del Perú, en contestación al que ha dado el General Bolívar, sobre los motivos que tiene para hacerle la guerra.* Lima, 1828.

———. Ministerio de Relaciones Exteriores. *Colección de los tratados, convenciones, capitulaciones, armisticios y otros actos diplomáticos y políticos celebrados desde la independencia hasta el día.* 14 vols. Lima, 1890–1919.

Newspapers

El Argos de Buenos Aires, 1821–25.

Boletín del Ejército del Sud del Perú Ausiliar de Bolivia [Potosí?], July 17, 1828.

El Cóndor de Bolivia (Chuquisaca), 1825–28.

Bibliography

Diário do Govêrno (Rio de Janeiro), 1823–24. Published under title of *Diário Fluminense*, 1824–29.

Gaceta de Colombia (Villa del Rosario de Cúcuta and Bogotá), 1821–29.

El Peruano (Lima), February 21, 1827.

Revêrbero Constitucional Fluminense (Rio de Janeiro), 1821–22.

O Tamoio (Rio de Janeiro), 1823.

Other Published Sources

Alincourt, Luiz de. "Rezultado dos trabalhos e indagações statisticas da Provincia de Matto-Grosso, por Luiz d'Alincourt, Sargento-Môr Engenheiro, encarregado da Commissão Statistica Topografica ácerca da mesma Provincia (Cuyabá 1828)." *Anais da Biblioteca Nacional do Rio de Janeiro*, III (1877–78), 68–161, 225–78; VIII (1880–81), 39–142.

"A annexação da província de Chiquitos," *Revista do Instituto Histórico de Mato Grosso*, IX (1927), 29–44.

Archivo Santander. 24 vols. Bogotá, [1913]–32.

Armitage, John. *The History of Brazil from the Period of the Arrival of the Braganza Family in 1808, to the Abdication of Don Pedro the First in 1831.* 2 vols. London, 1836.

[Bolívar, Simón.] *Cartas del Libertador.* 2nd ed. 8 vols. Caracas, 1964–1970.

Brazil. Ministério das Relações Exteriores. *Annaes do Itamaraty.* 7 vols. Rio de Janeiro, 1936–42.

———. ———. *Arquivo Diplomático da Independência.* 6 vols. Rio de Janeiro, 1922–25.

Bustos, Francisco Ignacio. *Exposición que hace el ministro de la República Arjentina de su conducta política en Bolivia.* [Chuquisaca, 1828].

Cacho, Fernando. "Ytinerario de un viaje por tierra desde el Río Janeyro hasta Lima (Perú) por Don Fernando Cacho Teniente Coronel al servicio de España Año 1818." In Félix Denegri Luna, *En torno a Ramón Castilla* (Lima, 1969), 35–139.

Cadena, Pedro Ignacio, comp. *Colección de tratados públicos de los Estados Unidos de Colombia.* 2 vols. Bogotá, 1883–84.

Campos, Raul Adalberto de, comp. *Legislação internacional do Brasil: Collectanea resumida de todas as leis e decretos dos Ministerios dos Negocios Estranjeiros e das Relações Exteriores, de 1808 a 1929, e de alguns dos outros, interessando as relações internacionales.* 2 vols. Rio de Janeiro, 1929.

"Correspondência do Barão de Mareschal." *Revista do Instituto Histórico e Geográfico Brasileiro*, CCCXIV (1977), 306–47.

Cortázar, Roberto, comp. *Cartas y mensajes de Santander.* 10 vols. Bogotá, 1953–56.

Bibliography

Cruz, Ernesto de la, ed. *Epistolario de D. Bernardo O'Higgins.* 2 vols. Madrid, 1920.

Dias, Floriano de Aguiar, ed. *Constituições do Brasil.* 2 vols. [Rio de Janeiro], 1975.

Forbes, John Murray. *Once años en Buenos Aires, 1820–1831: Las crónicas diplomáticas.* Compiled, translated, and edited by Felipe A. Espil. Buenos Aires, 1956.

Funes, Gregorio. *Ensayo de la historia civil del Paraguay, Buenos-Ayres y Tucumán.* 3 vols. Buenos Aires, 1816–17.

Gómez, Hernán F., ed. *Corrientes en la guerra con el Brasil.* Corrientes, Argentina, 1928.

Humphreys, R. A., ed. *British Consular Reports on the Trade and Politics of Latin America, 1824–1826.* London, 1940.

Iriarte, Tomás de. *Memorias.* 12 vols. Buenos Aires, 1944–69.

La Fuente, Antonio Gutiérrez de. *Manifiesto que di en Trujillo en 1824 sobre los motivos que me obligaron a deponer a D. José de la Riva-Agüero, y conducta que observé en ese acontecimiento.* Lima, 1829.

Lecuna, Vicente, ed. *Documentos referentes a la creación de Bolivia.* 2 vols. Caracas, 1924.

————, ed. *Relaciones diplomáticas de Bolívar con Chile y Buenos Aires.* 2 vols. Caracas, 1954.

Manning, William R., ed. *Diplomatic Correspondence of the United States Concerning the Independence of the Latin-American Nations.* 3 vols. New York, 1925.

Mello, Jeronymo de A. Figueira de. "A correspondencia do Barão Wenzel de Marschall (Agente diplomatico da Austria no Brasil, de 1821 a 1831)." *Revista do Instituto Histórico e Geográfico Brasileiro,* LXXVII (1914), 169–244; LXXX (1916), 5–148.

Miller, John. *Memoirs of General Miller, in the Service of the Republica of Peru.* 2nd ed. 2 vols. London, 1829.

O'Connor, F[rancis] Burdett. *Independencia americana.* Madrid, n.d.

O'Leary, Simón B., ed. *Memorias del general O'Leary.* 32 vols. Caracas, 1879–88.

Pinheiro, José Feliciano Fernandes. "Memorias do Visconde de S. Leopoldo." *Revista do Instituto Histórico e Geográfico Brasileiro,* XXXVII (1874), 5–69; XXXVIII (1875), 5–49.

Porras Barrenechea, Raúl, comp. *El Congreso de Panamá (1826).* Lima, 1930.

Restelli, Ernesto, comp. *La gestión diplomática del general de Alvear en el Alto Perú (Misión Alvear-Díaz Vélez, 1825–1827): Documentos del Archivo del Ministerio de Relaciones Exteriores y Culto.* Buenos Aires, 1927.

Rodríguez, Gregorio F., [comp.] *Contribución histórica y documental.* 3 vols. Buenos Aires, 1921.

Bibliography

Seckinger, Ron L. "A projetada aliança grã-colombiana-rioplatense contra o Brasil: Um documento inédito." *Mensário do Arquivo Nacional*, V (1974), 33–40.

Uribe, Antonio José, ed. *Anales diplomáticos y consulares de Colombia.* 9 vols. Bogotá, 1900–1959.

Webster, C. K., ed. *Britain and the Independence of Latin America, 1812–1830: Select Documents from the Foreign Office Archives.* 2 vols. London, 1938.

Wisner [de Morgenstern], Francisco. *El dictador del Paraguay, José Gaspar de Francia.* Edited by Julio César Chaves. 2nd ed. Buenos Aires, 1957.

PUBLISHED SECONDARY SOURCES

Alonso Eloy, Rosa, *et al. La oligarquía oriental en la Cisplatina.* Montevideo, 1970.

Argentine Republic. Ministerio de Relaciones Exteriores y Culto. *Catálogo de la biblioteca, mapoteca y archivo.* Buenos Aires, 1910.

Arnade, Charles. *The Emergence of the Republic of Bolivia.* Gainesville, Fla., 1957.

Bader, Thomas M. "The Chancellery and the Change-Purse: A Skeptic's View of the Applicability of a 'Balance of Power' Concept to Nineteenth-Century South America." *Proceedings of the Pacific Coast Council on Latin American Studies*, III (1974), 45–54.

Bákula, Juan Miguel. "El establecimiento de relaciones diplomáticas entre el Perú y el Brasil." *Revista Peruana de Derecho Internacional*, VII (1947), 82–113.

Barbosa, Francisco de Assis. "José Bonifácio e a política internacional." *Revista do Instituto Histórico e Geográfico Brasileiro*, CCLX (1964), 258–84.

Barreda Laos, Felipe. *General Tomás Guido, vida, diplomacia, revelaciones y confidencias.* Buenos Aires, 1942.

Basadre, Jorge. *Historia de la república del Perú, 1822–1933.* 6th ed. rev. 17 vols. Lima, [1968].

Belaúnde, Víctor Andrés. *Bolívar and the Political Thought of the Spanish American Revolution.* 1938; rpr. New York, 1967.

Bethell, Leslie. *The Abolition of the Brazilian Slave Trade: Britain, Brazil and the Slave Trade Question, 1807–1869.* Cambridge, England, 1970.

Beverina, Juan. *La guerra contra el imperio del Brasil: Contribución al estudio de sus antecedentes y de las operaciones hasta Ituzaingó.* Buenos Aires, 1927.

Bierck, Harold A., Jr. *Vida pública de don Pedro Gual.* Translated by Leopoldo Landaeta. Caracas, 1947.

Bibliography

Bomfim, M[anuel José do]. *O Brasil na América: Caracterização da formação brasileira*. Rio de Janeiro, 1929.

Burr, Robert N. "The Balance of Power in Nineteenth-Century South America: An Exploratory Essay." *Hispanic American Historical Review*, XXXV (1955), 37–60.

————. *By Reason or Force: Chile and the Balancing of Power in South America, 1830–1905*. Berkeley, Calif., 1965.

————. "Commentary on the Papers of Professors Hann and Bader." *Proceedings of the Pacific Coast Council on Latin American Studies*, III (1974), 55–72.

————. *The Stillborn Panama Congress: Power Politics and Chilean-Colombian Relations During the War of the Pacific*. Berkeley, Calif., 1962.

Bushnell, David. *El régimen de Santander en la Gran Colombia*. Translated by Jorge Orlando Melo. Bogotá, 1966.

————. "Santanderismo y bolivarismo: Dos matices en pugna." *Desarrollo Económico*, VIII (1968), 243–61.

Caillet-Bois, Ricardo R. "La misión Álvarez Thomas al Perú (1824–1826)." In *Segundo Congreso Internacional de Historia de América*. Vol. IV of 6 vols. Buenos Aires, 1938.

Calógeras, João Pandiá. *A política exterior do império*. 2 vols. Rio de Janeiro, 1927–28.

Campos, Raul Adalberto de, comp. *Relações diplomáticas do Brasil, contendo os nomes dos representantes diplomáticos do Brasil no estrangeiro e os dos representantes diplomáticos dos diversos paizes no Rio de Janeiro de 1808 a 1912*. Rio de Janeiro, 1913.

Cárcano, Miguel Ángel. *La política internacional en la historia argentina*. 6 vols. Buenos Aires, 1972–73.

Cardozo, Efraím. "Bolívar y el Paraguay." In *Segundo Congreso Internacional de Historia de América*. Vol. IV of 6 vols. Buenos Aires, 1938.

Checa Drouet, B[enigno]. *La doctrina americana del uti possidetis de 1810: Un estudio de derecho internacional público americano*. Lima, 1936.

Collier, Simon. *Ideas and Politics of Chilean Independence, 1808–1833*. Cambridge, England, 1967.

————. "Nationality, Nationalism, and Supranationalism in the Writings of Simón Bolívar." *Hispanic American Historical Review*, LXIII (1983), 37–64.

Colombia. Ministerio de Relaciones Exteriores. *Historia de la Cancillería de San Carlos*. Vol. I: *Pórtico*. Bogotá, 1942. (Only volume published.)

Costa, Emília Viotti da. "The Political Emancipation of Brazil." In *From*

Bibliography

Colony to Nation: Essays on the Independence of Brazil, edited by A. J. R. Russell-Wood. Baltimore, 1975.

Cruchaga Ossa, Alberto. *Estudios de historia diplomática chilena*. [Santiago], 1962.

Davis, Thomas Brabson. *Carlos de Alvear, Man of Revolution: The Diplomatic Career of Argentina's First Minister to the United States*. Durham, N.C., 1955.

Fernández, Juan J. *La república de Chile y el imperio del Brasil: Historia de sus relaciones diplomáticas*. [Santiago], 1959.

Fundação Getúlio Vargas. *Evolução do Ministério das Relações Exteriores*. [Rio de Janeiro, 1954.]

García Salazar, Arturo, and Jorge Linch. *Guía práctica para los diplomáticos y cónsules peruanos*. 2 vols. Lima, 1918.

González, Ariosto D. *La misión de Santiago Vázquez a Buenos Aires, 1829–1830*. Montevideo, 1950.

González, Julio César. "Las Provincias Unidas del Río de la Plata y el Congreso de Panamá." *Trabajos y Comunicaciones*, XII [1964], 29–91.

Guimarães, Argeu. *Diccionario bio-bibliographico brasileiro de diplomacia, política externa e direito internacional*. [Rio de Janeiro, 1938.]

Halperín-Donghi, Tulio. *The Aftermath of Revolution in Latin America*. Translated by Josephine de Bunsen. New York, 1973.

———. *Historia contemporánea de América Latina*. Madrid, 1969.

———. *Politics, Economics and Society in Argentina in the Revolutionary Period*. Translated by Richard Southern. Cambridge, England, 1975.

Hann, John Henry. "Brazil and the Río de la Plata, 1808–1828." Ph.D. dissertation, University of Texas, 1967.

———. "Burr's Model Applied: The Balance of Power in the Río de la Plata, Brazil's Role." *Proceedings of the Pacific Coast Council on Latin American Studies*, III (1974), 31–44.

Herrera, Luís Alberto de. *La misión Ponsonby*. 2 vols. [Montevideo], 1930.

Ireland, Gordon. *Boundaries, Possessions and Conflicts in South America*. Cambridge, Mass., 1938.

Kitchens, John William, Jr. "Colombian-Chilean Relations, 1817–1845: A Diplomatic Struggle for Pacific Coast Hegemony." Ph.D. dissertation, Vanderbilt University, 1969.

Lima, [Manoel de] Oliveira. *Historia diplomatica do Brazil: O reconhecimento do imperio*. Paris, [1901].

Lima, Nestor dos Santos. *La imagen del Brasil en las cartas de Bolívar*. [Caracas, 1978.]

Lofstrom, William L. "From Colony to Republic: A Case Study of Bureaucratic Change." *Journal of Latin American Studies*, V (1973), 177–97.

————. *The Promise and Problem of Reform: Attempted Social and Economic Change in the First Years of Bolivian Independence*. Ithaca, N.Y., 1972.

Lynch, John. *The Spanish-American Revolutions, 1808–1826*. New York, 1973.

Lyra, Heitor. "Correa da Camara no Prata." In Brazil, Ministério das Relações Exteriores, *Arquivo Diplomático da Independência*. Vol. V of 6 vols. Rio de Janeiro, 1922–25.

McBeth, Michael Charles. "The Politicians vs. the Generals: The Decline of the Brazilian Army During the First Empire, 1822–1831." Ph.D. dissertation, University of Washington, 1972.

Magalhães, Basílio de. *Expansão geographica do Brasil colonial*. 2nd ed. rev. São Paulo, 1935.

Manchester, Alan K. *British Preëminence in Brazil: Its Rise and Decline. A Study in European Expansion*. Chapel Hill, N.C., 1933.

Masur, Gerhard. *Simon Bolivar*. Albuquerque, N.M., 1948.

Mello, Arnaldo Vieira de. *Bolívar, o Brasil e os nossos vizinhos do Prata: Da questão de Chiquitos à guerra da Cisplatina*. Rio de Janeiro, 1963.

Monteiro, Tobias. *Historia do imperio: A elaboração da independência*. Rio de Janeiro, 1927.

————. *Historia do imperio: O primeiro reinado*. 2 vols. Rio de Janeiro, 1939–46.

Oliveira, João Gualberto de. *Gusmão, Bolívar e o princípio do "uti possidetis."* São Paulo, 1958.

Ovando Sanz, Jorge Alejandro. *La invasión brasileña a Bolivia en 1825: Una de las causas del Congreso de Panamá*. La Paz, 1977.

Parkerson, Philip T. "La misión diplomática de Andrés Santa Cruz en Chile, en 1828." *Presencia Literaria* (La Paz), June 17, 1974.

Pérez Acosta, Juan Francisco. *Francia y Bonpland*. Buenos Aires, 1942.

Piccirilli, Ricardo. *Rivadavia y su tiempo*. 2nd ed. 3 vols. Buenos Aires, [1960].

Pivel Devoto, Juan E. "La misión de Francisco J. Muñoz a Bolivia: Contribución al estudio de nuestra historia diplomática (1831–1835)." *Revista del Instituto Histórico y Geográfico del Uruguay*, IX (1932), 213–98.

————. *La misión de Nicolás Herrera a Rio de Janeiro (1829–1830): Contribución al estudio de nuestra historia diplomática*. Montevideo, 1932.

Ramos, R. Antonio. *La política del Brasil en el Paraguay bajo la dictadura del Dr. Francia*. 2nd ed. Buenos Aires, 1959.

Bibliography

René-Moreno, Gabriel. *Ayacucho en Buenos Aires y prevaricación de Rivadavia*. Madrid, n.d.

Rodrigues, José Honório. *Independência: Revolução e contra-revolução*. 5 vols. Rio de Janeiro, 1975–76.

Romêro, Marcos. *História da organização administrativa da Secretaria de Estado dos Negócios Estrangeiros e das Relações Exteriores, 1808–1951*. [Rio de Janeiro, 1951.]

Russell-Wood, A. J. R., ed. *From Colony to Nation: Essays on the Independence of Brazil*. Baltimore, 1975.

Saavedra, Carlos Gonzalo de. *El Deán Funes y la creación de Bolivia*. La Paz, 1972.

Schwartz, Stuart B. *Sovereignty and Society in Colonial Brazil: The High Court of Bahia and Its Judges, 1609–1751*. Berkeley, Calif., 1973.

Seckinger, Ron L. "The Chiquitos Affair: An Aborted Crisis in Brazilian-Bolivian Relations." *Luso-Brazilian Review*, XI (1974), 19–40.

———. "O estado brasileiro e a política externa no século XIX." *Dados*, No. 19 (1978), 111–33.

———. "South American Power Politics During the 1820s." *Hispanic American Historical Review*, LVI (1976), 241–67.

Segreti, Carlos S. A. "La misión diplomática del doctor Francisco Ignacio Bustos a Bolivia." *Trabajos y Comunicaciones*, X [1961], 165–203.

———. "El nacimiento de Bolivia." *Revista de la Universidad Nacional de Córdoba*, IX (1968) 55–98.

Silva, J. Francisco V. *El Libertador Bolívar y el Deán Funes en la política argentina: Revisión de la historia argentina*. Madrid, n.d.

Smith, Joseph, "New World Diplomacy: A Reappraisal of British Policy Toward Latin America, 1823–1850." *Inter-American Economic Affairs*, XXXII (1978), 3–24.

Soares, [Álvaro] Teixeira. *Diplomacia do império no Rio da Prata (até 1825)*. Rio de Janeiro, 1955.

Sousa, Octávio Tarquínio de. *História dos fundadores do império do Brasil*. 10 vols. Rio de Janeiro, 1957.

Stein, Stanley J., and Barbara H. Stein. *The Colonial Heritage of Latin America: Essays on Economic Dependence in Perspective*. New York, 1970.

Street, John. *Artigas and the Emancipation of Uruguay*. Cambridge, England, 1959.

Thévenin de Garabelli, Martha Campos. *La revolución oriental de 1822–1823: Su génesis*. Montevideo, 1972. One vol. to date.

Uricoechea, Fernando. *The Patrimonial Foundations of the Brazilian Bureaucratic State*. Berkeley, Calif., 1980.

Bibliography

Valladão, Alfredo. *Brasil e Chile na época do império: Amizade sem exemplo*. Rio de Janeiro, 1959.

Vásquez-Machicado, Humberto. "La invasión brasilera a Chiquitos y la diplomacia argentina de 1825." In *Segundo Congreso Internacional de Historia de América*. Vol. IV of 6 vols. Buenos Aires, 1938.

Vial Correa, Gonzalo. "La formación de las nacionalidades hispanoamericanas como causa de la independencia." *Boletín de la Academia Chilena de Historia*, No. 75 (1966), 110–44.

Villegas Basavilbaso, Benjamín. "La adquisición de armamentos navales en Chile durante la guerra del Brasil." *Boletín de la Academia Nacional de la Historia*, IV (1927), 133–47.

Williams, John Hoyt. *The Rise and Fall of the Paraguayan Republic, 1800–1870*. Austin, 1979.

———. "The Undrawn Line: Three Centuries of Strife on the Paraguayan-Mato Grosso Frontier." *Luso-Brazilian Review*, XVII (1980), 17–40.

Zubieta, Pedro A. *Apuntaciones sobre las primeras misiones diplomaticas de Colombia: Primero y segundo periodos—1809–1819–1830*. Bogotá, 1924.

Index

Index

Index

Index

Index